**7 – DAY
LOAN**

VIS
ME

KU-525-956

VISUAL METHODOLOGIES

An Introduction to the Interpretation of Visual Materials

second edition

Gillian Rose

SAGE Publications

London • Thousand Oaks • New Delhi

The edition first published 2007
First published 2001. Reprinted 2001, 2002, 2003 (twice), 2005 (twice), 2006

SAGE Publications Ltd
1 Oliver's Yard
55 City Road
London EC1Y 1SP

SAGE Publications Inc.
2455 Teller Road
Thousand Oaks, California 91320

SAGE Publications India Pvt Ltd
B-42, Panchsheel Enclave
Post Box 4109
New Delhi 110 017

British Library Cataloguing in Publication data

A catalogue record for this book is available from the British Library

ISBN 978 1 4129 2190 9
ISBN 978 1 4129 2191 6 (pbk)

Library of Congress Control Number

Typeset by C&M Digitals (P) Ltd., Chennai, India
Printed on paper from sustainable resources
Printed and bound in Great Britain by Cromwell Press, Trowbridge, Wiltshire

For Mauro, Giorgio and Lydia

contents

list of figures

acknowledgements

This book is based on a course I taught at the Graduate School for the Social Sciences, Edinburgh University, in 1996, 1997 and 1998. Most thanks must go to the students who took that course, for their enthusiastic engagement with the images I showed them and for their healthy scepticism towards methods textbooks. Robert Rojek has been a supportive editor, and Felicity Callard, Mike Crang and Don Slater were constructive readers for Sage. The first edition benefited from useful and pleasurable discussions in Edinburgh about matters visual and interpretive with Sue Smith, Charlie Withers and, especially, Mark Dorrian; the second edition is indebted to conversations with colleagues in the Geography Discipline at The Open University. My thanks to them all.

Figures

1.1. Reproduced with permission of the Conservative Party Archive Trust. © Bodleian Library, University of Oxford 2006

1.2 *Ways of Seeing,* by John Berger, 1972. Penguin Books

1.3 Robert Doisneau, 'An Oblique Look', 1948. Rapho, Paris

3.1 *Self-Portrait,* 1629 by Rembrandt Harmensz van Rijn, oil on panel. © Isabella Stewart Gardner Museum, Boston, Massachusetts, USA/Bridgeman Art Library

3.2 *Self-Portrait,* 1657 by Rembrandt Harmensz van Rijn. © the collection of the Duke of Sutherland, on loan to the National Gallery of Scotland

3.6 *Little Girl in a Blue Armchair,* 1878 oil on canvas by Mary Cassatt. The collection of Mr and Mrs Paul Mellon. Image © 2006 Board of Trustees, National Gallery of Art, Washington

4.1 'Adioukrou Woman', photograph © Carol Beckwith and Angela Fisher/photokunst

4.2, 4.3 *Reading National Geographic* by C.A. Lutz and J.L. Collins, 1993, University of Chicago Press

5.1, 5.6, 5.7 *Decoding Advertisements: Ideology and Meaning in Advertising* by Judith Williamson, 1978. Reproduced with permission of Marion Boyars

5.5 *Reading Ads Socially* by R. Goldman, 1992. Reproduced by permission of Routledge

6.1 *Women, Art and Power and Other Essays by* L. Nochlin, 1989, Thames & Hudson

6.2 © Buena Vista Television

6.3 © 1958 Universal City Studios, Inc. for Samuel Taylor and Patrica Hitchcock O'Connell as Trustees

6.4 *The Ambassadors* (Jean de Dinteville and Georges de Selve), 1533 by Hans Holbein the younger, oil on wood. © National Gallery, London

7.1 *The Arnolfini Portrait,* 1434 by Jan van Eyck, oil on oak. © National Gallery, London

7.2 Illustration to *The Bridge of Sighs,* 1878 by Gustave Dore. © The British Library Board. All rights reserved

7.3, 7.4 'Lost' and 'Found', c.1870 by W. Gray in W. Hayward, *London by Night.* © The British Library Board. All rights reserved

7.5 The River', 1850 by Hablot K. Browne (Phiz), engraving and etching in Charles Dickens, *David Copperfield,* No. 16 August 1850. © The British Library Board. All rights reserved

7.6 *Found Drowned,* 1848–50 (oil on canvas) by George Frederick Watts. © Trustees of the Watts Gallery, Compton, Surry, UK/Bridgeman Art Library

7.7 Map from *Life and Labour of the London Poor,* 1889 by Charles Booth. By permission of the London Topographical Society

7.8 *Police Illustrated News,* 17 November 1888. By permission of the British Library

9.1 Photograph © Martha Cooper in *Inside Culture: Art and Class in the American Home,* by D. Halle, 1993, University of Chicago Press

10.1 C. Pinney, *Camera Indica: The Social Life of Indian Photographs,* 1997, Reaktion Books

11.1 C. Suchar, 'Amsterdam and Chicago: seeing the macro-characteristics of gentrification' in C. Knowles and J. Sweetman (eds), *Picturing the Social Landscape: Visual Methods and Sociological Imagination,* 2004. Reproduced by permission of Routledge

11.2 T. Edensor, *Industrial Ruins: Space, Aesthetics and Modernity,* 2005, Berg

Every effort has been made to trace all the copyright holders, but if any have been overlooked, or if any additional information can be given, the publishers will be pleased to make the necessary arrangements at the first opportunity.

preface: introducing the second edition of this book

The first edition of this book was written mostly during 1999, and there can be no doubt that events in the intervening years have demonstrated the truth of the book's premise: that we need to learn to interpret visual images because they are an important means through which social life happens. Think of the pictures on tv screens, in newspapers and magazines, in art works and on websites, that have been generated by the attacks on the World Trade Centre in New York in September 2001; remember the furore in 2004 over photographs taken by US soldiers in the Abu Ghraib prison in Iraq, and the smaller scandal when a UK newspaper printed what it claimed were similar photos taken by British soldiers (which later turned out to be fakes); and recall thousands of Muslims all over the world protesting against what they saw as offensive cartoons published in a Danish magazine in 2006. Remember the photos published in newspapers showing the victims of bombs in Madrid in 2004 and London in 2005, and the makeshift shrines of candles, photos and other objects in memory of the victims of these and so many other violent attacks all around the world. Think of images of the tsunami that devastated much of the Indian Ocean's coastlines in December 2004: TV news reports, holiday-makers' videos and photographs, satellite imagery, pictures of missing people circulating on the internet, photos used in appeals for aid. Think of other 'global media events' (Dayan and Katz 1992): the opening ceremonies of Olympic Games, World Cup football matches, the coverage of what for some parts of the world was New Year 2000. And consider too the continuing importance of more everyday sorts of images: family snaps, billboard adverts, comics, birthday cards, photos taken on camera-phones.

So many images. And since the first edition of this book, several full-length discussions of 'visual culture' have been published (Cherry 2005; Dikovitskaya 2005; Evans 2006; Howells 2003; Rampley 2005; Sturken and Cartwright 2001), along with a journal devoted to its study: the *Journal of Visual Culture*. Indeed, 'visual culture studies' is now much more securely established as a field of study than it was seven years ago, with a range of academic scholars working hard to make sense of the proliferating field of the visual. Many are addressing, in different ways, questions of the power and effects of visual materials. But it also seems to me that there are three strands of work that don't often make an appearance in the emergent literature on visual culture that deserve more attention, and these are given new chapters in the second edition of this book. One is the argument, made increasingly often now, that researchers should work with visual materials that they have made rather than found, and Chapter 11 examines some studies with photographs generated by that claim. Another neglected strand is the well-established field of audience studies, discussed here in Chapter 9; and Chapter 10 looks at a number of studies by anthropologists who are interested in thinking less about what visual images or object mean, and more about what happens when things are done with them. All of these positions raise interesting questions for visual culture studies, questions that are both theoretical and methodological.

There remain remarkably few guides to possible methods of interpreting visual materials, and even fewer explanations of how to do those methods, despite the huge amount of academic work currently being published on things visual. This book has been joined by a few others (Banks 2001; Pink 2006; van Leeuwen and Jewitt 2001), it is true. But it is still unique in its attempt to discuss and evaluate systematically a wide range of methods for doing research with visual materials. It is addressed to the undergraduate student who has either found some intriguing visual materials to work with, or who wants to make some to work with, or who is excited by the visual culture literature and wants to do a research project that engages with some of its arguments.

A particular concern of mine is to encourage the grounding of interpretations of visual materials in careful empirical research. This is not because there is some essential truth lurking in each image, awaiting discovery (although we will encounter the latter claim in some of the early chapters of this book); as Stuart Hall says:

> It is worth emphasising that there is no single or 'correct' answer to the question, 'What does this image mean?' or 'What is this ad saying?' Since there is no law which can guarantee that things will have 'one, true meaning', or that meanings won't change over time, work in this area is bound to be interpretative – a debate between, not who is 'right' and who is 'wrong', but between equally plausible, though sometimes competing and contesting, meanings and interpretations. The best way to 'settle' such contested readings is to look again at the concrete example and try to justify one's 'reading' in detail in relation to the actual practices and forms of signification used, and what meanings they seem to you to be producing. (1997a: 9)

Interpreting images is just that, interpretation. As Hall suggests, it is therefore important to justify your interpretation. To do that you will need to have an explicit methodology, and this book will help you develop one. It provides a basic introduction to a range of methods that can be used to interpret visual images, and it provides enough references for you to develop more detailed methods if you need to.

It does not offer a neutral account of these different methods, though. There are significant differences between different theories of the visual. So the first chapter of this book addresses some aspects of current, more theoretical, debates about the visual. In that first chapter, I agree with the participants in those debates who argue that the interpretation of visual images must address questions of cultural meaning and power, and that position has certain implications for the way in which I subsequently assess the various methods I discuss. For example, while quantitative methods can be deployed in relation to these sorts of issues (as Chapter 4 will suggest), nonetheless this emphasis on meaning and significance suggests that qualitative methods are more appropriate. Indeed, every chapter here except the fourth explores qualitative methodologies. More broadly, the first chapter also makes some specific suggestions about why it is important to consider visual images, why it is important to be critical about visual images, and why it is important to reflect on that critique. These three issues are developed in Chapter 1 into three criteria for what I term a 'critical visual methodology'. By 'critical' I mean an approach that thinks about the visual in terms of the cultural significance, social practices and power relations in which it is embedded; and that means thinking about the power relations that produce, are articulated through and can be challenged by, ways of seeing and imaging. Those criteria then provide the means by which the various methods in this book are evaluated. For each method I ask, how useful is it in achieving a critical methodology for visual images?

Most chapters of this book focus on one method, and most chapters also focus on just one kind of visual imagery. Individual chapters look at paintings, photographs, films, televised soaps and adverts. Clearly, this is a narrow selection of visual things; there's nothing on video, or medical imaging, or maps, for example. And what about buildings, built landscapes, sculpture? There is nothing to prevent the methods discussed here being applied to other sorts of visual images and objects, however. Each chapter concentrates on one kind of visual thing and one method in order to offer a sustained and fairly detailed discussion of the issues each raises. In order to develop that detail, each chapter has boxes which ask you to *focus* on specific parts of the method. However, there are suggestions for *useful reading* at the end of the book which will help you to find your way around other visual media and genres, if you plan to use one of the methods discussed here on a different sort of imagery. The book also has a *list of key terms*. *Visual Methodologies* explores both theoretical and methodological issues, each of which has its own, sometimes rather obscure, vocabulary. To help you recognize the key terms of these vocabularies, the first time they are discussed in the text they are **highlighted in bold** and noted in the margin. To help you check your understanding of them, the list of key terms on pages 279–80 tells you where these terms are explored in the book.

To start using this book it is important to begin with Chapter 1, which will help you make sense of the other chapters. Chapter 2 explains how the book is organized in more detail, and will also help you to get the most out of the subsequent chapters. The following chapters then examine specific methods, and the concluding chapter rehearses the main arguments of the book and considers the usefulness of mixing different methods.

Finally, I'd like to comment on the limits of a book like this. This book offers some guidelines for investigating the meanings and effects of visual images. But the most exciting, startling and perceptive critics of visual images don't in the end depend entirely on their sound methodology, I think. They also depend on the pleasure, thrills, fascination, wonder, fear or revulsion of the person looking at the images and then writing about them. Successful interpretation depends on a passionate engagement with what you see. Use your methodology to discipline your passion, not to deaden it.

1
researching visual materials
towards a critical visual methodology

Choosing a research methodology means developing a research question and the tools to generate evidence for its answer; both of these should be consistent with a theoretical framework. This chapter explores recent debates about the visual to help you develop that framework. To do that, it:

- discusses a range of literature which explores the importance of the visual to contemporary Western societies;
- offers a broad analytical framework for understanding how images have social effects;
- suggests some criteria for a critical approach to visual materials;
- and sets up the approach to discussing methods that the rest of this book relies on.

1 an introductory survey of 'the visual'

Beginning in the 1970s, and over the following three decades, the social sciences experienced a significant change in their understanding of social life. This change is often described as the 'cultural turn'. That is, 'culture' became a crucial means by which many social scientists understood social processes, social identities, and social change and conflict. **Culture** is a complex concept, **culture** but, in very broad terms, the result of its deployment has been that social scientists are now very often interested in the ways in which social life is constructed through the ideas that people have about it, and the practices that flow from those ideas. To quote one of the major contributors to this shift, Stuart Hall:

> Culture, it is argued, is not so much a set of things – novels and paintings or TV programmes or comics – as a process, a set of practices. Primarily, culture is concerned with the production and exchange of meanings – the 'giving and taking of meaning' – between the members of a society or group

... Thus culture depends on its participants interpreting meaningfully what is around them, and 'making sense' of the world, in broadly similar ways. (Hall 1997a: 2)

Those meanings may be explicit or implicit, conscious or unconscious, they may be felt as truth or as fantasy, science or commonsense; and they may be conveyed through everyday speech, elaborate rhetoric, high art, television soap operas, dreams, movies or muzak; and different groups in a society will make sense of the world in different ways. Whatever form they take, these **representations** made meanings, or **representations**, structure they way people behave – the way you and I behave – in our everyday lives.

This sort of argument can take very diverse forms. But more recently, many writers addressing these issues argued that the visual is central to the cultural construction of social life in contemporary Western societies. We are, of course, surrounded by different sorts of visual technologies – photography, film, video, digital graphics, television, acrylics, for example – and the images they show us – TV programmes, advertisements, snapshots, public sculpture, movies, surveillance video footage, newspaper pictures, paintings. All these different sorts of technologies and images offer views of the world; they render the world in visual terms. But this rendering, even by photographs, is never innocent. These images are never transparent windows onto the world. They interpret the world; they display it in very particular ways. Thus a dis-**vision** tinction is sometimes made between vision and visuality. **Vision** is what the human eye is physiologically capable of seeing (although it must be noted that ideas about that capability have changed historically and will most likely con-**visuality** tinue to change: see Crary 1992). **Visuality**, on the other hand, refers to the way in which vision is constructed in various ways: 'how we see, how we are able, allowed, or made to see, and how we see this seeing and the unseeing therein' (Foster 1988: ix). Another phrase with very similar connotations to **scopic regime** visuality is **scopic regime**. Both terms refer to the ways in which both what is seen and how it is seen are culturally constructed.

For some writers, the visual is the most fundamental of all senses. Gordon Fyfe and John Law (1988: 2), for example, claim that 'depiction, picturing and seeing are ubiquitous features of the process by which most human beings come to know the world as it really *is* for them', and John Berger (1972: 7) suggests that this is because 'seeing comes before words. The child looks and recognizes before it can speak.' (Clearly these writers pay little attention to those who are born blind.) Other writers, however, prefer to historicize the importance of the visual, tracing what they see as the increasing saturation of Western societies by visual images. Many claim that this process has reached unprecedented levels, so that Westerners now interact with the world mainly through how we see it. Martin Jay (1993) has used the term **ocularcentrism** **ocularcentrism** to describe the apparent centrality of the visual to contemporary Western life.

This narrative of the increasing importance of the visual to contemporary Western societies is part of a wider analysis of the shift from premodernity to modernity, and from modernity to postmodernity (for example, see Mirzoeff 1999: 1–33). It is often suggested – or assumed – that in premodern societies, visual images were not especially important, partly because there were so few of them in circulation. This began to change with the onset of modernity. In particular, it is suggested that modern forms of understanding the world depend on a scopic regime that equates seeing with knowledge. Chris Jenks (1995), for example, makes this case in an essay entitled 'The Centrality of the Eye in Western Culture', arguing that 'looking, seeing and knowing have become perilously intertwined' so that 'the modern world is very much a "seen" phenomenon' (Jenks 1995: 1, 2).

> We daily experience and perpetuate the conflation of the 'seen' with the 'known' in conversation through the commonplace linguistic appendage of 'do you see?' or 'see what I mean?' to utterances that seem to require confirmation, or, when seeking opinion, by inquiring after people's 'views'. (Jenks 1995: 3)

Barbara Maria Stafford (1991), a historian of images used in the sciences, has argued that, in a process beginning in the eighteenth century, the construction of scientific knowledges about the world has become more and more based on images rather than on written texts; Jenks (1995) suggests that it is the valorization of science in Western cultures that has allowed everyday understandings to make the same connection between seeing and knowing. However, that connection was also made in other fields of modern practice. Richard Rorty (1980), for example, traces the development of this conflation of seeing with knowing to the intersection of several ideas central to eighteenth century philosophy. Judith Adler (1989) examines tourism and argues that, between 1600 and 1800, the travel of European elites was defined increasingly as a visual practice, based first on 'an overarching scientific ideology that cast even the most humble tourists as part of … the impartial survey of all creation' (Adler 1989: 24), and later on a particular appreciation of spectacular visual and artistic beauty. John Urry (1990) has sketched the outline of a rather different 'tourist gaze' which he argues is typical of the mass tourism of the nineteenth and twentieth centuries (see also Pratt 1992). Other writers have made other arguments for the importance of the visual to modern societies. The work of Michel Foucault explores the way in which many nineteenth century institutions depended on various forms of surveillance (1977) (Chapters 7 and 8 here examine the methodological implications of his work); and in his study of nineteenth century world fairs and exhibitions, Timothy Mitchell (1988) shows how European societies represented the whole world as an exhibition. Deborah Poole (1997) has traced how visions of that modernity were thoroughly racialized in the same period. In the twentieth century, Guy Debord (1977) claims that the world has turned into a 'society of the spectacle', and Paul Virilio (1994) argues that new visualizing technologies have created 'the vision machine' in which we are all **visual culture**   caught. The use of the term '**visual culture**' refers to the plethora of ways in which the visual is part of social life.

Thus it has been argued that modernity is ocularcentric. It is argued too that the visual is equally central to postmodernity; Nicholas Mirzoeff (1998: 4), for example, has proclaimed that 'the postmodern is a visual culture'. However, in postmodernity, it is suggested, the modern relation between seeing and true knowing has been broken. Thus Mirzoeff (1998) suggests that postmodernity is ocularcentric not simply because visual images are more and more common, nor because knowledges about the world are increasingly articulated visually, but because we interact more and more with totally constructed visual experiences. Thus the modern connection between seeing and knowledge is stretched to breaking point in postmodernity:

> Seeing is a great deal more than believing these days. You can buy an image of your house taken from an orbiting satellite or have your internal organs magnetically imaged. If that special moment didn't come out quite right in your photography, you can digitally manipulate it on your computer. At New York's Empire State Building, the queues are longer for the virtual reality New York Ride than for the lifts to the observation platforms. Alternatively, you could save yourself the trouble by catching the entire New York skyline, rendered in attractive pastel colours, at the New York, New York resort in Las Vegas. This virtual city will shortly be joined by Paris Las Vegas, imitating the already carefully manipulated image of the city of light. (Mirzoeff 1998: 1)

simulacrum   This is what Jean Baudrillard (1988) some time ago dubbed the **simulacrum**. Baudrillard argued that, in postmodernity, it is no longer possible to make a distinction between the real and the unreal; images had become detached from any certain relation to a real world with the result that we now live in a scopic regime dominated by simulations, or simulacra.

This story about the increasing extent and changing nature of visual culture in modernity and postmodernity is not without its critics, however (see, for example, the debates in the journal *October* [1996] and the *Journal of Visual Culture* [2001; 2003]). Two points of debate, for example, are the history and geography of this account. Jeffrey Hamburger (1997), to take just one example, argues that visual images were central to certain kinds of pre-modern, medieval spirituality, and Ella Shohat and Robert Stam (1998) have argued forcefully against the Eurocentrism that pervades many discussions of 'the visual'. The work of Hamburger (1997) and Shohat and Stam (1998), among others, makes it clear that if a narrative of increasing ocularcentrism in the West can be told, it must be much more nuanced, historically and geographically, than has so far been the case (see also Brennan and Jay 1996; Cheetham et al. 2005; Pinney 2003).

There are also debates about the social relations within which these visualities are embedded, and particularly about the effects of simulacra. Baudrillard, for example, has often been accused of uncritically celebrating the simulacrum without regard for the often very unequal social relations that can be articulated through it, and the work of Donna Haraway (1991) is taken by many as a salutary reminder of what is at stake in contemporary ocularcentrism (see also Sturken and Cartwright 2001; Lister and Wells 2001). Like many others, Haraway (1991) notes the contemporary proliferation of visualizing technologies in scientific and everyday use, and she characterizes the scopic regime associated with these technologies thus: 'vision in this technological feast becomes unregulated gluttony; all perspective gives way to infinitely mobile vision, which no longer seems just mythically about the god-trick of seeing everything from nowhere, but to have put the myth into ordinary practice' (Haraway 1991: 189). Haraway is concerned to specify the social power relations that are articulated through this particular form of visuality, however. She argues that contemporary, unregulated visual gluttony is available to only a few people and institutions, in particular those that are part of the 'history of science tied to militarism, capitalism, colonialism, and male supremacy' (Haraway 1991: 188). She argues that what this visuality does is to produce specific visions of social difference – of hierarchies of class, 'race', gender, sexuality and so on – while itself claiming not to be part of that hierarchy and thus to be universal. It is because this ordering of difference depends on a distinction between those who claim to see with universal relevance, and those who are seen and categorized in particular ways, that Haraway claims it is intimately related to the oppressions and tyrannies of capitalism, colonialism, patriarchy and so on. Part of Haraway's critical project, then, is to examine in detail how certain institutions mobilize certain forms of visuality to see, and to order, the world. This dominant visuality denies the validity of other ways of visualizing social difference, but Haraway insists that there are indeed other ways of seeing the world, and she is especially interested in efforts to see social difference in non-hierarchical ways. For Haraway, as for many other writers, then, the dominant scopic regime of (post)modernity is neither a historical inevitability, nor is it uncontested. There are different ways of seeing the world, and the critical task is to differentiate between the social effects of those different visions.

The particular forms of representation produced by specific scopic regimes are important to understand, then, because they are intimately bound into social power relations. Although we will later hear some misgivings about some of the results of this sort of argument (see section 4.2 in this chapter), Haraway's (1991) argument makes clear the necessity of understanding what social relations produce, and are reproduced by, what forms of visuality, and the next section explores this argument more fully.

Before doing so, however, it is important to note that there is a dispersed but persistent body of work in the social sciences that uses various kinds of images as ways of answering research questions (questions which may not be directly concerned with visuality or visual culture), not by examining images but by making them. Both anthropology and human geography have used visual images as research tools for as long as they have been established as academic disciplines, mostly photographs, diagrams and film in the case of anthropology, and photos, maps and diagrams in the case of geography. Visual sociology as a distinct sub-discipline is a more recent development; although the earliest sociological journals carried photographs for a short period before the First World War, it was not until the 1960s that a book by an anthropologist encouraged some sociologists to pick up their cameras again (Collier 1967). Researchers in these fields are taking heart from the current interest in questions of visuality to argue with greater conviction than ever for the analytical power of visual materials produced as part of a research project (see, for example, Banks 2001; Emmison and Smith 2000; Knowles and Sweetman 2004; Pink 2006; Prosser 1998; van Leeuwen and Jewitt 2001). However, when social scientists are making their own images, their concern for the power relations in which those images are embedded takes a specific form: it becomes a discussion of research ethics which reflects on the power dynamics between the researcher, the researched and the images. Chapter 11 of this book examines both the arguments for making visual images as a means of answering research questions, and the question of research ethics in relation to that making.

2 'visual culture': the social conditions and effects of visual objects

Making images as a way of answering a research question is relatively rare in studies of visual culture however. Instead, visual culture critics have concentrated their energies on critically examining the effects of visual images already out there in the world, already part of visual culture, and Chapters 3 to 10 of this book discuss a range of methods for understanding such 'found' images. This body of work has developed from several different theoretical positions (Barnard 2001; Bird et al. 1996; Evans and Hall 1999). Much of it is concerned to interpret the meaning of visual images, though some focuses more on practices of visuality or on the agency of visual objects; there are many historical studies, although some dispute the possibility of a fully historical account of an image's effect; some studies are more closely aligned with established academic disciplines like art history or cultural studies than others; some are structuralist and others post-structuralist; most of their methods are qualitative. This diversity obviously makes generalizing about studies of visuality a difficult task.

Nevertheless, I am going to suggest that there are five aspects of the recent literature that engage with visual culture that I think are valuable for thinking about the social effects of images.

The first point I take from the literature on (or against) 'visual culture' is its concern for the way in which images visualize (or render invisible) social difference. As Fyfe and Law (1988: 1) say, 'a depiction is never just an illustration ... it is the site for the construction and depiction of social difference'. One of the central aims of 'the cultural turn' in the social sciences was to argue that social categories are not natural but instead are constructed. These constructions can take visual form. This point has been made most forcefully by feminist and postcolonial writers who have studied the ways femininity and blackness have been visualized. An example would be Paul Gilroy's (1987: 57–9) discussion of a poster used by the Conservative Party in Britain's 1983 General Election, reproduced in Figure 1.1.

The poster shows a young black man in a suit, with 'LABOUR SAYS HE'S BLACK. TORIES SAY HE'S BRITISH' as its headline text. Gilroy's discussion is detailed but his main point is that the poster offers a choice between being black and being British, not only in its text but also in its image. The fact that the black man is pictured wearing a suit suggests to Gilroy that 'blacks are being invited to forsake all that marks them out as culturally distinct before real Britishness can be guaranteed' (Gilroy 1987: 59). Gilroy is thus suggesting that this poster asks its viewers not to see blackness. However, he also points out that the poster depends on other stereotyped images (which it does not show) of young black men, particularly as muggers, to make its point about the acceptability of this besuited man. This poster thus plays in complex ways with both visible and invisible signs of racial difference. Hence Fyfe and Law's general prescription for a critical approach to the ways images can picture social power relations:

> To understand a visualisation is thus to enquire into its provenance and into the social work that it does. It is to note its principles of inclusion and exclusion, to detect the roles that it makes available, to understand the way in which they are distributed, and to decode the hierarchies and differences that it naturalises. (Fyfe and Law 1988: 1)

Looking carefully at images, then, entails, among other things, thinking about how they offer very particular visions of social categories such as class, gender, race, sexuality, able-bodiedness and so on.

Secondly, writers on visual culture, among others, are concerned not only with how images look, but how images are looked at. This is a key point made by Maria Sturken and Lisa Cartwright's (2001) book on visual culture, which they entitle *Practices of Looking*. They argue that what is important about images is not simply the image itself, but how it is seen by particular spectators who look in particular ways. Sturken and Cartwright (2001) take

With the Conservatives, there are no 'blacks', no 'whites', just people.

Conservatives believe that treating minorities as equals encourages the majority to treat them as equals.

Yet the Labour Party aim to treat you as a 'special case', as a group all on your own.

Is setting you apart from the rest of society a sensible way to overcome racial prejudice and social inequality?

The question is, should we really divide the British people instead of uniting them?

WHOSE PROMISES ARE YOU TO BELIEVE?

When Labour were in government, they promised to repeal Immigration Acts passed in 1962 and 1971. Both promises were broken.

This time, they are promising to throw out the British Nationality Act, which gives full and equal citizenship to everyone permanently settled in Britain.

But how do the Conservatives' promises compare?

We said that we'd abolish the 'SUS' law.

We kept our promise.

We said we'd recruit more coloured policemen, get the police back into the community, and train them for a better understanding of your needs.

We kept our promise.

PUTTING THE ECONOMY BACK ON ITS FEET.

The Conservatives have always said that the only long term answer to our economic problems was to conquer inflation.

Inflation is now lower than it's been for over a decade, keeping all prices stable, with the price of food now hardly rising at all.

Meanwhile, many businesses throughout Britain are recovering, leading to thousands of new jobs.

Firstly, in our traditional industries, but just as importantly in new technology areas such as microelectronics.

In other words, the medicine is working.

Yet Labour want to change everything, and put us back to square one.

They intend to increase taxation. They intend to increase the National Debt.

They promise import and export controls.

Cast your mind back to the last Labour government. Labour's methods didn't work then.

They won't work now.

A BETTER BRITAIN FOR ALL OF US.

The Conservatives believe that everyone wants to work hard and be rewarded for it.

Those rewards will only come about by creating a mood of equal opportunity for everyone in Britain, regardless of their race, creed or colour.

The difference you're voting for is this:

To the Labour Party, you're a black person.

To the Conservatives, you're a British Citizen.

Vote Conservative, and you vote for a more equal, more prosperous Britain.

LABOUR SAYS HE'S BLACK. TORIES SAY HE'S BRITISH.

CONSERVATIVE ☒

Figure 1.1

Conservative Party election poster, 1983 (Gilroy 1987: 58)

their inspiration on this point from an influential book written in 1972 by John Berger, called *Ways of Seeing*. Berger's argument there is important because he makes clear that images of social difference work not simply by what they show but also by the kind of seeing that they invite. He uses the expression **'ways of seeing'** to refer to the fact that 'we never look just at one thing; we are always looking at the relation between things and ourselves' (Berger 1972: 9). His best-known example is that of the genre of female nude

ways of seeing

She is not naked as she is.
She is naked as the spectator sees her.

Often – as with the favourite subject of Susannah and the Elders – this is the actual theme of the picture. We join the Elders to spy on Susannah taking her bath. She looks back at us looking at her.

The mirror was often used as a symbol of the vanity of woman. The moralizing, however, was mostly hypocritical.

In another version of the subject by Tintoretto, Susannah is looking at herself in a mirror. Thus she joins the spectators of herself.

You painted a naked woman because you enjoyed looking at her, you put a mirror in her hand and you called the painting *Vanity*, thus morally condemning the woman whose nakedness you had depicted for your own pleasure.

The real function of the mirror was otherwise. It was to make the woman connive in treating herself as, first and foremost, a sight.

The Judgement of Paris was another theme with the same inwritten idea of a man or men looking at naked women.

50   51

Figure 1.2
a double-page spread from John Berger's Ways of Seeing *(Berger 1972: 50–1)*

painting in Western art. He reproduces many examples of that genre (see Figure 1.2), pointing out as he does so the particular ways they represent women: as unclothed, as vain, as passive, as sexually alluring, as a spectacle to be assessed.

Berger insists though on who it is that does the assessing, who this kind of image was meant to allure:

> In the average European oil painting of the nude, the principal protagonist is never painted. He is the spectator in front of the painting and he is presumed to be a man. Everything is addressed to him. Everything must appear to be the result of his being there. It is for him that the figures have assumed their nudity. (Berger 1972: 54)

Thus, for Berger, understanding this particular genre of painting means understanding not only its representation of femininity, but its construction of masculinity too. And these representations are in their turn understood as part of a wider cultural construction of gendered difference. To quote Berger again:

> One might simplify this by saying: *men act* and *women appear*. Men look at women. Women watch themselves being looked at. This determines not only most relations between women and men but also the relation of women to themselves. The surveyor of woman in herself is male: the surveyed, female.

Thus she turns herself into an object – and most particularly an object of vision: a sight. (Berger 1972: 47, emphasis in original)

While later critics would want to modify aspects of Berger's argument – most obviously by noting that he assumes heterosexuality in his discussion of masculinity and femininity – many critics would concur with his general understanding of the connection between image and spectator. Images work by producing effects every time they are looked at. Taking an image seriously, then, also involves thinking about how it positions you, its viewer, in relation to it.

Thirdly, there is the emphasis in the very term 'visual culture' on the embeddedness of visual images in a wider culture. Now, 'culture', as Raymond Williams (1976) famously noted, is one of the two or three most complicated words in the English language. It has many connotations. Most pertinent to this discussion is the meaning it began to be given in various anthropological books written towards the end of the nineteenth century. In this usage, culture meant something like 'a whole way of life', and even from the brief discussion in this chapter so far you can see that some current writers are using the term visual culture in just this broad sense. Indeed, one of the first uses of the term 'visual culture', by Svetlana Alpers (1983: xxv), was precisely to emphasize the importance of visual images of all kinds to many aspects of seventeenth century Dutch society. In this sort of work, it is argued that a particular, historically specific visuality was central to a particular, ocularcentric culture. In using the notion of culture in this broad sense, however, certain analytical questions may become difficult to ask. In particular, culture as a whole way of life can slip rather easily into a notion of culture as simply a whole, and the issue of difference becomes obscured. Barbara Maria Stafford's (1996) celebration of the visual in 'our' society has been criticized by Hal Foster (1996) in just these terms. Stafford never specifies who the 'we' to which she refers actually is, and she thus ignores this visuality's possible exclusions as well as the particularities of its inclusions.

In order to be able to deal with questions of social difference and the power relations that sustain them, then, a notion of culture is required that can also address questions of social difference, social relations and social power. One means of keeping these sorts of differentiations in the field of visual culture in analytical focus is to think carefully about just who is able to see what and how, and with what effects. Berger's (1972) work is in some ways exemplary here. An image will depend for its effects on a certain way of seeing, as he argued in relation to female nude painting. But this effect is always embedded in particular cultural practices that are far more specific than 'a way of life'. So Berger talks about the ways in which nude paintings were commissioned and then displayed by their owners in his discussion of the way of seeing which they express. Describing a seventeenth century English example of the genre, he writes:

Nominally it might be a *Venus and Cupid*. In fact it is a portrait of one of
the king's mistresses, Nell Gwynne ... [Her] nakedness is not, however, an
expression of her own feelings; it is a sign of her submission to the owner's
feelings or demands. (The owner of both the woman and the painting.) The
painting, when the king showed it to others, demonstrated this submission
and his guests envied him. (Berger 1972: 52)

It was through this kind of use, by those particular sorts of people interpreting it in that kind of way, that this kind of painting achieved its effects. The
seeing of an image thus always takes place in a particular social context that
mediates its impact. It also always takes place in a specific location with its
own particular practices. That location may be a king's chamber, a Hollywood
cinema studio, an avant-garde art gallery, an archive, a sitting room, a street.
These different locations all have their own economics, their own disciplines,
their own rules for how their particular sort of spectator should behave,
including whether and how they should look, and all these affect how a particular image is seen too (for an early example of this sort of approach, see
Becker 1982). These specificities of practice are crucial in understanding how
an image has certain effects.

Fourthly, much of this work in visual culture argues that the particular
'audiences' (that might not always be the appropriate word) of an image will
bring their own interpretations to bear on its meaning and effect. Not all
audiences will be able or willing to respond to the way of seeing invited by a
particular image and its particular practices of display (Chapter 9 will discuss
this in more detail).

Finally, in all of this work there is an insistence that images themselves
have their own agency. In the words of Carol Armstrong (1996: 28), for
example, an image is 'at least potentially a site of resistance and recalcitrance,
of the irreducibly particular, and of the subversively strange and pleasurable',
while Christopher Pinney (2004: 8) suggests that the important question is
'not how images "look", but what they can "do"'. In the search for an
image's meaning, it is therefore important not to claim that it merely reflects
meanings made elsewhere – in newspapers, for example, or gallery catalogues. It is certainly true that visual images very often work in conjunction
with other kinds of representations. It is very unusual, for example, to
encounter a visual image unaccompanied by any text at all, whether spoken or
written (Armstrong 1998; Wollen 1970: 118); even the most abstract painting
in a gallery will have a written label on the wall giving certain information
about its making, and in certain sorts of galleries there are sheets of paper giving a price too, and these make a difference to how spectators will see that
painting. So although virtually all visual images are **multimodal** in this way –   **multimodal**
they always make sense in relation to other things, including written texts and
very often other images – they are not reducible to the meanings carried by
those other things. The colours of an oil painting, for example, or what

Barthes (1982) called the *punctum* of a photograph (see Chapter 5, section 3.3), will carry their own peculiar kinds of visual resistance, recalcitrance, argument, particularity, strangeness or pleasure.

Thus I take five major points from current debates about visual culture as important for understanding how images work: an image may have its *own visual effects* (so it is important to look very carefully at images); these effects, through the *ways of seeing* mobilized by the image, are crucial in the production and reproduction of visions of *social difference*; but these effects always intersect with the *social context of viewing* and with *the visualities spectators bring* to their viewing.

3 towards a critical visual methodology

Given this general approach to understanding the importance of images, I can now elaborate on what I think is necessary for a 'critical approach' to interpreting found visual images. (The implications of this approach in relation to the production of images as part of a research project are somewhat different, as I've already suggested, and will be discussed in Chapter 11.) A critical approach to visual culture:

- takes images seriously. While this might seem rather a paradoxical point to insist on, given all the work I have just mentioned that addresses visualities and visual objects, art historians of all sorts of interpretive hues continue to complain, often rightly, that social scientists do not look at images carefully enough. I argue here that it is necessary to look very carefully at visual images, and it is necessary to do so because they are not entirely reducible to their context. Visual representations have their own effects.
- thinks about the social conditions and effects of visual objects. As Griselda Pollock (1988: 7) says, 'cultural practices do a job which has major social significance in the articulation of meanings about the world, in the negotiation of social conflicts, in the production of social subjects'. Cultural practices like visual representations both depend on and produce social inclusions and exclusions, and a critical account needs to address both those practices and their cultural meanings and effects.
- considers your own way of looking at images. This is not an explicit concern in many studies of visual culture. However, if, as section 2 just argued, ways of seeing are historically, geographically, culturally and socially specific; and if watching your favourite movie on a DVD for the umpteenth time at home with a group of mates is not the same as studying it for a research project; then, as Mieke Bal (1996, 2003; Bal and Bryson 2001) for one has consistently argued, it is necessary to reflect on how you as a critic of visual images are looking. As Haraway (1991: 190) says, by thinking carefully about where we see from, 'we might become answerable for what we learn how to see'. Haraway also comments that this is not a straightforward task (see also Rogoff 1998; Rose 1997). Several of the chapters will return to this issue of reflexivity in order to examine what it might entail further.

The aim of this book is to give you some practical guidance on how to do these things; but I hope it is already clear from this introduction that this is not simply a technical question of method. There are also important analytical debates going on about visualities. In this book, I use these particular criteria for a critical visual methodology to evaluate both theoretical arguments and the methods discussed in Chapters 3 to 10.

Having very briefly sketched a critical approach to images that I find useful to work with and which will structure this book's accounts of various methods, the next section starts more explicitly to address the question of methodology.

4 towards some methodological tools: sites and modalities

As I have already noted, the theoretical sources which have produced the recent interest in visual culture are diverse. This section will try to acknowledge some of that diversity, while also developing a framework for approaching the almost equally diverse range of methods that critics of visual culture have used.

Interpretations of visual images broadly concur that there are three **sites** at which the meanings of an image are made: the site(s) of the **production** of an image, the site of the **image** itself, and the site(s) where it is seen by various **audiences**. I also want to suggest that each of these sites has three different aspects. These different aspects I will call **modalities**, and I suggest that there are three of these that can contribute to a critical understanding of images:

sites
production
image
audiences
modalities

- **technological.** Mirzoeff (1998: 1) defines a visual technology as 'any form of apparatus designed either to be looked at or to enhance natural vision, from oil paintings to television and the Internet'.

  technological

- **compositional.** Compositionality refers to the specific material qualities of an image or visual object. When an image is made, it draws on a number of formal strategies: content, colour and spatial organization, for example. Often, particular forms of these strategies tend to occur together, so that, for example, Berger (1972) can define the Western art tradition painting of the nude in terms of its specific compositional qualities. Chapter 3 will elaborate the notion of composition in relation to paintings.

  compositional

- **social.** This is very much a shorthand term. What I mean it to refer to are the range of economic, social and political relations, institutions and practices that surround an image and through which it is seen and used.

  social

These modalities, since they are found at all three sites, also suggest that the distinctions between sites are less clear than my subsections here might imply.

Many of the theoretical disagreements about visual culture, visualities and visual objects can be understood as disputes over which of these sites and

Figure 1.3

modalities are most important, how and why. The following subsections will explore each site and its modalities further, and will examine some of these disagreements in a little detail. To focus the discussion, and to give you a chance to explore how these sites and modalities intersect, I will often refer to the photograph reproduced in Figure 1.3. Take a good look at it now and note down your immediate reactions. Then see how your views of it alter as the following subsections discuss its sites and modalities.

4.1 the site of production

All visual representations are made in one way or another, and the circumstances of their production may contribute towards the effect they have.

Some writers argue this case very strongly. Some, for example, would argue that the *technologies* used in the making of an image determine its form, meaning and effect. Clearly, visual technologies do matter to how an image looks and therefore to what it might do and what might be done to it. Here is Berger describing the uniqueness of oil painting:

> What distinguishes oil painting from any other form of painting is its special ability to render the tangibility, the texture, the lustre, the solidity of what it depicts. It defines the real as that which you can put your hands on. (Berger 1972: 88)

For a particular study it may be important to understand the technologies used in the making of particular images, and at the end of the book you will find some references which will help you do that.

In the case of the photograph here, it is perhaps important to understand what kind of camera, film and developing process the photographer was using, and what that made visually possible and what impossible. The photograph was made in 1948, by which time cameras were relatively lightweight and film was highly sensitive to light. This meant that, unlike in earlier periods, a photographer did not have to find subjects that would stay still for seconds or even minutes in order to be pictured. By 1948, the photographer could have stumbled on this scene and 'snapped' it almost immediately. Thus part of the effect of the photograph – its apparent spontaneity, a snapshot – is enabled by the technology used.

Another aspect of this photograph, and of photographs more generally, is also often attributed to its technology: its apparent truthfulness. Here, though, it must be noted that critical opinion is divided. Some critics (for example Roland Barthes, whose arguments are discussed in section 3.2 of Chapter 5, and Christopher Pinney, discussed in Chapter 10) suggest that photographic technology does indeed capture what was really there when the shutter snapped. Others find the notion that 'the camera never lies' harder to accept. From its very invention, photography has been understood by some of its practitioners as a technology that simply records the way things really look. But also from the beginning, photographs have been seen as magical and strange (Slater 1995). This debate has suggested to some critics that claims of 'truthful' photographic representation have been constructed. Chapter 8 will look at some Foucauldian histories of photography which make this case with some vigour. Maybe we see the Doisneau photograph as a snapshot of real life, then, more because we expect photos to show us snippets of truth than because they actually do. But this photo might have been posed: the photographer who took this one certainly posed others which nevertheless have the same 'real' look (Doisneau 1991). Also, as Griselda Pollock (1988: 85–7) points out in her discussion of this photograph, its status as a snapshot of real life is also established in part by its content, especially the boys playing in the street, just out of focus; surely if it had been posed those boys would have been in focus? Thus the apparently technological effects on the production of a visual image need careful consideration, because some may not be straightforwardly technological at all.

The second modality of an image's production is to do with its *compositionality*. Some writers argue that it is the conditions of an image's production that govern its compositionality. This argument is perhaps most effectively made in relation to the **genre** of images a particular image fits (perhaps rather uneasily) into. Genre is a way of classifying visual images into certain groups. Images that belong to the same genre share certain features. A particular genre will share a specific set of meaningful objects and locations,

genre

and, in the case of movies for example, have a limited set of narrative problematics. Thus John Berger can define 'female nude painting' as a particular genre of Western painting because these are pictures which represent naked women as passive, available and desirable through a fairly consistent set of compositional devices. A certain kind of traditional art history would see the way that a particular artist makes reference to other paintings in the same genre (and perhaps in other genres) as he or she works at a canvas as a crucial aspect of understanding the final painting. It helps to make sense of the significance of elements of an individual image if you know that some of them recur repeatedly in other images. You may need to refer to other images of the same genre in order to explicate aspects of the one you are interested in. Many books on visual images focus on one particular genre.

The photograph under consideration here fits into one genre but has connections to some others, and knowing this allows us to make sense of various aspects of this rich visual document. The genre the photo fits most obviously into, I think, is that of 'street photography'. This is a body of work with connections to another photography genre, that of the documentary (Hamilton 1997; see also Pryce 1997 for a discussion of documentary photography). Documentary photography originally tended to picture poor, oppressed or marginalized individuals, often as part of reformist projects to show the horror of their lives and thus inspire change. The aim was to be as objective and accurate as possible in these depictions. However, since the apparent horror was being shown to audiences who had the power to pressure for change, documentary photography usually pictures the relatively powerless to the relatively powerful. It has thus been accused of voyeurism and worse. Street photography shares with documentary photography the desire to picture life as it apparently is. But street photography does not want its viewers to say 'oh how terrible' and maybe 'we must do something about that'. Rather, its way of seeing invites a response that is more like, 'oh how extraordinary, isn't life richly marvellous'. This seems to me to be the response that this photograph, and many others taken by the same photographer, asks for. We are meant to smile wryly at a glimpse of a relationship, exposed to us for just a second. This photograph was almost certainly made to sell to a photo-magazine like *Vu* or *Life* or *Picture Post* for publication as a visual joke, funny and not too disturbing for the readers of these magazines. This constraint on its production thus affected its genre.

The third modality of production is what I have called the *social*. Here again, there is a body of work that argues that these are the most important factors in understanding visual images. Some argue that it is the economic processes in which cultural production is embedded that shape visual imagery. One of the most eloquent exponents of this argument is David Harvey. Certain photographs and films play a key role in his 1989 book *The Condition of Postmodernity*. He argues that these visual representations exemplify postmodernity. Like many other commentators, Harvey defines postmodernity in part through the importance of visual images to postmodern culture, commenting on 'the mobilization of fashion, pop art, television and other forms of media image, and the variety of urban life styles that have become part and parcel of daily life under capitalism' (Harvey 1989: 63). He sees the qualities of this mobilization as ephemeral, fluid, fleeting and superficial: 'there has emerged an attachment to surface rather than roots, to collage rather than in-depth work, to superimposed quoted images rather than worked surfaces, to a collapsed sense of time and space rather than solidly achieved cultural artefact' (Harvey 1989: 61). And Harvey has an explanation for this which focuses on the latter characteristics. He suggests that contemporary capitalism is organizing itself in ways that are indeed compressing time and collapsing space. He argues that capitalism is more and more 'flexible' in its organization of production techniques, labour markets and consumption niches, and that this has depended on the increased mobility of capital and information; moreover, the importance of consumption niches has generated the increasing importance of advertising, style and spectacle in the selling of goods. In his Marxist account, both these characteristics are reflected in cultural objects – in their superficiality, their ephemerality – so that the latter are nothing but 'the cultural logic of late capitalism' (Harvey 1989: 63; Jameson 1984).

To analyse images through this lens you will need to understand contemporary economic processes in a synthetic manner. However, those writers who emphasize the importance of broad systems of production to the meaning of images sometimes deploy methodologies that pay rather little attention to the details of particular images. Harvey (1989), for example, has been accused of misunderstanding the photographs and films he interprets in his book – and of economic determinism (Deutsche 1991).

Other accounts of the centrality of what I am calling the social to the production of images depend on rather more detailed analyses of particular industries which produce visual images. David Morley and Kevin Robins (1995), for example, focus on the audiovisual industries of Europe in their study of how those industries are implicated in contemporary constructions of 'Europeanness'. They point out that the European Union is keen to encourage a Europe-wide audiovisual industry partly on economic grounds, to compete with US and Japanese conglomerates. But they also argue that the EU has a cultural agenda too, which works at 'improving mutual knowledge among European peoples and increasing their consciousness of the life and destiny they have in common' (Morley and Robins 1995: 3), and thus elides differences within Europe while producing certain kinds of differences between Europe and the rest of the world. Like Harvey, then, Morley and Robins pay attention to both the economic and the cultural aspects of contemporary cultural practices. Unlike Harvey, however, Morley and Robins do not reduce the latter to the former. And this is in part because they rely on a more fine-grained analytical method than Harvey, paying careful attention to particular companies and products, as well as understanding how the industry as a whole works.

Another aspect of the social production of an image is the social and/or political identities that are mobilized in its making. Peter Hamilton's (1997) discussion of the sort of photography of which Figure 1.3 is a part explores its dependence on certain postwar ideas about the French working class. Here though I will focus on another social identity articulated through this particular photograph. Here is a passage from an introduction to a book on street photography that evokes the 'crazy, cockeyed' viewpoint of the street photographer:

> It's like going into the sea and letting the waves break over you. You feel the power of the sea. On the street each successive wave brings a whole new cast of characters. You take wave after wave, you bathe in it. There is something exciting about being in the crowd, in all that chance and change. It's tough out there, but if you can keep paying attention something will reveal itself, just a split second, and then there's a crazy cockeyed picture! ... 'Tough' meant it was an uncompromising image, something that came from your gut, out of instinct, raw, of the moment, something that couldn't be described in any other way. So it was TOUGH. Tough to like, tough to see, tough to make, tough to understand. The tougher they were the more beautiful they became. It was our language. (Westerbeck and Meyerowitz 1994: 2–3)

This rich passage allows us to say a bit more about the importance of a certain kind of identity to the production of the photograph under discussion here. To do street photography, it says, the photographer has to be there, in the street, tough enough to survive, tough enough to overcome the threats posed by the street. There is a kind of macho power being celebrated in that account of street photography, in its reiteration of 'toughness'. This sort of photography also endows its viewer with a kind of toughness over the image because it allows the viewer to remain in control, positioned as somewhat distant from and superior to what the image shows us. We have more information than the people pictured, and we can therefore smile at them. This particular photograph even places a window between us and its subjects; we peer at them from the same hidden vantage point just like the photographer did. There is a kind of distance established between the photographer/ audience and the people photographed, then, reminiscent of the patriarchal way of seeing that has been critiqued by Haraway (1991), among others (see section 1 of this chapter). But since this toughness is required only in order to record something that will reveal itself, this passage is also an example of the photograph being seen as a truthful instrument of simple observation, and of the erasure of the specificity of the photographer himself; the photographer is there but only to carry his camera and react quickly when the moment comes, just like our photographer snapping his subject. Again, this erasure of the particularity of a visuality is what Haraway (1991) critiques as, among other things, patriarchal. It is therefore significant that of the many photographers whose work is reproduced in that book on street photography, very few are women. You need to be a man, or at least masculine, to do street photography, apparently. However, this passage's evocation of 'gut' and 'instinct' is interesting in this respect, since these are qualities of embodiment and non-rationality that are often associated with femininity. Thus, if masculinity might be said to be central to the production of street photography, it is a particular kind of masculinity.

Finally, it should be noted that there is one element active at the site of production that many social scientists interested in the visual would pay very little attention to: the individual often described as the author (or artist or director or sculptor or so on) of the visual image under consideration. The notion that the most important aspect in understanding a visual image is what its maker intended to show is sometimes called **auteur theory**. However, most **auteur theory** of the recent work on visual matters is uninterested in the intentionality of an image's maker. There are a number of reasons for this (Hall 1997b: 25; see also the focus in Chapter 3, section 3). First, as we have seen, there are those who argue that other modalities of an image's production account for its effects. Secondly, there are those who argue that, since the image is always made and seen in relation to other images, this wider visual context is more significant for what the image means than what the artist thought they were doing. Roland Barthes (1977: 145–6) made this argument when he proclaimed 'the death of the author'. And thirdly, there are those who insist that the most important site at which the meaning of an image is made is not its author, or indeed its production or itself, but its audiences, who bring their own ways of seeing and other knowledges to bear on an image and in the process make their own meanings from it. So I can tell you that the man who took this photograph in 1948 was Robert Doisneau, and that information will allow you, as it allowed me, to find out more information about his life and work. But the literature I am drawing on here would not suggest that an intimate, personal biography of Doisneau is necessary in order to interpret his photographs. Instead, it would read his life, as I did, in order to understand the modalites that shaped the production of his photographs.

4.2 the site of the image

The second site at which an image's meanings are made is the image itself. Every image has a number of formal components. As the previous section suggested, some of these components will be caused by the *technologies* used to make, reproduce or display the image. For example, the black and white tonalities of the Doisneau photo are a result of his choice of film and processing techniques. Other components of an image will depend on *social* practices. The previous section also noted how the photograph under discussion might look the way it does in part because it was made to be sold to particular magazines. More generally, the economic circumstances under which Doisneau worked were such that all his photographs were affected by them. He began working as a photographer in the publicity department of a pharmacy, and then worked for the car manufacturer Renault in the 1930s (Doisneau 1990). Later he worked for *Vogue* and for the Alliance press agency. That is, he very often pictured things in order to get them sold: cars, fashions. And all his life he had to make images to sell; he was a freelance photographer needing to make a living from his photographs. Thus his photography showed commodities and was itself a commodity (see Ramamurthy 1997 for a discussion of photography and commodity culture). Perhaps this accounts for his fascination with objects, with emotion, and with the emotions objects can arouse. Just like an advertiser, he was investing objects with feelings through his images, and, again like an advertiser, could not afford to offend his potential buyers.

However, as section 2 above noted, many writers on visual culture argue that an image may have its own effects which exceed the constraints of its production (and reception). Some would argue, for example, that it is the particular qualities of the photographic image that make us understand its technology in particular ways, rather than the reverse; or that it is those qualities that shape the social modality in which it is embedded rather than the other way round. The modality most important to an image's own effects, however, is often argued to be its *compositionality*.

Pollock's (1988: 85) discussion of the Doisneau photograph is very clear about the way in which aspects of its compositionality contribute towards its way of seeing (she draws on an earlier essay by Mary Ann Doane [1982]). She stresses the spatial organization of looks in the photograph, and argues that 'the photograph almost uncannily delineates the sexual politics of looking'. These are the politics of looking that Berger explored in his discussion of the Western tradition of female nude painting. 'One might simplify this by saying: *men act* and *women appear*', says Berger (1972: 47). In this photograph, the man looks at an image of a woman, while another woman looks but at nothing, apparently. Moreover, Pollock insists, the viewer of this photograph is pulled into complicity with these looks.

> it is [the man's] gaze which defines the problematic of the photograph and it erases that of the woman. She looks at nothing that has any meaning for the spectator. Spatially central, she is negated in the triangulation of looks between the man, the picture of the fetishized woman and the spectator, who is thus enthralled to a masculine viewing position. To get the joke, we must be complicit with his secret discovery of something better to look at. The joke, like all dirty jokes, is at the woman's expense. (Pollock 1988: 47)

Pollock is discussing the organization of looks in the photograph and between the photograph and us, its viewers. She argues that this aspect of its formal qualities is the most important for its effect (although she has also mentioned the effect of spontaneity created by the out-of-focus boys playing in the street behind the couple, remember).

Such discussions of the compositional modality of the site of the image can produce persuasive accounts of a photograph's effect on its viewers. It is necessary to pause here, however, and note that there is a significant debate among critics of visual culture about how to theorize an image's effects. As I've already noted, some critics, often art historians, are concerned that many discussions of visual culture do not pay enough attention to the specificities of particular images. As a result they argue, visual images are reduced to nothing more than reflections of their cultural context. Pollock (1988: 25–30) herself has argued against such a strategy, and indeed her interpretation of the Doisneau photograph depends absolutely on paying very close attention to its visual and spatial structure and effects. However, hers is only one way to approach the question of an image's effects, and other critics advocate other ways. Caroline van Eck and Edward Winters (2005), for example, argue that the essence of a visual experience is its sensory qualities, qualities studiously ignored by Pollock, in her essay on Doisneau at least. Van Eck and Winters (2005: 4) emphasize that 'there is a subjective "feel" that is ineliminable in our seeing something', and that appreciation of this 'feel' should be as much part of understanding images as the interpretation of their meaning, even though they find it impossible to convey fully in words (see also Elkins 1998, Corbett 2005). Moreover, emerging from some critical quarters is a certain hesitation about full-on criticism of images' complicity with dominant ways of seeing class, 'race', gender, sexuality and so on. W.J.T. Mitchell (1996: 74), for example, has called this sort of work 'both easy and ineffectual' because it changes nothing of what it criticizes. Michael Ann Holly (in Cheetham, Holly and Moxey 2005: 88) has also worried that the urge to study visual culture simply in order to critique it seems 'to have sacrificed a sense of awe at the power of an overwhelming visual experience, wherever it might be found, in favour of the "political" connections that lie beneath the surface of this or that representation'. 'To me,' Holly continues, 'that's neither good "research" nor serious understanding.' Holly even suggests that the theoretical rigour with which so many visual culture studies are conducted may also have a deadening effect on images. 'There are many times', she says, 'when I yearn for something that is "in excess of research"' (Cheetham et al. 2005: 88).

What might this 'something in excess of research' be for which Holly yearns? All of these suspicions about the 'political' critique of images depend on claims that, in one way or another, visual materials have some sort of agency which exceeds, or is different from, the meanings brought to them by their producers and their viewers, including their visual culture critics. This is an interesting thread twisting its way through studies of visual culture, since it suggests that culture – understood as cultural meanings and practices – may not be an adequate term to address fully all aspects of visualities. For if we agree that images can have their own effects, this is not always because they produce their own meanings. Rather, it may also be because they do something unique to their visuality which is also something excessive to meaning itself (hence van Eck and Winter's [2005: 4] suggestion that it might not be possible to describe this effect in words). There are different understandings of this excess beyond the cultural, though. For van Eck and Winter (2005), as we have noted, it is the sensory and experiential nature of seeing (see also Mitchell 1996). For Ernst van Alphen (2005: 194–5), it is an image doing its own thinking, which presents puzzles to us on its own terms so that it becomes 'not only the object of framing – which, obviously, is also true and important – but it also functions, in turn, as a frame for cultural thought'. For Alfred Gell (1998: 6), it is about the way that art objects (specifically) are 'a system of action, intended to change the world rather than encode symbolic propositions about it'. For now, though, it is enough to note that there are a range of ways in which visual culture theorists have conceptualized the workings of the site of the image itself; subsequent chapters will develop their methodological implications.

4.3 the site of audiencing

You might well not agree with Pollock's interpretation of the Doisneau photograph, and I will discuss some of the other interpretations of the image made by students in some of my classes in this section. Your disagreement, though, is the final site at which the meanings and effects of an image are made, for you are an audience of that photograph and, like all audiences, you bring to it your own ways of seeing and other kinds of knowledges. John Fiske (1994), for one, suggests that this is the most important site at which an

audiencing   image's meanings are made, and uses the term **audiencing** to refer to the process by which a visual image has its meanings renegotiated, or even rejected, by particular audiences watching in specific circumstances. Once again, I would suggest that there are three aspects to that process.

The first is the *compositionality* of the image. Several of the methods that we will encounter in this book assume that the formal arrangement of the elements of a picture will dictate how an image is seen by its audiences. The notion of ways of seeing assumes just this. So too does Pollock when she claims that the Doisneau image is always seen as a joke against the woman, because the organization of looks by the photograph coincides with, and reiterates, a scopic regime that allows only men to look. It is important, I think, to consider very carefully the organization of the image, because that does have an effect on the spectator who sees it. There is no doubt, I think, that the Doisneau photograph pulls the viewer into a complicity with the man and his furtive look. But that does not necessarily mean the spectator sympathizes with that look. Indeed, many of my students often comment that the photograph shows the man (agreeing with Pollock, then, that the photograph is centred on the man) as a 'lech', a 'dirty old man', a 'voyeur'. That is, they see him as the point of the photograph, but that does not make the photograph an expression of a way of seeing that they approve of. Moreover, that man and his look might not be the only thing that a particular viewer sees in that photograph, as I'll suggest in a moment. Thus audiences make their own interpretations of an image.

Those theories that privilege the *technological* site at which an image's meanings are made similarly often imply that the technology used to make and display an image will control an audience's reaction. Again, this might be an important point to consider. How does seeing a particular movie on a television screen differ from seeing it on a large cinema screen with 3D glasses? How different is a reproduction in a book of an altarpiece from seeing the original in a church? Clearly at one level these are technological questions concerning the size, colour and texture, for example, of the image. At another level though they raise a number of other, more important questions about how an image is looked at differently in different contexts. You don't do the same things while you're flicking through a book of renaissance altarpieces at home as you do when you're in a church looking at one. While you're looking at a book you can be listening to music, eating, comparing one plate to another, answering the phone; in a church you may have to dress a certain way to get in, remain quiet, not get very close, not actually be able to see it at all well, let alone touch the image. Again, the audiencing of an image thus appears very important to its meanings.

The *social* is thus perhaps the most important modality for understanding the audiencing of images. In part this is a question of the different social practices which structure the viewing of particular images in particular places. Visual images are always practised in particular ways, and different practices are often associated with different kinds of images in different kinds of spaces. A cinema, a television in a living room and a canvas in a modern art gallery do not invite the same ways of seeing. This is both because, let's say, a Hollywood movie, a TV soap and an abstract expressionist canvas do not have the same compositionality or depend on the same technologies, but also because they are not done in the same way. Popcorn is not sold by or taken into galleries, generally, and usually soaps are not watched in contemplative, reverential isolation. Different ways of relating to visual images define the cinema and the gallery, for example, as different kinds of spaces. You don't applaud a sculpture the way you might do a film, for example, but applauding might depend on the sort of film and the sort of cinema you see it in. This point about the spaces and practices of display is especially important to bear in mind given the increasing mobility of images now; images appear and reappear in all sorts of places, and those places, with their particular ways of spectating, mediate the visual effects of those images.

Thus, to return to our example, you are looking at the Doisneau photograph in a particular way because it is reproduced in this book and is being used here as a pedagogic device; you're looking at it often (I hope – although this work on audiences suggests you may well not be bothering to do that) and looking at in different ways depending on the issues I'm raising. You would be doing this photograph very differently if you had been sent it in the format of a postcard (and many of Doisneau's photographs have been reproduced as greetings cards, postcards and posters). Maybe you would merely have glanced at it before reading the message on its reverse far more avidly; if the card had been sent by a lover, maybe you would see it as some sort of comment on your relationship ... and so on.

There is actually surprisingly little discussion of these sorts of topics in the literature on visual culture, even though 'audience studies', which most often explore how people watch television and videos in their homes, has been an important part of cultural studies for some time. There is also an important and relevant body of work in anthropology that treats visual images as objects, often as commodities, and sees what effects they have when such objects are gifted, traded or sold in different contexts. Chapters 9 and 10 of this book will explore these two approaches to the site of audiencing in more detail. As we will see, especially in Chapter 9, these approaches can rely on research methods that pay little attention to the images themselves. This is because many of those concerned with audiences argue that audiences are the most important aspect of an image's meaning. They thus tend, like those studies which privilege the social modality of the site of production of imagery, to use methods that do not address visual imagery directly.

The second and related aspect of the social modality of audiencing images concerns the social identities of those doing the watching. As Chapter 9 will discuss in more detail, there have been many studies which have explored how different audiences interpret the same visual images in very different ways, and these differences have been attributed to the different social identities of the viewers concerned.

In terms of the Doisneau photograph, it seemed to me that as I showed it to students over a number of years, their responses have changed in relation to some changes in ways of representing gender and sexuality in the wider visual culture of Britain from the late 1980s to the late 1990s. When I first showed it, students would often agree with Pollock's interpretation, although sometimes it would be suggested that the man looked rather henpecked and that this somehow justified his harmless fun. It would have been interesting to see if this opinion came significantly more often from male students than female, since the work cited above would assume that the gender of its audiences in particular would make a difference to how this photo was seen. As time went on, though, another response was made more frequently. And that was to wonder what the woman is looking at. For in a way, Pollock's argument replicates what she criticizes: the denial of vision to the woman. Instead, more and more of my students started to speculate on what the woman in the photo is admiring. Women students began quite often to suggest that of course what she is appreciating is a gorgeous semi-naked man, and sometimes they say, maybe it's a gorgeous woman. These later responses depended on three things, I think. One was the increasing representation over those few years of male bodies as objects of desire in advertising (especially, it seemed to me, in perfume adverts); we were more used now to seeing men on display as well as women. Another development was what I would very cautiously describe as 'girlpower'; the apparently increasing ability of young women to say what they want, what they really really want. And a third development might have been the fashionability in Britain of what was called 'lesbian chic'. Now of course, it would take a serious study (using some of the methods I will explore in this book) to sustain any of these suggestions, but I offer them here, tentatively, as an example of how an image can be read differently by different audiences: in this case, by different genders and at two slightly different historical moments.

There are, then, two aspects of the social modality of audiencing: the social practices of spectating and the social identities of the spectators. Some work, however, has drawn these two aspects of audiencing together to argue that only certain sorts of people do certain sorts of images in particular ways. Sociologists Pierre Bourdieu and Alain Darbel (1991), for example, have undertaken large-scale surveys of the visitors to art galleries, and have argued that the dominant way of visiting art galleries – walking around quietly from painting to painting, appreciating the particular qualities of each one, contemplating them in quiet awe – is a practice associated with middle-class visitors to galleries. As they say, 'museum visiting increases very strongly with increasing level of education, and is almost exclusively the domain of the cultivated classes' (Bourdieu and Darbel 1991: 14). They are quite clear that this is not because those who are not middle-class are incapable of appreciating art. Bourdieu and Darbel (1991: 39) say that, 'considered as symbolic goods, works of art only exist for those who have the means of appropriating them, that is, of deciphering them'. To appreciate works of art you need to be able to understand, or to decipher, their style – otherwise they will mean little to you. And it is only the middle classes who have been educated to be competent in that deciphering. Thus they suggest, rather, that those who are not middle-class are not taught to appreciate art; that although the curators of galleries and the 'cultivated classes' would deny it, they have learnt what to do in galleries and they are not sharing their lessons with anyone else. Art galleries therefore exclude certain groups of people. Indeed, in other work Bourdieu (1984) goes further and suggests that competence in such techniques of appreciation actually defines an individual as middle-class. In order to be properly middle-class, one must know how to appreciate art, and how to perform that appreciation appropriately (no popcorn please).

The Doisneau photograph is an interesting example here again. Many reproductions of his photographs could be bought in Britain from a chain of shops called Athena (which went out of business some time ago). Athena also sold posters of pop stars, of cute animals, of muscle-bound men holding babies and so on. Students in my classes would be rather divided over whether buying such images from Athena was something they would do or not – whether it showed you had (a certain kind of) taste or not. I find Doisneau's photographs rather sentimental and tricksy, rather stereotyped – and I rarely bought anything from Athena to stick on the walls of the rooms I lived in when I was a student. Instead, I preferred postcards of modernist paintings picked up on my summer trips to European art galleries. This was a genuine preference but I also know that I wanted the people who visited my room to see that I was ... well, someone who went to European art galleries. And students tell me that they often think about the images with which they decorate their rooms in the same manner. We know what we like, but we also know that other people will be looking at the images we choose to display. Our use of images, our appreciation of certain kinds of imagery, performs a social function as well as an aesthetic one. It says something about who we are and how we want to be seen.

These issues surrounding the audiencing of images are often researched using methods that are quite common in qualitative social science research: interviews, ethnography and so on. This will be explored in Chapters 9 and 10. However, as I have noted above, it is possible and necessary to consider the viewing practices of one spectator without using such techniques because that spectator is you. It is important to consider how you are looking at a particular image and to write that into your interpretation, or perhaps express it visually. Exactly what this call to reflexivity means is a question that will recur throughout this book.

5 summary

Visual imagery is never innocent; it is always constructed through various practices, technologies and knowledges. A critical approach to visual images is therefore needed: one that thinks about the agency of the image, considers the social practices and effects of its viewing, and reflects on the specificity of that viewing by various audiences including the academic critic. The meanings of an image or set of images are made at three sites – the sites of production, the image itself and its audiencing – and there are three modalities to each of these sites: technological, compositional and social. Theoretical debates about how to interpret images can be understood as debates over which of these sites and modalities is most important for understanding an image, and why. These debates affect the methodology that is most appropriately brought to bear on particular images; all of the methods discussed in this book are better at focusing on some sites and modalities than others.

With these general points in mind, the next chapter explains some different ways to use this book.

Further reading

Stuart Hall in his essay 'The work of representation' (1997b) offers a very clear discussion of recent debates about culture, representation and power. A useful collection of some of the key texts that have contributed towards the field of visual culture has been put together by Jessica Evans and Stuart Hall as *Visual Culture: The Reader* (1999). Sturken and Cartwright's *Practices of Looking* (2001) is an excellent overview of both theoretical approaches to visual culture, and of many of its empirical manifestations in the affluent world today.

2
how to use this book

The previous chapter's discussion of what could constitute a critical visual methodology might have seemed rather abstract. However, it plays a key role in this book, because it provides the criteria with which I will assess the strengths and weaknesses of the methods this book examines. Each of these methods is discussed in one of the following chapters (apart from Chapter 11, which discusses several different methods) by examining some particularly revealing examples of its application. But how, you may be wondering, do you start to work out which of these methods is best suited to your particular research concerns? In other words, how are you going to make use of this book?

I imagine that the users of this book might be of two broad types: those that approach it comprehensively, and those that approach it selectively.

Some readers may want to read this book from beginning to end, evaluating all the methods it discusses, carefully assessing my arguments, and reaching their own decision about which method best suits their purposes. You are my 'comprehensive readers'. I am sure many authors dream of such thorough and attentive readers; however, authors are also readers themselves, and we know that there is another, and probably far more common approach to books: reading them selectively. If you are a selective reader, that might be because you already have a sense of what your analytical approach to visual culture is and, therefore, which sites and modalities you want to investigate. Or, you might be a selective reader because you've already found some images you want to work with, and you want to know what's the best method to work on them with. The next two sections suggest how each of you might best use this book.

1 reading this book selectively on the basis of sites and modalities

If you are doing this, you have already done enough preparatory reading to have a sense of which site(s) of visuality you are interested in, whether that is the production of image, the image itself, or its audiencing, and you want to know which methods are most appropriate for focusing on it. After all, if you think that the audience is the most important site at which the meaning of an image is made, and that the social is that site's most important modality (these are theoretical choices), there is no point inadvertently choosing a method that focuses mostly on the production processes or the technologies of the image you are concerned with.

Almost all the methods discussed here focus on some sites and modalities and not others. There are very few studies of visual culture that attempt to examine all the sites and modalities outlined in the previous chapter in equal depth; most are driven by their theoretical logics to concentrate on one site in particular. Some of those that do examine more than one site suffer (I think) from a certain analytical incoherence, as I suggest in Chapter 4; others, like those examined in Chapter 10, are analytically coherent but researchers rarely have the time, resources or inclination to pursue all sites and modalities. Thus, for both practical and theoretical reasons, engaging with the debates in visual culture means deciding which site and which modalities you think are most important in explaining the effect of an image.

Figure 2.1 is an attempt to suggest which of the various methods discussed in this book focus most directly on which sites and modalities. Locate the site/modality you're most interested in on the diagram, and see what methods it suggests are most appropriate. You can then turn to the appropriate chapter.

It is important to realize, though, that you do not then have to slavishly follow the method indicated in Figure 2.1. For example, if you're interested in the site of audiencing in its social modality, the obvious methodological route would be to follow audience studies and use a combination of interviews and ethnography. However, they are not the only productive methodologies that might be deployed; Charles Goodwin (2001), for example, uses ethnomethodology (a method not in fact discussed in this book) to produce a very fine-grained account of how looking is structured in highly skilled ways by people in their everyday interactions. Nonetheless, beginning with the sort of method most commonly used with the materials you are interested in will at least give you a starting point for thinking about what method might work best for you.

2 reading this book selectively on the basis of having found some images

On the other hand, you may want to read this book selectively because you've found some images that you want to explore, or you have a question about some aspect of contemporary or historical ways of seeing that you want to try to answer. In which case, you might find it most helpful to begin by looking at the method that has been used most often in relation to the material you have.

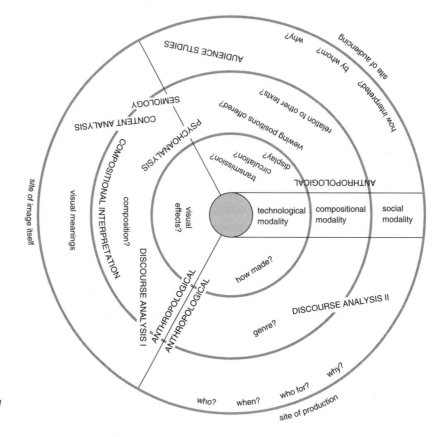

Figure 2.1
*sites, modalities
and methods for
interpreting found
visual materials*

Many of the methods discussed in this book tend to have been applied more to some sorts of images than others. Sometimes there is a fairly obvious, if not always watertight, reason for this. For example, the anthropological approach to images as visual objects examined in Chapter 10 has looked more at photographs and fine artworks than at other kinds of visual materials. This is for two reasons, I think. One is that these scholars found much of their theoretical inspiration in anthropological theories of exchange, and hence are very interested in the mobility of visual objects; and certain sorts of photos and artworks are obviously objects that can and do travel particularly easily and often. A second reason is that this work has a strong interest in the impact of colonialism on patterns and processes of exchange, and anthropological photographs and the trade in so-called 'primitive' or indigenous art are excellent examples with which to work towards a postcolonial reading of visual culture. Other examples of particular methods being deployed in relation to specific sorts of visual materials are less easy to understand, however. For example, audience studies, discussed in Chapter 9, have focused almost entirely on the audiencing of TV programmes and videos. Why? I don't

Table 2.1   *Found visual materials and the methods usually used*
for interpretation

television programmes	audience studies
fine art paintings	compositional interpretation
advertising, fine art paintings	semiology
films	psychoanalysis
photographs and fine art objects	an anthropological approach
institutions that display visual images and objects, for example museums and art galleries	discourse analysis II
a wide range of still and moving images, including book illustrations, maps, photographs, paintings and cartoons	discourse analysis I
any sort of images when there are large numbers of them	content analysis

know. I cannot see any particular reason why this should be the case; indeed, examining the interpretive work done by audiences of films or glossy magazines or museum exhibits would seem to be just as valid, given the theoretical arguments underpinning audience studies.

Even when there do seem to be good reasons why a method is applied to one sort of visual material rather than another, though, it is important to think carefully before deciding that you too will apply the same method to the same sorts of materials. It may be that approaching the same visual images from a different methodological direction will yield more interesting results. For example, many semiotic or discourse analyses of domestic photography – those photos snapped by ordinary people of their families and when they are on holiday – decry their conventional subject matter. However, some anthropologists have examined just why the banality of such photos matters to the people who make and live with them, and their work suggests that critiques of the cultural meanings of their content may be somewhat beside the point. Chapter 10 discusses this further.

Bear all that in mind as you look at Table 2.1, which lists the methods discussed in this book and the sorts of images to which they have been most often applied. If you already have some images you want to work with, find them (or something like them) in this list, see what methods have been used to interpret them, and start with the chapters on those methods. Remember that you do not *have* to use those methods – they might only provide a starting point for thinking methodologically.

It is obvious from this table that, to repeat a point made in the preface, there are many sorts of visual objects that this book does not examine. Again, this can only serve as encouragement to sever any automatic link between a method and an image. A method should be used for its interpretive possibilities, not because of conventional ways of using it.

3 why you should also read books other than this one

If you want to interpret visual materials successfully, there are at least two other sorts of reading you need to be doing.

First, you will have to engage with the theoretical arguments underpinning the method you eventually choose. Methods do not work in isolation; they depend on understandings of how meaning is made, and you will need to appreciate those understandings in order to make the method work well.

Secondly, there is another sort of preparation that is needed, regardless of theoretical starting point, methodological implications or visual materials. All of these methods require some sorts of contextual knowledge about the imagery you are interested in. It is always important to know something about all aspects of the image you want to research; even if the audience is your main analytical focus, it is often useful to know something about the production of the image too. So before you utilize any of the methods the following chapters discuss, look at the bibliographies at the end of the book to help you find some background material, and use the other resources at your disposal too: libraries, databases, reading lists and so on. Search for what others have written on the medium in which you are interested and on the genres which you think are relevant to the images you are concerned with. If you have an 'artist' of some kind as the producer of your images, look for what has been written on him or her.

4 how each chapter works

In terms of the practicalities of using this book, each chapter shares a similar structure:

- at the opening of each chapter a box tells you what key examples are discussed by the chapter;
- the chapter proper then starts with a more or less brief introduction to the method and its theoretical context;
- the context is then elaborated in more detail;
- the method is described; particular aspects of some methods are given special attention in some chapters;
- each chapter ends with an assessment of its method's strengths and weaknesses in relation to the critical visual methodology discussed in Chapter 1;
- and finally there is a summary, which lists what sorts of visual materials the method is most often applied to, the sites and modalities it addresses most directly, the method's key terms, and its strengths and weaknesses as I have assessed them.

The repetition of this structure for each method will make the book easy to use, I hope.

5 a quick word on finding, referencing and reproducing your images

If you have not already found the images with which you want to research, the possibilities are endless. There are contemporary exhibitions, galleries, magazines, cinemas, TV shows, videos and web pages; there are historical archives and museums. Lois Swan-Jones (1999) offers a useful guide to *Art Information on the Internet*, and there is also the *Picture Researcher's Handbook* (Evans and Evans 2001; see also Eakins and Loving 1985). The key texts listed in the bibliographies at the end of this book may also provide some ideas. If you find just one image that intrigues you, that's a good start. You can find more related images by searching for published work on the artist who made that first image, or on the genre to which it belongs. If it is a historical image, contact its owners, and make use of archivists; they are almost always extremely helpful and knowledgable.

Once you have found your images, there are a number of considerations to bear in mind in relation to their eventual use in your essay or dissertation. First, you need to be able to *reference* them in as clear a manner as you would reference any other source material. That is, you need to record as much of the following sort of information as possible. For a painting, for example, you will need the name and date of the artist who made the image, the title of the piece, the date of its creation, the materials from which it is made, its dimensions, its condition, its current location and its accession number (if it is now in a collection). For an advertisement in a magazine, you might need the name, date, volume number and place of publication of the magazine, plus the number of the page on which the advert appeared and its size; or, if you know about the whole campaign of which this advert is a part, you need to make systematic reference to the different parts of that campaign. For a website, you need its address and the date you accessed it.

Secondly, you need to consider the precise *format* in which you will interpret your images. In particular, how much material beyond the image itself will you need? Surrounding text can make a big difference to a picture's interpretation. The Doisneau photograph discussed in Chapter 1, for example, has been given three different titles by the various books in which it has been reproduced: 'A Sidelong Glance', 'Painting by Wagner in the window of the Galerie Romi, Rue de Seine, Paris 6e, 1948', 'An Oblique Look'. Each encourages a rather different interpretation. Other aspects of an image's format are important too. If you are studying a painting, is it important that you see the original, or is a reproduction good enough? Should you be concerned with its original site of display, or is seeing it in a gallery adequate? If it is an advertisement, how important is it to know what was printed next to it in a magazine? Some of these concerns depend, again, on what theoretical position you are adopting. Knowing where an advert appeared in a magazine would be more important if you were using discourse analysis (Chapter 7), for example, than if you were using compositional interpretation (Chapter 3) or content analysis (Chapter 4). However, they can be crucial regardless of your particular method.

When you come to write up your research, you should also consider the relation between your own text and the images you have been working with. It is always important to show the reader what you are discussing. But do you want to use the images simply to illustrate your argument? Do you want to try to convey something of their own agency? Do you want them to make their own arguments, by making a photo-essay for example? In *Ways of Seeing*, John Berger (1972) offers essays consisting entirely of images; you might feel that some of the things you want to say about your images are better shown as a photo-essay. Or you could annotate your images with text and other images as John Berger (1972) also does (see Figure 1.2 in Chapter 1 and Chapter 11, section 3.2).

Finally, it is always useful to bear in mind how you might *reproduce* the images you are researching. Don't crop or otherwise tamper with the reproduction without making your intervention clear to your reader (if you have cut an image down to show a small part of it, say it is a 'detail' of the work). Colour photocopying remains an excellent way to reproduce published images for essays (even black and white photographs are better copied this way because the various shades of grey are much better preserved). Scanning printed images into digital format, or using images downloaded from the web, is also very useful: digital images can easily be cropped if necessary and inserted into written text. If you have the skills, you may even want to consider producing your work as a website or in CD or DVD format: Samantha Warren (2002) suggests, rightly, that these digital formats permit much higher standards of visual reproduction than do printed social science journals, and of course they also allow you to integrate moving images into your work.

If these sorts of reproductions are for private research purposes only, there is usually no problem with copyright. However, if you think you might publish your work, then you will often be legally obliged to obtain permission from its copyright holders to reproduce it. Rosemary Eakins and Elizabeth Loving (1985: 8–15) have a guide to pictures and the law. Reproduction for publication often entails paying a fee to the copyright holders too, and you will need your sources clearly recorded to do this.

And now, on to the nitty-gritty of interpreting visual materials.

3
'the good eye'
looking at pictures using compositional interpretation

key example a review written by a journalist of an exhibition of seventeenth century paintings in the National Gallery, London.

1 compositional interpretation: an introduction

The first criterion for a critical approach to visual imagery outlined in section 3 of Chapter 1 was the need to take images seriously. That is, it is crucial to look very carefully at the image or images in which you are interested, because the image itself has its own effects. These effects are always embedded in social practices, of course, and may well be negotiated by the image's audiences; nevertheless, it seems to me that there is no point in researching any aspect of the visual unless the power of the visual is acknowledged. As Norman Bryson (1991: 71) says of paintings, 'the power of the painting is there, in the thousands of gazes caught by its surface, and the resultant turning, and the shifting, the redirecting of the discursive flow'. Paintings, like other visual images, catch the gazes of spectators and affect them in some way, and they do so through how they look.

But how can you describe how an image looks? This chapter explores one approach which offers a detailed vocabulary for expressing the appearance of an image. I have chosen to call this approach 'compositional interpretation'. This is a term I have invented for describing an approach to imagery that has developed through certain kinds of art history. I need to invent a term because the method has tended to be conveyed by example rather than by explication (some exceptions to this generalization include Acton 1997; Gilbert 1995; O'Toole 1994; Taylor 1957). This method depends on what Irit Rogoff (1998: 17) calls 'the good eye'; that is, a way of looking at paintings that is not methodologically explicit but which nevertheless produces a specific way of describing paintings. The 'good eye' pays attention to what it sees as high Art, and refuses to be either methodologically or theoretically explicit. It thus functions as a kind of visual **connoisseurship**.

connoisseurship

> Connoisseurship involves the acquisition of extensive first-hand experience
> of works of art with the aim, first, of attributing works to artists and schools,
> identifying styles and establishing sources and influences, and second, of
> judging their quality and hence their place in a canon. (Fernie 1995: 330)

Developing the 'good eye' of a connoisseur requires a lot of a certain
kind of what the previous chapter described as 'contextual information'.
Specifically, you need a lot of knowledge about particular painters, about the
kinds of painting they did, about the sorts of visual imagery they were looking at and being inspired by. All this is then used by the 'good eye' to assess
paintings for their 'quality'. Thus compositional interpretation claims to look
at images for 'what they are', rather than for, say, what they do or how they
were or are used. The 'good eye' therefore looks mostly at the site of an *image
itself* in order to understand its significance, and pays most (although not
exclusive) attention to its *compositional* modality.

As this is an approach long-established in art history, it is usually used in
relation to one of the sorts of objects that art historians have traditionally
studied: paintings. This chapter will mostly follow that practice, although section 4 will introduce some terms for describing the compositional modality of
moving images. Its case study of compositional interpretation is a review written by Adrian Searle in 1999 for the *Guardian* newspaper of an exhibition of
self-portraits by Rembrandt van Rijn, a Dutch painter who was born in 1606
and died in 1669. Most of this review is reprinted, with two of its five illustrations, below.

'I can think of no room of paintings in the world so moving'.
Adrian Searle is astounded by Rembrandt's self-portraits.

It is night in the National Gallery. The lights are off. The machines that sniff the
humidity and check the temperature are quietly ticking over, the alarm system is
primed. The guards make their rounds, and outside in Trafalgar Square the club-
bers are waiting for the night bus home. From tomorrow morning the queues will
be forming for the exhibition 'Rembrandt By Himself', which brings together almost
all of Rembrant's self-portraits, the paintings, etchings and drawings he made of
himself over the entirety of his artistic career. But for now I imagine Rembrandt's
self-portraits, looking out into the twilit empty rooms in the Sainsbury Wing. I know
they're there.

I think of his ghost, with what Picasso called 'that elephant's eye of his', that
bulbous nose and the head with its curls spilling from under a mob cap, a turban, a
plumed beret, a helmet. Rembrandt young, porcine and adenoidal; Rembrandt old
as the painter-king. Rembrandt grimacing open-mouthed into a mirror as he draws
on an etching-plate. Rembrandt dressed as an Oriental Potentate, Rembrandt in a
cloak and Rembrandt as a beggar. I think of his multiple selves looking out into the
dark, painting himself as though he were already a figure from history ...

on the image itself, and although it pays most attention to its compositionality, it also pays some attention to its *production*. Usually a note is made of aspects of the *social* modality of its production: who commissioned it, why, who painted it, and what then happened to it before it ended up in its current location (the various owners and locations of a painting are known as its **provenance** **provenance**). And connoisseurship also involves exploring the *compositional* modality of its production.

But attention is usually focused mostly on the *technological* modality of the making of an image. As the discussion of technologies in the previous chapter noted, it can be important to know with what material and technique an image is made because that can affect the impact an image has. Joshua Taylor (1957) provides some very useful discussions of the various technologies that have been used to produce pictorial images. He explores the particular qualities of both certain media – drawing, paintings, graphic arts, sculpture and architecture – and the different ways in which these can be deployed. His discussion of painting, for example, examines the techniques of fresco, watercolour, tempera, oil, encaustic and collage. James Monaco (2000) examines the technologies of moving images in similar detail. However, as Taylor (1957: 70) himself notes, the only reason for paying much attention to the technologies of an image's production is 'when a knowledge of the technique helps in describing the particular characteristics of the work'.

---

focus

Where does Searle's essay refer to the effect of their use of oil paints on Rembrandt's portraits? What effects does his description of the oils have?

---

3 doing compositional interpretation: the compositionality of the image itself

Compositional interpretation pays most attention to the compositionality of the image itself. This section breaks down the compositionality seen by the 'good eye' into a number of components. This is a schematic device, however, since in practice few of these components are completely distinct from each other. **composition** Indeed, the notion of **composition** refers to all these elements in combination.

3.1 content

When looking at an image for itself, a starting point could be its content. What does the image actually show? This might seem a very obvious question not

Looking at late Rembrandt, we think we can tell how it is to be old, to have been old then, in 1669, prematurely aged at 63. What we are looking at is an old man with old skin in an old painting with a cracked and sallow surface, Rembrandt in the soft yellowing light, the last bright highlights in his eyes. It is almost impossible to look at Rembrandt's paintings of himself without regarding them as the artist's meditations on mortality, as a dialogue with himself conducted with a heart-breaking truthfulness and candour. That is how we are accustomed to read these self-portraits, we look into their painted space, now three-and-a-half centuries old. We think we are looking at the painter as much as the paintings, seeing the man himself in his own self-image, and in the brush-work that created it. The paint molten, distressed, frank, concentrated, cursory, darkened, yellowed, translucent and papery. The painted surface at times as worn and slovenly as an old man's table, as though the painting itself were evidence of human fortitude and endurance. The catalogue essays can't dispel this view, but they set Rembrandt's self-portraiture within a context that tempers our projected existential feelings about it. It is odd, isn't it, that Rembrandt painted himself so often in clothing from the dressing-up box of the previous century – a rag-bag property-box of costumes, outlandish headgear, brocades and cloaks – and yet that he should also be a painter whose timelessness and contemporaneity continues to strike us so forcibly …

Figure 3.1
Rembrandt van Rijn, Self-Portrait, *1629*

But what scholarship cannot do, finally, is to dispel the disquiet Rembrandt's paintings arouse, the sense that Rembrandt was both unrepeatable and inescapable as a painter of himself. He painted and drew with a candour – at least, we suppose it was candour – about what was happening to his appearance as he got older. Perhaps he saw himself as a 'type', no less than his paintings were 'types', and saw his own face as a vessel of universal characteristics – melancholia and black bile marking his like a map …

Later, he tries on all manner of costumes, and grows in stature and solidity with every one. He paints the spots on this cheek and that inescapable great nose. He goes on to paint himself in all his guises, but he ends up painting himself, both with a sort of grandeur, and with what we can only see as humility.

Figure 3.2

Rembrandt van Rijn, Self-Portrait, *1657*

'Rembrandt By Himself' is undoubtedly going to be a block-buster, although it is a much smaller show than Monet at the Royal Academy, with only 30 painted self-portraits by the artist – over some of which, the question of attribution still hangs – as well as his numerous etchings of himself, in numerous states, and works by Rembrandt's pupils, and paintings which might be seen as precursors to the artist's works, such as the National's 'Portrait Of A Man', by Titian, assumed by some to be Titian himself.

Apart from the two self-portraits by Carel Fabritius, Rembrandt's most talented pupil (who was accidentally blown up when a gunpowder factory exploded in Delft), most of these works are unnecessary to the show. They are makeweights. But there's nothing to truly argue with here. I can think of no other room of paintings in the world at this moment (apart from the room of Goya's black paintings in the Prado) so moving and disquieting as the central gallery of the Rembrandt show, containing the self-portraits of the last half of his career. Standing in this room I realised that you can't review Rembrandt. Rembrandt reviews you.

extracted from the *Guardian*, 8 June 1999, page 12 of arts supplement

I will return to this review in sections 2 and 3 of this chapter.

As a method for developing a critical visual methodology along the lines sketched in the previous chapter, compositional interpretation has its limitations. Visual images do not exist in a vacuum, and looking at them for 'what they are' neglects the ways in which they are produced and interpreted through particular social practices. Bryson makes this clear when he adds two qualifications to his comments quoted above about the power of the painting. First, he says, 'my ability to recognise an image … is … an ability which presupposes competence within the social, that is socially constructed, codes of recognition' (Bryson 1991: 65). Secondly, 'the social formation isn't … something which supervenes or appropriates or utilizes the image so to speak *after* it has been made; rather, painting … unfolds from within the social formation from the beginning' (Bryson 1991: 66). Moreover, compositional interpretation does not reflect on its own practices. This chapter will therefore be able to pay little attention to these two aspects of a critical visual methodology.

Despite these absences, compositional interpretation remains a useful method because it does offer a way of looking very carefully at the content and form of images. The successful deployment of many of the other methods discussed in this book – methods which I think are more appropriate for a critical visual methodology – nonetheless relies, initially, on the detailed scrutiny of the image itself. Nigel Whitely (1999) complains that too often in the social sciences this initial stage is neglected and the power of the image is subordinated to the theoretical debates in which its interpretation is embedded. He insists that compositional interpretation should be undertaken seriously, and that it should then be 'conjoined to other types of analysis so that the visual scrutiny of what can literally be seen can be studied in relation to reception, meaning and content' (Whitely 1999: 107). This chapter will offer some suggestions about how to achieve that 'visual scrutiny' adequately; and in order to be helpfully explicit, I will occasionally draw on writers whose work has in many ways distanced itself from more traditional art history approaches, but who still offer useful methodological pointers. So this chapter will:

- explore the key terms used by compositional interpretation to describe the compositional modality of an image itself;
- discuss the method's reliance on certain implicit ideas about high Art;
- assess the usefulness of compositional interpretation for a critical visual methodology.

2 doing compositional interpretation: technologies and the production of the image

Despite its lack of methodological explicitness, then, compositional interpretation is a very particular way of looking at images. It focuses most strongly worth spending much time on. And for some images it will indeed be a very simple question. For others, though, it will not. For example, some viewers of the Doisneau photograph reproduced as Figure 1.3 need a bit of time to work out that the photographer is inside the gallery looking out into the street. Moreover, some images picture particular religious, historical, mythological, moral or literary themes or events, as Acton (1997) discusses (and section 3.2 in Chapter 7 will explore a method whose aim is to decode the conventional-ized visual symbols used to refer to such themes and events: iconography). Take some time to be sure you are sure about what you think an image is showing.

3.2 colour

Colour is another crucial component of an image's compositionality. Taylor (1957) offers three ways of describing the colours of a painting:

- **hue**. This refers to the actual colours in a painting. Thus the dominant   **hue**
  hues used in the Rembrandt portraits reproduced for Searle's review are browns, blues, and flesh.
- **saturation**. Saturation refers to the purity of a colour in relation to its   **saturation**
  appearance in the colour spectrum. Thus saturation is high if a colour is used in a vivid form of its hue, and low if it is nearly neutral. The blues and flesh colours in the review's illustrations are low, but the browns are high: rich and intense.
- **value**. This refers to the lightness or darkness of a colour. If a colour is in   **value**
  its near-white form, then its value is high; if in its near black form, its value is low. The browns, blacks and some of the blues in the illustrations have low value: they are all dark. But other blues, and flesh colours, seem to have quite high value.

These terms can describe the colours used in a painting. But it is also necessary to describe the effects of the colours in an image. Colour can be used to *stress* certain elements of an image, for example. The flesh colours in par-ticular in the illustrations to Searle's essay seem to have quite high value, because they are often where the light falls in the painting; but of course since these are portraits, the high value of the face colours serves to draw our atten-tion to the point of portrait paintings, the face.

There is also the question of how *harmonious* the colour combination of a painting is. There have been many theories about what colours combine most harmoniously with each other, and John Gage (1993) offers a very full account of the different ways in which colour has been understood 'from antiquity to abstraction', as the subtitle of this book says. For our purposes here, however, it is sufficient to consider whether the colours of a painting rely on contrasts or on the blending of similar value or saturation hues. The Rembrandt illustrations appear very harmonious since they have a limited range of colours which blend into each other; even the blue is a muted contrast to the brown since, like the browns, it is mostly of low saturation. Gunther Kress and Theo van Leeuwen (1996: 163–5) also suggest that the combination of hues, values and saturations of an image affect how realistic audiences will imagine that image to be. If the colours look the same as a colour photograph of the same subject would, then our sense of its realism is heightened, they suggest.

Colour can also work to suggest an effect of distance in a painting, especially in landscape paintings. In that genre, the hues used often become more bluish as a means of suggesting the way a landscape recedes. This is known **atmospheric perspective**   as **atmospheric perspective**.

3.3 spatial organization

All images have their space organized in some way, and there are two related aspects of this organization to consider: the organization of space 'within' an image, and the way the spatial organization of an image offers a particular viewing position to its spectator. This offer is part of an image's way of seeing.

First, the spatial organization within the image (Acton [1997: 1–24] has a useful discussion of this). Take a look at the *volumes* of an image. How are these arranged in relation to each other? Are some volumes connected in some way to others by vectors, while others are left isolated? How? What about the *lines* of the volumes and their connections? Which directions do they follow? Are they fluid curves or jagged fragments? What sort of *rhythm* do they have: static or dynamic? What are the effects of these things? Kress and van Leeuwen (1996: 79–118) have an interesting discussion of images such as diagrams, flow charts and maps that explores how their elements are conventionally structured in relation to each other.

Then consider the space in which these volumes are placed. Acton (1997: 25–50) suggests thinking about width, depth, interval and distance. Is this space simple, or complicated? In answering this question, it is important to understand something about perspective, which is the method used in Western art to make a two-dimensional image look as if it shows three-dimensional space. Perspective, like colour, has a long history in Western discourse, and there is more than one kind of system of perspective (Andrews 1995; Edgerton 1975; Elkins 1994; Kress and van Leeuwen 1996). Section 3.2 has already mentioned that colour can be used to convey distance in land-**geometrical perspective**   scape painting. This section considers **geometrical perspective**, and this too has its variations. However, there are some basic principles which provide starting points for thinking about the space represented by an image. Perspective depends on a geometry of rays of vision, and your eye is central to this geometry (several perspective systems assume that the viewer of a scene is a single point and thus that you only have one eye). The level of your eye is always the same as the horizon of a painting. It is also the level at which the rays of vision converge at what is called the vanishing point. Figure 3.3

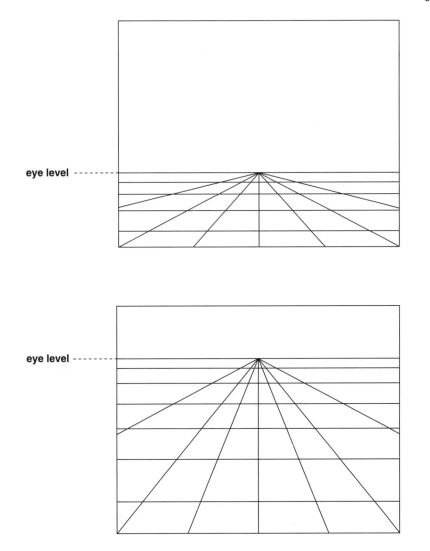

Figure 3.3
*geometrical
perspective*

shows what difference your eye level makes to the representation of a paved area, if you were sitting, first, on the ground and then on a high wall, according to this kind of perspective.

Now let's see what happens if some basic building blocks appear in this scene, one close to us and one further apart (Figure 3.4).

Finally, Figure 3.5 shows what happens if there are two different eye levels and two different vanishing points in an image of blocks.

Paintings can have different effects depending on their manipulation of this kind of perspective. In relation to Figure 3.5, for example, since one eye is assumed to be normal in this geometrical system, the space constructed with two eye levels seems strange and incoherent. Other paintings try to shift the spectator's point of view through their use of perspective. For example,

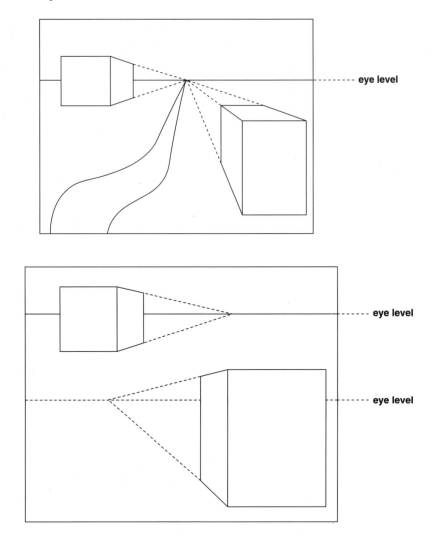

Figure 3.4
geometrical
perspective

Figure 3.5
geometrical
perspective

using a very low eye level might represent the way a child sees the world, and Pollock (1988: 65) suggests that Mary Cassatt painted some of her canvases with this effect in mind (see Figure 3.6).

Or a low eye level might suggest that the painting was made to be seen from below, and this is the case with, for example, Masaccio's crucifixion, painted in about 1427 as a fresco on the wall of the church of Santa Maria Novella in Florence, where the congregation would sit beneath it (Edgerton 1975). Perspective thus provides a means of representing three-dimensional space on a two-dimensional surface. It dominated Western painting for centuries, from its first explication in the fifteenth century to its rejection by some painters in the early twentieth. Although now it is only one means among many of organizing its space, it can provide a benchmark for thinking about the representation of space in any particular image.

Figure 3.6
Mary Cassatt,
Little Girl in a
Blue Armchair,
1878

focus

How do the Rembrandt portraits use geometrical perspective? Do we look down on the painted figure, or up to him?

A useful way to explore these aspects of the spatial organization within an image is to try to draw a summary diagram of the image you are looking at (see Taylor (1957) and Kress and van Leeuwen (1996: 47) for some examples). Look for lines that show the edges of things; extend them, and see where and how they intersect. The Rembrandt illustrations reproduced here are perhaps too simple in terms of their spatial organization to make this a worthwhile exercise; but you might try making a simplified version of the painting reproduced as Figure 7.1, which is a marriage portrait of Giovanni Arnolfini and Giovanna Cenami and was painted in 1434 by Jan van Eyck. Try extending the lines of the floorboards, the windowsill and the bedstead, for example. James Elkins (1991) has explored the use of perspective in this painting through just such a diagram of its converging and diverging lines. Compare his to yours.

This discussion of perspective brings us to the second aspect of the spatial organization of an image that it is necessary to consider. This is the way in which the picture also offers a particular position to its viewers. We have already seen this process at work in our discussion of the Doisneau photograph in Chapter 1. The elements 'inside' that photo are arranged in such a way that they construct a particular viewing position 'outside' the photo (and this makes the distinction between 'inside' and 'outside' difficult to sustain). The Doisneau photograph aligns the spectator with the look of the man. Michael Ann Holly (1996) has argued that it is this positioning of the viewer that is most important when thinking about how visual images have

logic of figuration   their own effects. This positioning she calls the **logic of figuration** of an image. In relation to the painting in Figure 3.6, for example, we can say that its logic of figuration places us low down in the painted room, inviting us to adopt a child's point of view. In asking 'what the work of art does for us', Holly (1996: xiv) argues that it is the spatial and temporal organization of a painting that structures its effects most profoundly; 'legislated and predicted by the spatial and temporal organisation of the visual field: we stand where the works tell us to stand and we see what they choose to reveal', she says (Holly 1996: 9). Kress and van Leeuwen (1996: 119) talk in similar terms about the ways images can be seen as 'designing the position of the viewer' through, in part at least, their spatial organization. Holly examines this effect through a discussion of early renaissance paintings and 'a few classic cultural histories from the nineteenth and twentieth centuries' (Holly 1996: xiii), suggesting that the histories, in their panoramic sweep, reflect the rules of perspective through which the paintings were constructed. (These are not uncontroversial claims, however; Chapter 9 in particular will emphasize that particular spectators may not take up the position offered to them by an image.)

Kress and van Leeuwen (1996: 119–58) also explore the effects of the spatial organization of visual images on the position of the viewer. Like Holly, they examine the effects of geometrical perspective in some detail. They suggest, for example, that the *angle* between the spectator and what is pictured produces particular effects, with frontal angles engaging the viewer more with what is pictured than oblique angles (Kress and van Leeuwen 1996: 140–6). They also explore the effects of apparent differences in *height* between the spectator of an image and what is pictured: if the viewer is positioned by the image's perspective to look down on it, Kress and van Leeuwen (1996: 146–8) argue, they are given some sort of power over its subject matter; if they look up to it, then they are positioned as in some way inferior to it; and if they look at it at the same level, then a relationship of equality between spectator and pictured is suggested. They also look at other aspects of the spatial organization of images, such as *distance*, suggesting, for example, that pictures of people in close-up usually offer a relation of intimacy between the person pictured and the spectator (Kress and van Leeuwen 1996: 130–5). Searle assumes this in his discussion of the Rembrandt portraits. However, an exception to this latter claim suggests that these sort of generalizations must always be carefully examined in relation to specific images: think, for example, of the use of police mugshots in newspaper reports of crimes, where the close-up format of the mugshot suggests precisely a big difference between the person pictured – the criminal – and the person looking – the innocent newspaper reader. In this case, too, though, the spatial organization of the composition is a crucial element of the relationship between an image and its audiences.

Mieke Bal (1991: 158–60), on the other hand, advocates concentrating less on the *spatial* organization of an image, and more on the *visual* organization of looks and gazes in her notion of the **focalizers** of an image. She points out that all paintings have a range of viewers: addressed, implied and represented. Each focalizes – or looks – in their own way (see also Kress and van Leeuwen 1996: 121–35). They look in a particular way, at specific things. The relations of looks between them – who can see what and how – can tell us much about how the image works to catch our gaze. For if an external focalizer – a spectator – can look in the same way at the same things as a focalizer in the picture, then the spectator's identification with the image will be strong, says Bal. An example of this sort of analysis is Pollock's (1988) account of the Doisneau photograph that was discussed in Chapter 1. Pollock examined the structure of the looks in the photograph and the way in which the look of the spectator was incorporated into these.

focalizers

Thus the spatial organization of an image is not innocent. It has effects. It can produce a specific relation between image and spectator.

focus

What position are we offered by the logic of figuration and the focalizers of the Rembrandt portraits? What account does Searle give of this position?

Through their use of geometrical perspective, the Rembrandt portraits position us as looking at the same level as the painter; we neither look down onto his image nor up at it. In that spatial sense we are at the same level as him. And we look at him in the way that he seems to be looking at us: directly.

Searle develops this sense of directness and equality between the artist's self-image and our view of it in particular ways. Searle says that these are paintings done by a man in dialogue with himself; we as

(Continued)

(Continued)

spectators are now in the place of the mirror that Rembrandt must have used to make these pictures of himself. But he also suggests that Rembrandt's face is 'a vessel of universal characteristics' that he painted with 'candour'; the artist's honesty, his directness in confronting his own image and now us, mean that his portraits touch us now in 'moving and disquieting' ways. Indeed, such is the strength of Rembrandt's gaze, Searle eventually claims that he is reviewing us, not the other way round.

Thus Searle glosses aspects of the spatial organization and focalization of these portraits in specific ways. He gives a particular meaning to them. He suggests that they are an expression not only of Rembrandt's qualities – his honesty – but also of ours – since in looking at his portraits we are forced to confront the fact that we too will age and die. His honesty in confronting his ageing makes us honest and face ours. Thus he claims the portraits' power depends on showing the commonalities between us in the early twenty-first century and Rembrandt in the seventeenth.

3.4 light

The light shown in an image is clearly related to both its colours and its spaces. What *type* of light a painting represents – candlelight, daylight, electric light – will clearly affect the saturation and value of its hues. And the illusion that geometrical perspective realistically represents three-dimensional space can be enhanced or called into question by the use of light *sources*. The apparent realism of the Arnolfini portrait (see Figure 7.1) is increased, for example, by the dominant source of light coming from the window and the way all the shadows in the painting are consistent with this. Light can also be used to *highlight* certain elements of a painting, as we have seen in the case of the Rembrandt portraits.

3.5 expressive content

Finally in this section, I want to mention a more elusive aspect of this approach to images because, despite its rather uncertain methodological status, it is crucial to this mode of interpretation and to many others. That is the evocation in writing of the 'feel' of an image, or what, after Taylor, I will call its **expressive content**. Taylor (1957: 43–4) describes an image's expressive content as 'the combined effect of subject matter and visual form'. Separate consideration of expressive content is necessary because breaking an image

expressive content

into its component parts – spatial organization, colour, content, light – does not necessarily capture the look of an image. Instead, what may be needed is some imaginative writing that tries to evoke its affective characteristics. As an example, here is the art historian Erwin Panofsky writing about the Arnolfini portrait reproduced as Figure 7.1:

> In a comfortably furnished interior, suffused with a warm, dim light, Giovanni Arnolfini and his wife are standing represented in full-length ... The husband gingerly holds the lady's right hand in his left while raising his right in a gesture of solemn affirmation. Rather stiffly posed and standing as far apart as the action permits, they do not look at each other yet seem to be united by a mysterious bond ... (Panofsky 1953: 201–2)

Panofsky uses terms like 'comfortably', 'gingerly' and 'solemn' which would be difficult to produce relying solely on the list of concerns this chapter has offered, yet they seem necessary elements in any description of this painting.

The expressive content of an image is always necessary to consider. However, section 4.2 in Chapter 1 suggested that not all visual culture critics agree on its significance, and it may be important that your reaction to it does not obscure other issues concerning the meaning of the image.

focus

Return to Searle's review one more time. The expressive content of the Rembrandt portraits is central to his discussion of them. Pick out the moments in his text when he evokes it.

Searle's efforts to articulate the expressive content of the Rembrandt self-portraits are particularly interesting because they explicitly reject (or marginalize) other ways of relating to the paintings. What does Searle imply are unimportant in understanding the portraits, compared to the impact of their expressive content?

Searle suggests that both the gallery and the catalogue become somewhat irrelevant next to the extraordinary effects of the portraits. This tactic is typical of the connoisseurship central to the 'good eye'. Only the 'quality' of the paintings matters; everything else – all the other sorts of interpretive apparatus brought to bear on them – is insignificant.

(Continued)

(Continued)

But of course Searle too is bringing an interpretive apparatus to bear on the portraits; the 'good eye' is itself an interpretive technique. This apparatus assumes that only the paintings are important, to begin with. But his discussion of them also draws on at least two other assumptions regarding great art. One is that it is produced by something called **genius**: a marvellously gifted individual who can rise above the specificities of his circumstances to touch what are apparently the fundamental concerns of human life (see Battersby [1994] for a critique of the notion of genius, particularly the way it is a masculinized category). And the other is that art – **Art** – can speak directly to this humanity in everyone.

genius

Art

Victor Burgin summarizes these definitions of Art and genius thus:

ART is an activity characteristic of humanity since the dawn of civilisation. In any epoch the ARTIST, by virtue of special gifts, expresses that which is finest in humanity ... the visual artist achieves this through modes of understanding and expression which are 'purely visual' ... This special characteristic of art necessarily makes it an autonomous sphere of activity, completely separate from the everyday world of social and political life. The autonomous nature of visual art means that questions asked of it may only be properly put, and answered, in its own terms – all other forms of interrogation are irrelevant. (Burgin 1986: 30, emphasis in original)

Hence Searle's assertion that galleries and catalogues are irrelevant in relation to the Rembrandt portraits; because these portraits are Art, only his, and our, humanity matters. In this view, art is seen as cross-cultural, with universal appeal. In the introduction to their book on *Visual Culture* (1994), Norman Bryson, Michael Ann Holly and Keith Moxey make clear the difference between approaches to visual images that depend on this notion of Art, and the approach to visual images that the contributors to their book adopt:

Instead of seeking to promote and sustain the value of 'great' art by limiting discussion to the circumstances of the work's production and to speculation about the extraordinary impulses that may have characterized the intentions of its makers, these contributors examine the work performed by the image in the life of culture ... Instead of applying a Kantian aesthetic, according to which value is an intrinsic characteristic of the work of art, one

(Continued)

(Continued)

capable of being perceived by all human beings regardless of their location in time and place – a recognition that depends only on one's status as a human being – these writers betray an awareness that the aesthetic value of a work depends on the prevailing cultural conditions. They invest the work with value by means of their appreciation of its meaning both in the cultural horizon of its production and its reception. (Bryson, Holly and Moxey 1994: xvi)

Thus, while the connoisseurship usually accompanying the exercise of 'the good eye' denies the cultural specificity of Art, the notion of visual culture addresses that specificity directly.

A question remains, though. Is it possible to retain a sense of the power of (some) images, of their often visceral impact, if it is assumed only that 'the aesthetic value of a work depends on the prevailing cultural conditions'?

4 the compositional interpretation of moving images

Thus far, compositional interpretation has been described as a method for describing paintings, but the same terms could be used to describe other sorts of still images too: photographs, for example. Some aspects of moving images – film, television and video, for example – can also be described using the terminology of compositional interpretation. Some of the terms used in the previous sections are conventionally given other names when used in relation to moving images, however, and moving images also require a further set of terms to describe their dynamic qualities. Monaco offers a detailed vocabulary for describing the spatial and temporal organization of moving images, and this section will draw on his very useful discussion (Monaco 2000: 152–225).

Monaco's discussion begins with a basic distinction between the spatial organization of a film, which is called its **mise-en-scène**, and its temporal organization, or its **montage**. Monaco (2000: 179) suggests that mise-en-scène is a result of decisions about what to shoot and how to shoot it, while montage is how the shots are presented. His descriptive vocabulary is divided between each of these. Two further considerations in interpreting many moving images is the sound that accompanies them, and, in the case of films that tell a story, their narrative structure.

mise-en-scène

montage

4.1 mise-en-scène

Monaco (2000) suggests that what is shot involves looking at how the film frame is used, and that how it is shot concerns the structure of the shots themselves.

screen ratio

There are three aspects of the framing of scenes that Monaco (2000) calls attention to. The first of these is the **screen ratio**. The screen ratio is the ratio between the height of the projected image and its width: that is, the screen ratio describes the shape of the screen. In classic Hollywood movies – those made in the Hollywood studio system of the 1930s, 1940s and 1950s – the screen ratio was 1:33. Monaco (2000: 184) suggests that this proportion facilitated directors and audiences focusing on faces and dialogue. In the 1950s, the arrival of widescreen with screen ratios 2:33 or more was paralleled by more landscape shots, location shooting and action movies. The

screen frame

second aspect of framing, according to Monaco (2000), is how the **screen frame** works. If the action is filmed in such a way that the space beyond the screen frame is important, then the screen frame is *open*. Open screen frames are often used in horror and thriller films, where the suspense builds because the audience knows or suspects some one or some thing is lurking outside the screen frame, outside what we or the film's characters can actually see. If, on the other hand, the scene makes no reference to the space beyond its own frame, the screen frame is *closed*. A closed screen frame can be used to suggest a particular mood or emotion. For example, in Steven Soderbergh's film *Ocean's Eleven*, one of the characters is making money in LA teaching poker to film stars. There is a long scene early in the film of one of his lessons, and the confined space of its closed screen frame manages to imply how restrictive and boring the character finds his work. Finally, Monaco (2000: 186–7,

screen planes

192) discusses the **screen planes**. There are three of these, and they intersect. The *frame plane* is how forms are distributed across the screen; the *geographical plane* is how forms are distributed in three-dimensional space; and the *depth plane* is how the apparent depth of the images is perceived.

multiple images

superimpositions

Also in relation to the frame, Monaco (2000) points out that a frame can contain **multiple images** if it is split, or images can shown as **superimpositions**, through techniques such as double exposure. Sometimes this is done as a sort of visual in-joke (as when the film *The Incredible Hulk* uses multiple images to reference the original source of the Hulk story, which was a comic). Sometimes it is done to make a connection between different characters: in *Ocean's Eleven* after the first few minutes of the film have introduced us to one main character, a wipe to the right stops half-way across the screen (the next section explains wipes), revealing the second main character eating a burger; for a moment their two images are seen side-by-side, before a second wipe to the right obscures the first character and takes us into the second character's story and how the two meet to work together again.

shot

distance

The second aspect of moving images' mise-en-scène is their shots. **Shot distance** refers to how much of a figure is shown by a particular shot, and a shot can be an *extreme long shot* (where the figure is in the far distance), a *long shot*, or a *full, three-quarters, medium, head and shoulders* or *close-up* shot. Monaco (2000) tentatively suggests some of the effects that the frequent use of one or other of these sorts of shots might produce in a particular film. The repeated use of close-ups, for example, may produce a sense of claustrophobic intensity, while long shots may imply alienation and emptiness. However, as was noted in section 3.3 of this chapter and as Monaco himself comments, these sorts of generalizations about the effects of the spatial organization of images always need to be assessed carefully in relation to specific images.

The **focus** of shots is also important. *Deep focus* is when the foreground, middle ground and background of a shot – all of the frame's geographical plane – are in focus. *Shallow focus* is when one of these grounds is more in focus than others. Shallow focus is sometimes used to direct attention to a particular character or event in a scene; for example, in *Ocean's Eleven*, again, there is a dialogue scene between the two main characters in which the focus repeatedly shifts from one to the other as they talk with each other. Focus can also be *sharp* or *soft*. Monaco comments that certain kinds of focusing may have particular effects. Soft focus may be used to create a romantic or nostalgic feel to a scene, for example. But again, the precise effects of a particular kind of focus may not correspond to these sorts of generalizations.

focus

The **angle** of shots also needs to be considered. The angle of *approach*, for example: is it square or oblique? The angle of *elevation* matters too: it can be overhead (looking right down onto the scene), high angle, eye level or low angle (looking up at the scene). The shot may also *roll*, which is when the horizon of the image tilts, although Monaco notes that this is rare since it disrupts the union between camera and audience that cinema especially very often tries to maintain.

angle

The **point of view** adopted by shots is also crucial to a film's effects. The camera may adopt the point of view of a particular character, for example, and in Chapter 6 we will see what use Hitchcock made of this device in his film *Vertigo*. The *reverse-angle* shot is a particular case of the camera adopting characters' points of view. It is very often used to show a conversation between two people: one is seen talking or listening from approximately the other's viewpoint as the other listens or talks. An example of this technique was the conversation between villain Robert de Niro and cop Al Pacino in Michael Mann's *Heat*: their conversational confrontation in the movie was shot entirely with reverse angles so the viewer never saw the two men in the same frame together, an indication of the divisions between them perhaps. The camera may also adopt what Monaco (2000: 211) calls the *'third person'* shot, in which 'the camera often seems to take on a character of its own, separate from those of the characters'. In classic Hollywood movies, the opening point of view is very often a particular sort of this third person shot. It is an *establishing* shot, which works to give the audience the information they need about place, time and character before the narrative begins.

point of view

Finally, Monaco offers a number of terms that refer to the way that the camera itself moves in film images. The camera can revolve while remaining stationary, or it can physically move. There are three kinds of shots possible when the camera revolves (Monaco 2000: 97): the **pan**, when the camera

pan

moves along a horizontal axis, perhaps along the horizon of a landscape; the
tilt   **tilt**, when it moves along a vertical axis, perhaps moving from the head to the
roll   feet of a character; and the **roll**, which has already been noted. When the cam-
tracking   era itself moves, the shot is a **tracking** shot if the line it follows is horizontal,
crane   and a **crane** shot if the line it follows is vertical. An example of a tracking shot
mentioned by Monaco (2000: 219) is the opening shot of Robert Altman's
film *The Player*. This is a very long tracking shot which is also an establishing shot, as it moves through the lot of a Hollywood studio introducing loca-
zoom   tion and characters to the audience. Finally, there is the **zoom** shot, which is
similar to a tracking shot but is made by a stationary camera. In a zoom shot,
the figure in a scene remains the same size while the surroundings they are
moving through change in size.

4.2 montage

Montage refers to how the shots of a film are put together; that is, how they
editing   are presented. Another term for montage is **editing**. As Monaco (2000) comments, the vocabulary for describing different montage techniques is much
less well-developed than that which can be used to describe frames and shots.

In classic Hollywood cinema, and in many of its commercial products
today, the principle behind montage is the maintainance of an impression of
both narrative flow and spatial coherence. The kind of editing used to achieve
continuity cutting   this is known as **continuity cutting**. Shots are edited in order to allow the clear
development of the story and to maintain a realistic representation of the
spaces which the narrative occupies. There are many ways in which this is
done, and as audiences of films we take many of them for granted.
Establishing shots and reverse angles, for example, are seen as realistic ways
of showing place and characters. Editing techiques like *jump cuts*, for example, when two completely unrelated images are spliced together, were rare in
classic Hollywood cinema, because we do not perceive the world like that
(although as Monaco [2000] comments, many of the techniques we see as
representing realistically how we see the world bear little resemblance to how
we do actually look).

cut   The jump cut is one sort of connection, or **cut**, that can be made between
shots. It is an example of an *unmarked cut*, where one image ends and
another starts. Other sorts of connections are the *fade*, where an image fades
to black, the *dissolve*, which superimposes a fade in over a fade out, the *iris*,
in which the image is reduced in size by an encroaching border circle, and the
wipe, mentioned in the previous section, where one image removes another.
Ocean's Eleven has a striking dissolve cut too, which fades out of focus (not
to black) on a bunch of red balloons being sold in a street in Las Vegas and
fades in again to the same bunch of balloons being carried through a casino.
The *rhythm* of cuts, determined by how long each shot is held, may also be
important in considering a film's effects. Jose Arroyo (2000) comments on the

effects of a certain rhythm of cuts in the film *Mission: Impossible*, in a scene where our hero is suspended by wires from the ceiling of a high-security room, attempting to steal a computer disk; as he hangs, a bead of sweat drops from him onto the pressure-sensitive floor. This is filmed in a series of short, sharp cuts, to build suspense, interspersed with longer slow motion shots, as the sweat drop falls. Arroyo (2000: 25) says that 'the cominbined effect [of these shots] is sublime. The slow motion fixes our gaze with awe; the quick cuts rush us headlong into terror'. Indeed, Monaco comments that a series of progressively shorter scenes is a technique often used to accumulate tension as a narrative climax develops. Monaco (2000: 220–4) also spends some time on the complicated schema for describing montage developed by Christian Metz, a rare example of an attempt to formulate a typology for all montage possibilities and rather elaborate as a result.

focus

Steven Sodebergh's film *Ocean's Eleven* is a slick Hollywood thriller, superbly shot and edited to maintain the flow of its story, which follows a group of con-men as they attempt to steal millions of dollars from the vault of a Las Vegas casino. (The soundtrack is also crucial to its flow and style, and section 4.3 below will emphasize the importance of sound to movies.)

Watch *Ocean's Eleven* on DVD. Choose a chapter at random and describe it using the vocabulary presented in sections 4.1 and 4.2.

You will have found that describing all the shots and edits of even a small part of a film is very time-consuming. This raises an interesting question for the compositional interpretation of moving images: how do you choose which shots and edits to discuss when you are describing the film?

4.3 sound

Sound is crucial to many moving images, especially movies. Monaco (2000) suggests that there are three types of sound: *environmental*, *speech* and *music*. Environmental sounds are noise effects, whether 'real' or artificial, and Monaco (2000: 213) comments that they can be crucial to a movie's expressive content. The music soundtrack of a movie is also fundamental to its effect. A final example from *Ocean's Eleven* makes this point. The opening scene has one of the main characters, Danny Ocean, in prison, facing his parole board. When asked what he intends to do if he is given parole, he doesn't answer; instead, the soundtrack begins that will accompany the gang throughout their con, clearly suggesting that Danny has planned the con already and it is what he will do if released.

Monaco (2000: 214–15) also suggests three overlapping ways in which the relation between the sound and the image of a film can be considered. The *source* of the sound can be in or out of the frame. *Parallell* sound is sound that is actual, synchronous with and related to the image. In contrast, *contrapuntal* sound is commentative, asynchronous and opposes the image.

4.4 a summary of Monaco's schema

To summarize Monaco's descriptive vocabulary, the mise-en-scène can be understood in terms of its:

- *frame:*
  - *screen ratio*
  - *screen frame*: open or closed
  - *screen planes*: frame plane, geographical plane and depth plane
  - *multiple images*
  - *superimpositions*

- *shots*:
  - *shot distance*: extreme long shot, long shot, full, three-quarters, medium, head and shoulders, close-up shot
  - *shot focus*: deep or shallow, sharp or soft
  - *shot angle*: angle of approach, angle of elevation, angle of roll
  - *point of view*: character, third person, establishing, reverse angle
  - *pans*, *tilts*, *zooms* and *rolls*, when the camera remains in one position
  - *tracking* and *crane* shots, when the camera itself moves

  The montage of a moving image can be described with reference to its:

- *cuts*:
  - *type of cut*: unmarked, fade, dissolve, iris, jump
  - *rhythm*

The sounds of moving images can be described by considering their:

  - *type*: music, environmental sound, speech
  - *relation to the image*: source, parallel, contrapuntal

Finally, there is one thing that Monaco (2000) pays little attention to but which is central to some kinds of film and to criticism of those films: **narrative structure**. What is the story that a movie tells? What happens to its characters? Section 6 in Chapter 6 will discuss an interpretation of a film that pays close attention to the structure of its story as well as to its visual representation.

narrative structure

5 compositional interpretation: an assessment

Compositional interpretation offers ways of describing the content, colour, spatial organization, light and expressive content of a still image, and the mise-en-scène, montage, sound and (less centrally) the narrative structure of a moving image. This is very useful as a first stage of getting to grips with an image that is new to you, and it remains useful as a way of describing the visual impact of an image. In its concern for the spatial organization of an image, moreover, compositional interpretation may also begin to say something about an image's possible effects on a spectator.

However, in relation to the criteria for a critical visual methodology spelled out in Chapter 1, compositional interpretation has many shortcomings. It does not encourage discussion of the production of an image (other than of its technological or compositional modalities), nor of how it might be used, understood and interpreted by various viewers. Mark Garrett Cooper (2002) has argued in relation to film that the sort of approach outlined in section 4 here has difficulty engaging with the broader cultural meanings and resonances of particular films. And with its unproblematized concern for visual images 'as they are', it does not allow for a reflexivity that considers the particularity of any intepretation. Thus compositional interpretation can end up relying on notions of connoisseurship, or genius, or Art, for example, as Searle's essay does, which simply cannot get to grips with the concerns of the previous chapter about the specificities of particular visualities. It thus needs to be combined with other methodologies in order to address these latter sorts of issues. In his discussion of film, for example, Monaco (2000) also uses terms drawn from semiology (see Chapter 5) to explore how films carry meanings.

summary

- *associated with:*
  Compositional interpretation can (and should) be used in relation to any sort of image, but its roots lie in a certain tradition of art history, and it continues to be used on its own most often in relation to paintings.

- *sites and modalities:*
  Compositional interpretation pays some attention to the production of images, especially their technologies, but is mostly concerned with the image itself in its compositional modality.

- *key terms:*
  According to compositional analysis, some of the key components of a still image are its *content, colour, spatial organization, light and expressive content*. Moving images can be described in terms of their *mise-en-scène, montage, sound and narrative structure*.

- *strengths and weaknesses for a critical visual methodology:*
  This method demands careful attention to the image, which is crucial for any discussion of images. A disadvantage of this method is its uninterest in the social practices of visual imagery.

Further reading

Joshua Taylor's *Learning to Look* (1957) is very useful for still art images, while James Monaco's *How to Read a Film* (2000) is excellent for approaching film, television and video images (and also covers far more ground than just compositional interpretation). For an account of the inadequacies of this approach, and for an elaboration by an art historian of some of the issues raised in the previous chapter, see Michael Baxandall's book on *Painting and Experience in Fifteenth Century Italy* (1972). This book was one of the earliest efforts to show that 'social history and art history are continuous, each offering necessary insights into the other' (Baxandall 1972: v).

4
content analysis
counting what you (think you) see

key example a book by Catherine Lutz and Jane Collins which analyses nearly 600 of the photographs published in the magazine *National Geographic* between 1950 and 1986.

1 content analysis: an introduction

This chapter discusses a method of analysing visual images that was originally developed to interpret written and spoken texts: content analysis. In one way, content analysis stands in sharp contrast to the method examined in the previous chapter. Whereas compositional interpretation is methodologically silent, relying instead on that elusive thing called 'the good eye', content analysis is methodologically explicit. Indeed, it is based on a number of rules and procedures that must be rigorously followed for the analysis of images or texts to be reliable (on its terms). Don Slater puts the contrast between these two methods into the broader context of social science and humanities research more generally. Speaking of the post-Second World War period, he says:

> The main line of development in (particularly Anglo-Saxon) social science was structured by the ideals of quantification and natural science methodology. In this context, social research which relied on cultural meanings as data was seen as shaky and subjective, incapable of rigorous control. Moreover, whereas interpretive, qualitative approaches to social *action* secured footholds in social science, cultural *texts* seemed to belong in the domain of literary or art criticism, which were irredeemably woolly and had more to do with refined 'cultural appreciation' than with any tradition of sustained analysis and investigation. (Slater 1998: 233–4)

Whereas what I have called 'compositional interpretation' would have been seen as one version of 'refined cultural appreciation', content analysis was concerned to analyse cultural texts in accordance with 'the ideals of quantification and natural science methodology'. It was first developed in the interwar period by social scientists wanting to measure the 'accuracy' of the new mass media, and was given a further boost during the Second World War, when its methods were elaborated in order to detect implicit messages from German domestic radio broadcasts (Krippendorf 1980). Hence its explicit methodology, through which, it was claimed, analysis would not be woolly but would be rigorous, reliable and objective.

Some discussions of content analysis argue that its definition of 'reliable' equates reliability with quantitative methods of analysis (Ball and Smith 1992; Neuendorf 2002; Slater 1998). However, as Krippendorf (1980) makes clear in his discussion of content analysis, content analysis also involves various qualitative procedures (see also Weber 1990). Instead of focusing on the question of quantification, Krippendorf's definition of content analysis emphasizes two different aspects of what might be called 'natural science methodology': replicability and validity (these terms will be defined in sections 2.2 and 2.3 of this chapter respectively). 'Content analysis', he says, 'is a research technique for making replicable and valid inferences from data to their context' (Krippendorf 1980: 21). In line with the broad approach to visual images outlined in Chapter 1, he insists that content analysis is a way of understanding the symbolic qualities of texts, by which he means the way that elements of a text always refer to the wider cultural context of which they are a part. Content analysis aims to analyse those references in any one group of texts in a replicable and valid manner.

Nonetheless, studies using content analysis do tend to use lots of numbers to make their points. This is because, in its concern for replicability and validity, content analysis offers a number of techniques for handling large numbers of images with some degree of consistency. In their study of nearly 600 of the photographs used in the magazine *National Geographic* over nearly three decades, for example, Catherine Lutz and Jane Collins decided to use content analysis for just this reason. Their defence of content analysis suggests that content analysis can be useful for the visual critical methodology outlined in Chapter 1 of this book:

> Although at first blush it might appear counterproductive to reduce the rich material in any photograph to a small number of codes, quantification does not preclude or substitute for qualitative analysis of the pictures. It does allow, however, discovery of patterns that are too subtle to be visible on casual inspection and protection against an unconscious search through the magazine for only those which confirm one's initial sense of what the photos say or do. (Lutz and Collins 1993: 89)

This passage is worth expanding on. First, like Krippendorf, these authors are insisting that content analysis can include qualitative interpretation. Content analysis and qualitative methods are not mutually exclusive. Secondly, Lutz and Collins are suggesting that content analysis can reveal empirical results that might otherwise be overwhelmed by the sheer bulk of material under analysis, and their own study seems to provide evidence for this. And finally, they suggest that content analysis prevents a certain sort of 'bias'. Clearly they are not referring to the sort of bias that worried some of the early proponents of content analysis; they are not concerned that their work is subjective, 'woolly' or informed by social theory, for example. Rather, like Christopher Pinney (2003), working in a very different tradition (see Chapter 10), they are concerned to avoid searching through photographs in order only to confirm what they think they already know about the photos. They are suggesting that this danger can be avoided by using the rules of content analysis, which force a researcher to be methodologically explicit rather than rely unknowingly on 'unconscious' strategies. Being so up-front about your research procedures is a sort of reflexive research strategy, then. Lutz and Collins's argument thus coincides at this point with the third criterion for a critical visual methodology that Chapter 1 outlined: the need to be as methodologically explicit as possible in order to make your own way of seeing as evident as possible. This chapter will assess the efficacy of content analysis as part of a critical visual methodology by using Lutz and Collins's (1993) book as its case study of a content analysis.

Content analysis would also appear to have some disadvantages in relation to visual images, however. There are aspects of visual imagery which it is not well-equipped to address. It focuses almost exclusively on the *compositional* modality of the site of the *image* itself. It therefore has very little to say about the production or the audiencing of images. In this sense, it is paradoxically very much like compositional interpretation, which has little to say about those two sites of meaning-making either. Its uninterest in audiencing feeds into its proponents' faith in the replicability of content analysis, as we will see in section 2.3; critics like Michael Ball and Gregory Smith (1992) and Don Slater (1998) suggest that the different ways different people interpret the same text has to be ignored if replicability is to be achieved. Finally, some of its critics also argue that content analysis cannot satisfactorily deal with the cultural significance of images either. This latter criticism, it seems to me, depends on how successfully the links between the content of the images undergoing content analysis and their broader cultural context are made. If those links are tenuous, then this final criticism is valid.

This chapter examines content analysis by:

- exploring its claims to replicability and validity;
- describing its procedural rules;
- assessing the usefulness of the kinds of evidence it produces, using the criteria for a critical visual methodology outlined in Chapter 1.

2 four steps to content analysis

The method of content analysis is based on counting the frequency of certain visual elements in a clearly defined sample of images, and then analysing those frequencies. Each aspect of this process has certain requirements in order to achieve replicable and valid results.

2.1 finding your images

As with any other method, the images chosen for a content analysis must be appropriate to the question being asked. Lutz and Collins describe their research question thus:

> Our interest was, and is, in the making and consuming of images of the non-Western world, a topic raising volatile issues of power, race, and history. We wanted to know what popular education tells Americans about who 'non-Westerners' are, what they want, and what our relationship is to them. (Lutz and Collins 1993: xii)

Given that research question, they then explain why they chose *National Geographic* as an appropriate source of images:

> After much consideration, we turned to the examination of *National Geographic* photographs as one of the most culturally valued and potent media vehicles shaping American understandings of, and responses to, the world outside the United States. (Lutz and Collins 1993: xii)

They point out that *National Geographic* is the third most popular magazine subscribed to in the USA, and that each issue is read by an estimated 37 million people worldwide, and that in its reliance on photography it reflects the importance of the visual construction of social difference for contemporary Western societies.

Unlike many other of the methods this book will discuss, however, content analysis places further strictures on the use of images. To begin with, content analysis must address all the images relevant to the research question. This raises questions for content analysts about the *representativeness* of the available data. If, for example, you are interested in tracing the increasing acceptability of facial hair on bourgeois men in the nineteenth century, you may decide that the most appropriate source of images for assessing this acceptability are the popular magazines that those men would have been reading. If, however, you find that a twenty-year run of the best-selling of those magazines is missing from the archive you have access to, you face a serious problem in using content analysis: your analysis cannot be representative since your set of relevant images is incomplete.

Ensuring that the images you use are representative does not necessarily entail examining every single relevant image, however. Almost all content analyses rely on some sort of sampling procedure. This is because most content analyses work with large datasets; this chapter has already noted that this is one of the strengths of content analysis. Sampling in content analysis is subject to the same concerns it would be in any quantitative study. It should

Figure 4.1
'Adioukrou
Woman', an
image from
National
Geographic
magazine

be both *representative* and *significant*. There are a number of sampling strategies described in Krippendorf (1980) and Weber (1990). They include:

- *random*. Number each image from 1 onwards, and use a random number
  table to pick out a significant number of images to analyse.
- *stratified*. Sample from subgroups that already exist in the dataset, choosing your image from within each subgroup again using a clear sampling
  strategy.
- *systematic*. Select every third or tenth or nth image. Be careful that the
  interval you are using between images does not coincide with a cyclical
  pattern in your source material, otherwise your sample will not be representative. For example, in a study of weekday newspaper advertisements,
  choosing every sixth paper might mean that every paper in your sample
  contains the weekly motoring page, which might mean that your sample
  will contain a disproportionate number of adverts for cars.
- *cluster*. Choose groups at random and sample from them only.

Which sampling method you choose – or which combination of methods –
will depend on the implications of your research question. If you wanted to
sample the full range of TV programmes in order to explore how often people
with disabilities were given airtime, you might use a stratified sampling

procedure as described by Krippendorf (1980: 67): this involves 'stratifying a whole year's programming into weekdays and time slots and then randomly selecting for each time slot 1 out of the 52 possibilities'.

---

focus

If you were interested in the representation of Edinburgh in contemporary picture postcards, a random sample would be an appropriate sampling strategy. But this raises some interesting questions about how you access a representative random sample of that sort of imagery. How would you do that?

Would you go into every shop in Edinburgh's main tourist street – the Royal Mile – and buy five cards at random? Would you contact all the postcard manufacturers and ask them to send you copies or catalogues of their current postcards, and select from there?

Think about what you want your postcards to be representative of. While the latter method would be more representative of current postcard production, the former would be more representative of the cards most often on sale.

There are no hard and fast rules for deciding what size your sample should be. Sample size depends on the amount of variation among all the relevant images. If there is absolutely no variation, a sample of one will be representative. If though there are a whole range of extreme variations, the sample size must be large enough to contain examples of those extremes. There are also practical considerations in considering sample size. The sample should not be so large that it overwhelms the resources you have available for analysing it. In their study of *National Geographic*, Lutz and Collins chose one photo at random from each of the 594 articles on non-Western people published between 1950 and 1986 (Lutz and Collins 1993: 88). This was a stratified sampling procedure, since they were choosing an image from subgroups, in this case the groups of photos contained in each article; and they had two research assistants to help them analyse the large number of images that resulted from this procedure.

2.2 devising your categories for coding

Having selected a sample of images to work with, the next stage is to devise a set of categories for coding the images. 'Coding' means attaching a set of descriptive labels (or 'categories') to the images. This is a crucial stage. As

Slater (1998: 236) notes, much of the rigour of classic content analysis relies on the structure of categories used in the coding process, because the categories should be apparently objective in a number of ways and therefore only describe what is 'really' there in the text or image. More recent users of content analysis like Lutz and Collins (1993) develop their categories in relation to their theoretical concerns so that their categories are immediately more obviously interpretive. This is one of their tactics that allows them to make their claim that content analysis and qualitative analysis are not mutually exclusive.

The **coding categories** used must have a number of characteristics regardless of their putative status as descriptive or interpretive, however. They must be: **coding categories**

- *exhaustive*. Every aspect of the images with which the research is concerned must be covered by one category.
- *exclusive*. Categories must not overlap.
- *enlightening*. As Slater (1998: 236) says, the categories must produce 'a breakdown of imagery that will be analytically interesting and coherent'.

Achieving a list of coding categories that satisfies these criteria is extremely difficult. When faced with a large number of images, their sheer richness is likely to be overwhelming. For advertisements or TV programmes, the written or spoken text will also need coding, and so too may background music. As Lutz and Collins (1993: 89) say, the process of reducing the rich material in any photograph to a series of codes is just that: a reduction in which much will be lost. The key point to remember, though, is that the images must be reduced to a number of component parts which can be labelled in a way that has some analytical significance. That is, the codes used must depend on a theorized connection between the image and the broader cultural context in which its meaning is made. 'Theorized', because making this connection entails drawing on a theoretical and empirical understanding of the images under consideration. Thus the connection between text, context and code requires careful thought, and it is on the integrity of this link that the codes can be judged **valid** (Krippendorf 1980: 129). A starting point is the research question driving the content analysis. What coding categories does that suggest? Some may be obvious. For more, though, it is necessary to return to the wider theoretical and empirical literature from which the research question has been formulated. Are there arguments there that suggest other codes? This return to the broader context of the research question will hopefully ensure that the categories eventually decided upon are 'enlightening'. Further codes might suggest themselves from the familiarity you already have with this particular set of images. Does anything strike you as interesting, unusual or unexpected about them that might bear further analysis? **valid**

The coding categories developed by Lutz and Collins (1993: 285) depend on a particular theoretical literature about 'power, race, and history'. Each of the 598 photographs in their sample was coded for:

1 world location
2 unit of article organization (region, nation-state, ethnic group, other)
3 number of photographs including Westerners in an article
4 smiling in a photograph
5 gender of adults depicted
6 age of those depicted
7 aggressive activity or military personnel or weapons shown
8 activity level of main foreground figures
9 activity type of main foreground figures
10 camera gaze of main person photographed
11 surroundings of people photographed
12 ritual focus
13 group size
14 Westerners in photograph
15 urban versus rural setting
16 wealth indicators in photograph
17 skin colour
18 dress style ('Western' or local)
19 male nudity
20 female nudity
21 technological type present (simple handmade tools, machinery)
22 vantage (point from which camera perceives main figures)

---

focus

Think about these categories. Are they exhaustive? Are they exclusive?

Lutz and Collins (1993) are fairly clear about the connection between these coding categories and their initial research question. Their question is formulated by drawing on a large body of work that examines how the West has seen and pictured people in the non-Western world. Some of the key texts they cite include Sarah Graham-Brown's (1988) book on photographs of women taken by European travellers in the Near East, Sander Gilman's (1985) study of racial stereotypes, Elizabeth Edwards's (1992) edited collection on anthropologists' uses of photography in the nineteenth century and Christopher Lyman's (1982) work on photographs of native American peoples. Drawing on this body of work, they argue that, in very broad terms, Westerners have represented non-Western peoples as everything that the West is not. (Hence their use of the term 'non-Western'.) This structure of representation is complex; it draws on a wide range of discourses and varies both historically and geographically, and Lutz and Collins address various aspects of this complexity in their book. However, to take one example of how their codes connect to this understanding of certain parts and peoples of the world as the opposite of the West, much of the literature they draw on suggests that, historically, non-Western peoples have been represented by Westerners as 'natural'. The West sees itself as technologically advanced but therefore also alienated from nature; thus non-Westerners are represented as technologically less advanced and as closer to nature. Non-Westerners are thus often pictured as using little or so-called primitive technologies, for example, being more spiritual, more in tune with the environment and their bodies, wearing fewer clothes. These analyses inform a number of Lutz and Collins's codes: 12 (ritual focus), 15 (urban versus rural setting), 19 and 20 (male and female nudity) and 21 (technological type present). Given the way their codes flow from a wider set of ideas about power and representation, it is clear that many of their codes are likely to be enlightening, and so it proves. For example, they point out that *National Geographic* represents non-Western people as either natural or as modern, but very rarely as both. It is as if non-Westerners can only be the opposite of, or the same as, the West.

As well as being enlightening, though, exhaustiveness and exclusivity must also be considered when coding categories are being formulated. The only way to ensure that the categories fulfil these latter two requirements is to try them out on the images. Putting the initial categories to use in a trial run on a few of your sample images will almost certainly reveal overlaps between categories and relevant elements of images not covered by categories. The categories must be revised and tried again until they are exhaustive and exclusive. Oddly, the list of codes used by Lutz and Collins (1993), at least as it is reproduced in their book, do not seem to fulfil these other requirements of content analysis coding. There seem to me to be some examples of overlap, for example. Thus 'surroundings of people photographed' seems to overlap with 'urban versus rural setting'; and perhaps 'ritual focus' overlaps with 'dress style', since ritual would only be seen as such (on the theoretical arguments that Lutz and Collins draw on) if it was in local dress.

2.3 coding the images

Now, Lutz and Collins only offer the list of categories as I have reproduced it. Presumably the list they actually worked with had its categories defined much more fully. One would hope so, otherwise there are more ambiguities in their list; if 'world location' is taken to imply which country the article was picturing, then there is a potential overlap with 'unit of article organization'. My queries about the Lutz and Collins categories raise the issue that content analysis tries to obviate, which is that different coders might interpret what seem to be the same codes in different ways.

In order to avoid this possibility, according to content analysis, the coding categories must be completely unambiguous. They must be so clearly defined that different researchers at different times using the same categories would code the images in exactly the same way. This, it is claimed, makes the

replicable   coding process **replicable**. A content analysis should take various steps to ensure this replicability. Codes must be defined as fully as possible and a pilot study should ensure that two different coders using the same codes produce the same results from the same set of images. If they do not, the codes must be refined so that they do. Further tests of coder reliability may also take place during the research process, as Philip Bell (2001) discusses at some length. Lutz and Collins (1993: 88) say that the photographs in their study were coded independently by two coders, with 86 per cent agreement between them after the final codes had been agreed. The disagreements were resolved by discussion, they say. Their categories must therefore have been defined much more fully than the list they reproduce in their book.

Then the coding proper begins. The application of any set of coding categories must be careful and systematic. Each image must be carefully examined and all the relevant codes attached to it. This process is both tedious and extremely important. It needs a great deal of attention, otherwise the danger of 'unconscious' lapses looms, but it can also be rather boring.

Practically, there are different ways to record your coding. You might do it manually, with an index card for each image on which you note the codes you think are relevant to it (perhaps in some abbreviated form). Or you might be able to set up a computer spreadsheet to record this information. The advantage of the latter is that it might make subsequent quantitative analysis easier, especially if you want to do more than just count up totals (see section 2.4).

2.4 analysing the results

The sample of images is now coded. Each image has a number of codes attached to it. The next stage is to count them, in order to produce a quantitative account of their content.

The simplest way to count the codes is to produce frequency counts, which can be absolute or relative (the latter expressed as a percentage of the total number of images, for example). If you are using a spreadsheet, producing frequency counts is very easy; make sure that you don't count everything simply for the sake of it, though. Choose the important frequencies

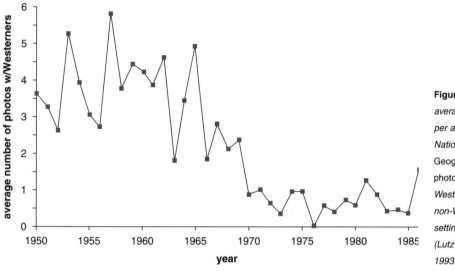

Figure 4.2

*average number
per article of
National
Geographic
photographs with
Westerners in
non-Western
settings, 1950–86
(Lutz and Collins
1993: 40)*

only, deciding which are important by referring to the broader theoretical and empirical framework with which you are working.

A common use of frequencies is to compare them with some other value, and Kimberley Neuendorf (2002: 167–90) offers a useful guide to a range of ways of doing this. A comparison can be made across time, for example. Lutz and Collins (1993: 40) do this for their code 3 (number of photographs including Westerners in an article). (This code too seems rather odd: their codes were apparently applied to one photograph randomly chosen per article, but this code refers not to a photograph but to the article.) This shows a striking decrease in the number of times Westerners were shown in *National Geographic* photographs after the mid-1960s (see Figure 4.2).

In making sense of this drop, Lutz and Collins again turn to their contextual understanding of the *National Geographic*. They suggest that, unlike some other photo-magazines, *National Geographic* consistently avoids presenting images of conflict. Yet the 1960s were a period of conflict both in the USA and elsewhere, and of conflict moreover focusing on precisely the issues of 'race, power, and history'. Both the civil rights movement in the USA and anti-colonial struggles elsewhere in the world, particularly in Vietnam, made the relations between West and non-West, black and white, especially troubled. The *National Geographic* responded by removing pictures that showed West and non-West, black and white, in contact. Thus the illusion of social harmony could be preserved. Lutz and Collins (1993: 120) also compare frequency counts across space, pointing out that the distribution of *National Geographic* articles does not follow the distribution of world population, but rather the geopolitical interests of the USA (see Figure 4.3).

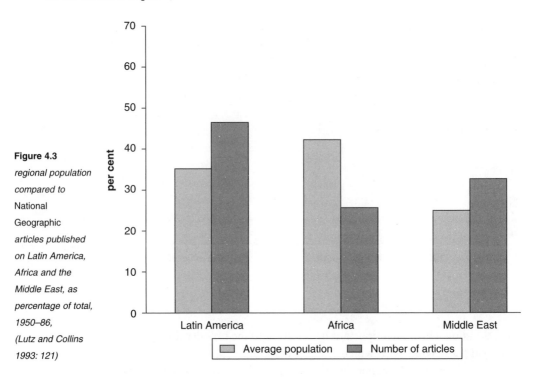

Figure 4.3

regional population compared to National Geographic *articles published on Latin America, Africa and the Middle East, as percentage of total, 1950–86, (Lutz and Collins 1993: 121)*

focus

Figures 4.2 and 4.3 reproduce some of Lutz and Collins's (1993) results. Representing these forms of analysis visually, as they do, is often more striking for a reader than a list of numbers. But there are standard ways of designing graphs and charts in order to show quantitative results (Edward Tufte [1983] provides a useful discussion and assessment of these). These visual ways of presenting quantitative data themselves have a certain effect.

How do figures 4.2 and 4.3 strike you? Are they particularly persuasive because they seem to be 'scientific'?

A more sophisticated analysis can be developed by exploring the relations between different coding categories. This can be done qualitatively and quantitatively. Quantitative measures of possible relationships between categories include associations, cross-tabulations and correlations between two variables, and multivariate analyses between more. Krippendorf (1980) offers guidance here. Lutz and Collins use quantitative correlations at certain points in their book. They note, for example, that 'ritual tends to be depicted in color (χ^2 = 3.008, df = 1, p = .083)' (Lutz and Collins 1993: 94). The correlation between colour and ritual suggests that these are exotic people living spectacular lives; as they say, 'color is the vehicle of spectacle' (Lutz and Collins 1993: 94).

But Lutz and Collins (1993) mostly seem to rely on qualitative interpretations of the relations between their categories. They say that from their content analysis of *National Geographic*, four overarching themes emerged. These were the depiction of Third World people as exotic, idealized, naturalized and sexualized. Now, none of these themes appears directly in the list of coding categories deployed by Lutz and Collins. Instead, they were reached by amalgamating some of those codes on the basis of the theoretical and empirical literature their study was drawing on. Thus 'idealized' was formed from a number of codes: 'smiling in a photo', 'group size', 'aggressive activity ... ', and 'wealth indicators'. Given the number of smiling portraits, the prevalence of pictures of small groups, the rarity of pictures of aggression, and the dominance of pictures of work and middle-class social groups, Lutz and Collins conclude that Third World people are presented as 'idealized': 'gentle natives and wars without brutalized bodies' (Lutz and Collins 1993: 98). Thus non-Westerners are not shown as ill or very poor or hungry or deformed: instead they are given the qualities that the North American *National Geographic* would like to see: happy, not too badly off, hard-working, content. In this way, Lutz and Collins elaborate the symbolic meanings carried by *National Geographic*.

Thus content analysis is a technique the results of which need interpreting through an understanding of how the codes in an image connect to the wider context within which that image makes sense. To do that requires not just quantitative skills but also qualitative ones. Even an advocate of quantitative, computerized content analysis like Robert Weber (1990: 69) has to acknowledge that 'time, effort, skill, and art are required to produce results, interpretations, and explanations that are valid and theoretically interesting'.

3 content analysis: an assessment

Content analysis offers a clear method for engaging systematically with large numbers of images. And it is not simply a quantitative method; clearly, every stage of content analysis, from formulating the research question, to developing coding categories, to interpreting the results, entails decisions about meaning and significance. While Ball and Smith (1992) and Bell (2001) suggest that content analysis is pretty much useless for understanding the cultural meaning of the visual components it analyses, the case study explored in this chapter disputes this claim. Lutz and Collins (1993) suggest that, especially if the coding of images is carefully formulated, content analysis can indeed be used to interpret the cultural meaning of images.

However, to the extent that content analysis does indeed depend on quantitative analysis, some difficult questions about the relevance of content analysis to a critical visual methodology remain. First, it is important to remember numbers do not translate easily into significance. There is a tendency in content analysis to assume that if something occurs very often, it is more important than something that occurs rarely. As Weber (1990: 72) and Ball and Smith (1992) note, this is not necessarily the case. Something that is kept out of the picture may nonetheless be extremely significant to its meaning. An example here would be the election poster analysed by Gilroy (1987: 57–9) (see section 2 in Chapter 1). I am not making the point here that there is a single reality which visual images only selectively represent. Rather, I mean to suggest that certain representations of what is visible depend on other things being constructed as their invisible opposite; and content analysis is incapable of addressing these invisibilized others.

Moreover, content analysis does not discriminate between occurrences of a code: that is, it cannot discriminate between an aspect of an image that exemplifies a code perfectly, and one that is only a weak example of it. Thus simple frequencies may be problematic to interpret. A further problem arises when the difficulty content analysis has in handling the context of its coded image components is considered. Content analysis breaks an image into parts and has no way of handling any interconnections that may exist between its parts, other than by statistical correlation. This is probably not the best way to understand how an image works. Lutz and Collins (1993) demonstrate this when they turn, not to statistical tests, but to theoretical accounts, to pull together some of their codes into overarching themes that form the basis of their analysis of the *National Geographic* photographs.

There is also another problem produced by the fragmentation of an image when it undergoes content analysis, which is the inability of content analysis to articulate what compositional interpretation would call the expressive content of an image. It is very hard to evoke the mood of an image through codes.

Finally, there are the broader issues in analysing visual images that content analysis cannot address. Content analysis focuses on the image itself. But there are the two other sites at which an image's meanings are made: the site of its production, and the site of its audiencing. Content analysis simply ignores both of these. Indeed, as section 1.3 pointed out, in its concern for coder replicability, content analysis assumes that different viewers can see the same image in the same way, and as a method it therefore has no interest in audience creativity. Lutz and Collins (1993) try to overcome these absences by using other research methods to access the way meaning is made at these other sites. At the site of *National Geographic* production, they conducted interviews with the magazine's photographers and editors, to gain an understanding of the social and compositional modalities of production. And at the site of *National Geographic* audiencing, they conducted group interviews with *National Geographic* readers in which they discussed particular photographs. What they found was that at each site, the meanings given to the photographs varied. However, what they do not discuss is the relationship between these three sites. Moreover, further issues are raised if we recall their description of their own content analysis; they gave it the status of the 'discovery of patterns that are too subtle to be visible on casual inspection' and suggested that it gave 'protection against an unconscious search through the magazine for only those which confirm one's initial sense of what the photos say or do' (Lutz and Collins 1993: 89). Lutz and Collins have apparently 'discovered' patterns (which implies that they have uncovered a pre-existing and therefore, perhaps, more real *National Geographic* way of seeing) and have removed any unconscious interpretive predilections. This removes any need on their part to be reflexive in any way other than by reporting their method in detail; any more considered reflexivity is not part of content analysis because content analysis assumes it is an objective method. But what does that suggest about the other meaning-makers Lutz and Collins interviewed? That their interpretations are more unconscious? Less valid? More 'woolly', perhaps? Lutz and Collins (1993) deny that they are implying this. But their defence of content analysis leaves that lingering impression nonetheless. Maybe the natural science legacy of content analysis is harder to leave behind than Lutz and Collins hope.

summary

- *associated with:*
  Content analysis is used to analyse large numbers of images. Most typically it is used in relation to mass media images found in newspapers and magazines or on television.

- *sites and modalities:*
  Content analysis focuses most on the image itself in its compositional modality.

- *key terms:*
  Key terms for content analysis are *validity* and *replicability*, in relation to the development and use of *coding categories*.

- *strengths and weaknesses as a critical visual methodology:*
  Content analysis provides clear guidelines for dealing with large numbers of images consistently and systematically. But it has no way of dealing with those sites at which the meanings of images are made other than that of the image itself. Nor, apart from its methodological explicitness, does it demand reflexivity on the part of the researcher.

Further reading

For a clear discussion of content analysis, consult Kimberley Neuendorf's *The Content Analysis Guidebook* (2002).

5
semiology
laying bare the prejudices beneath
the smooth surface of the beautiful

key example Judith Williamson's highly influential book on adverts, published
in 1978 and called *Decoding Advertisements*.

1 semiology: an introduction

This chapter examines an approach to visual images which has been much
more prominent than either compositional interpretation or content analysis
in the development of the debates about the visual that were briefly reviewed
in Chapter 1. This method is semiology (sometimes also called semiotics). Its
prominence is due in part to the fact that semiology confronts head on the
question of how images make meanings. It is not simply descriptive, as compositional interpretation appears to be; nor does it rely on quantitative esti-
mations of significance, as content analysis at some level has to. Instead,
semiology offers a very full box of analytical tools for taking an image apart
and tracing how it works in relation to broader systems of meaning. Semiology
is also influential as an approach to interpreting the materials of visual culture because it draws upon the work of several major theorists whose impact
on the social sciences since the 1960s has been immense. Judith Williamson's
(1978) classic semiological study *Decoding Advertisements*, which is this
chapter's key example of semiology put to work to interpret visual materials,
cites Althusser, Barthes, Benjamin, Berger, Brecht, Foucault, Freud, Gramsci,
Lacan, Lévi-Strauss, Marx and Saussure at the end of her book, and this is a
roll-call of many of the twentieth century's most important critical writers.
Especially significant to Williamson, as we will see, are those writers central
to structuralist traditions of social theory.

Semiology is thus embedded in a rich and complex series of ideas
whose implications are still actively debated; hence there are different
analytical emphases within semiology, which this chapter will briefly touch

on. The most important tool in any semiological box, though, is the 'sign': semiology means 'the study of signs'. As Mieke Bal and Norman Bryson (1991: 174) say in their defence of semiology, 'human culture is made up of signs, each of which stands for something other than itself, and the people inhabiting culture busy themselves making sense of those signs'. Semiology has an elaborate analytical vocabulary for describing how signs make sense, and this is one of its major strengths. A semiological analysis entails the deployment of a highly refined set of concepts which produce detailed accounts of the exact ways the meanings of an image are produced through that image.

Semiology offers a certain kind of analytical precision, then. As was noted in the previous chapter, so too does content analysis. And, again like content analysis, a certain sort of semiology claims to be a scientific approach to the analysis of meaning. Content analysis is said to be a science because it is quantitative, replicable and valid. These are not the grounds on which the advocates of semiology as a science claim semiology as a science, however. Semiologists depend on a definition of science that contrasts scientific knowledge with **ideology** (this distinction is usually elaborated with reference to the **ideology** Marxist theorist Louis Althusser). Ideology is knowledge that is constructed in such a way as to legitimate unequal social power relations; science, instead, is knowledge that reveals those inequalities. This use of the term ideology is evidence of the formative influence of Marxism on semiology. Marx and Engels famously claimed in *The German Ideology* that 'the ideas of the ruling class are in every age the ruling ideas', and here are Robert Hodge and Gunther Kress defining ideology in the introduction to their book *Social Semiotics*:

> In contemporary capitalist societies as in most other social formations there are inequalities in the distribution of power and other goods. As a result there are divisions in the social fabric between rulers and ruled, exploiters and exploited: such societies exhibit characteristic structures of domination. In order to sustain these structures of domination the dominant groups attempt to represent the world in forms that reflect their own interests, the interests of their power. (Hodge and Kress 1988: 3)

Ideology is those representations that reflect the interests of power. In particular, ideology works to legitimate social inequalities, and it works at the level of our subjectivity:

> ideology is the meaning made necessary by the conditions of society while helping to perpetuate those conditions. We feel a need to belong, to have a social 'place'; it can be hard to find. Instead, we may be given an imaginary one. (Williamson 1978: 13)

Williamson's use of the term 'imaginary' is multi-layered, but for the moment we can understand it as contrasting the imaginary with the real: she is contrasting the imaginary social positions produced by ideology with the actual social relations produced by capitalism as revealed by scientific knowledge. Semiology, then, is centrally concerned with the social effects of meaning.

Williamson (1978) argues that one of the most influential ideological forms in contemporary capitalist societies is advertising. She claims that advertisements are ubiquitous and thus appear autonomous, so that they have 'a sort of independent reality that links them to our own lives' (Williamson 1978: 11). Robert Goldman agrees. 'Ads saturate our lives', he says, and he goes on, 'yet, because ads are so pervasive and our reading of them so routine, we tend to take for granted the deep social assumptions embedded in advertisements: we do not ordinarily recognise them as a sphere of ideology' (Goldman 1992: 1). Both Williamson and Goldman choose to use semiology as a method that can help them penetrate the apparent autonomy and reality of adverts, in order to reveal their ideological status. Williamson describes her understanding of adverts thus:

> in our society, while the real distinctions between people are created by their role in the *process* of production, as workers, it is the *products* of their own work that are used, in the false categories invoked by advertising, to obscure the real structure of society by replacing class with the distinctions made by the consumption of particular goods. Thus instead of being identified by what they produce, people are made to identify themselves with what they consume ... we are made to feel that we can rise or fall in society through what we are able to buy, and this obscures the actual class basis that still underlies social position. The fundamental differences in society are still class differences, but use of manufactured goods as a means of *creating* classes or groups form an overlay on them. This overlay is ideology. (Williamson 1978: 13)

It is evident in this passage that Williamson is happy to make a clear distinction between the 'real' structures of society – class relations – and the 'false' knowledge of social differences offered by adverts. And that false knowledge is, for Williamson, ideological. She uses semiology, described as a science (Williamson 1978: 9), to dissect the workings of ideology. Hence Margaret Iversen's (1986: 84) description of semiology as 'laying bare the prejudices beneath the smooth surface of the beautiful'.

Some semiologists writing more recently, however, are much more circumspect than Williamson in claiming that their knowledges are scientifically true. Hodge and Kress (1988) suggest that any knowledge that sanctions a particular form of social organization must be described as ideological. Thus knowledge that legitimates the social position of dominant groups is ideological; but so too are those knowledges of other possibilities for social organization that are held by dominated groups. To capture this 'double and contradictory' notion of ideology, they prefer to use the term 'ideological complex': 'a functionally related set of contradictory versions of the world, coercively imposed by one social group on another on behalf of its own distinctive interests or subversively offered by another social group in attempts at resistance in its own interests' (Hodge and Kress 1988: 3). The implication of this argument is that the critical goals of semiology are just as ideological as the adverts or whatever that are being critiqued; the difference between them is in the social effects of the knowledges each depends on, not its truth status. Bal and Bryson (1991) offer another version of this argument, simply pointing out that since all knowledge depends on signs, all knowledge is vulnerable to semiological reinterpretation, including that of the semiologists themselves. Elsewhere Bal (1996) has described this as a process of 'double exposure'. When a critic writes about, let's say, a video, not only is the video interpreted and exposed to interpretation; the interpretation is also on display, exposing the critic's ideas to interpretation by others. As she says, there are 'intricacies between ... academic subjectivity and the subject matter it purports to analyse' (Bal 1996: 7). Bal therefore acknowledges the importance of the third criterion outlined in Chapter 1 for a critical visual methodology, and tries to be reflexive about her own viewing practices. Although Williamson (1978) offers a personal account of why she was interested in writing about adverts in the preface to her book, *Decoding Advertisements* is not reflexive in the way that Bal (1996) advocates.

Williamson's (1978) account of ideology focuses on class relations in both their 'real' and 'false' forms. In her book though she also recognizes the centrality of gender to how adverts are constructed, and another development in more recent semiological studies is the way in which the construction of many forms of social difference are explored: class, gender, race, ablebodiedness and so on. Semiology assumes that these constructions of social difference are articulated through images themselves. Section 1 of Chapter 3 has already quoted Norman Bryson making this point, and it is now possible to see the theoretical inspiration for his remarks:

> The social formation isn't, then, something which supervenes or appropriates or utilises the image so to speak *after* it has been made; rather painting, as an activity of the sign, unfolds within the social formation from the beginning. And from the inside – the social formation is inherently and immanently present in the image and not a fate or an external which clamps down on an image that might prefer to be left alone. (Bryson 1991: 66)

Many semiological studies therefore tend to concentrate on the *image itself* as the most important site of its meaning. Its focus on signs means that semiology always pays very careful attention to the *compositional* modality of that site; but its concern for the social effects of an image's meaning mean that some attention is also paid to the *social* modality of that site. However, and again more recently, there have been some efforts to emphasize what this book is calling the social modality at other sites. Bal and Bryson (1991: 184), for example, emphasize above all the site of an image's *audiencing*, arguing that semiology 'is centrally concerned with reception', and Hodge and Kress (1988) have developed what they call 'social semiotics' as a way of emphasizing what this book is calling the social modality at all sites of meaning-making. This chapter will consider their arguments in section 4.

This introduction is suggesting, then, that semiology can fulfil the criteria for a critical visual methodology that were outlined in the first chapter of this book. It offers a range of tools for looking at images carefully; it is centrally concerned with the ways in which social difference is created; and at least some of its practitioners advocate a reflexivity in its deployment. However, as a method it also has its drawbacks. Semiology is conceptually elaborate. Each semiological term carries substantial theoretical baggage with it, and there is a tendency for each semiological study to invent its own analytical terms. This terminological precision accounts for the analytical precision of semiology. It also accounts, however, for a certain density of terminology that is not always easy for the novice to grasp; Michael Ball and Gregory Smith (1992) are not the only ones to see this as one of the disadvantages of this method. Don Slater (1998) offers another criticism: that for all its analytical richness, semiology does not offer a clear method for its application. This chapter therefore focuses more on suggesting some ways to do semiology than on elaborating its theoretical implications. This chapter will:

- examine the central importance of 'the sign' to semiology;
- explore the connections made by semiology between signs and broader structures of meaning;
- look at some work which attempts to consider the social modalities of the production and audiencing of images;
- offer an assessment of the strengths and weaknesses of semiology as a method for a critical visual methodology.

2 choosing images for a semiological study

Semiological studies require extensive knowledge of the type of image the case studies will examine. Judith Williamson (1978: 9) tells her readers that she arrived at the University of California at Berkeley to take a course on popular culture in the mid-1970s with 'a bulging file of advertisements collected over many years' that eventually provided the illustrations for her book, and Goldman (1992: 2) says he was 'watching ads for over a decade' before writing his book. However, neither suggest they had a rigorous sampling procedure, as a content analyst would; nor do either say how they chose which of these many adverts to discuss in detail as examples in their books. This is because semiologists choose their images on the basis of how conceptually interesting they are, it seems. There is no concern among semiologists to find images that are statistically representative of a wider set of images, for example, as there is in content analysis. Images are interpreted in close relation to semiological theory, and the discussion of particular images is often directed at exemplifying analytical points. Thus semiology very often takes the form of detailed case studies of relatively few images, and the case study stands or falls on its analytical integrity and interest rather than on its applicability to a wide range of material.

3 the sign and its meaning-making processes

The 'sign' is the most fundamental unit of semiology. The sign is a unit of meaning, and semiologists argue that anything that has meaning – an advert, a painting, a conversation, a poem – can be understood in terms of its signs and the work they do. Signs make meaning in complex ways, and much of the technical vocabulary of semiology describes the precise ways in which signs make sense.

3.1 what is a sign?

Semiological understanding of the sign depends in part on the work of Ferdinand de Saussure, and in particular on his *Course on General Linguistics*. Saussure wanted to develop a systematic understanding of how language works, and he argued that the **sign** was the basic unit of language. **sign** The sign consists of two parts, which are only distinguishable at the analytical level; in practice they are always integrated into each other. The first part of the sign is the **signified**. The signified is a concept or an object, let's **signified** say 'a very young human unable to walk or talk'. The second part of the sign is the **signifier**. The signifier is a sound or an image that is attached to **signifier** a signified; in this case, the word 'baby'. The point that Saussure made with this distinction between signifier and signified, and which semiological analysis depends upon, is that there is no necessary relationship between a particular signifier and its signified. We can see this if we think of the way in which different languages use different words for the same signified: 'baby' in English is 'bimbo' or bimba' in Italian, for example. Moreover, the same signifier can have different meanings; 'baby' can also be a term of endearment between adults, for example, and in English 'bimbo' does not refer to babies at all but is rather a term that stereotypes certain kinds of adult women. Whatever stability attaches to a particular relationship between a signifier and signified does not depend on an inherent connection between them, then. Instead, Saussure argued that it depends upon the difference between that particular sign and many others. Thus one meaning of 'baby' in English depends for its significance not on a necessary relation between the word 'baby' and 'very young humans unable to walk or talk', but rather on the difference between the sign 'baby' and other signs such as 'toddler', 'child', 'kid', 'teenager', 'adolescent', 'adult' and so on. The actual object in the world that the sign is related to is called **referent**   the sign's **referent**.

The distinction between signifier and signified is crucial to semiology, because it means that the relation between meanings (signifieds) and signifiers is not inherent but rather is conventional, and can therefore be problematized. While 'a sign is always thing-plus-meaning' (Williamson 1978: 17), the connection between a certain signifier and a certain signified can be questioned; and the relations between signs can also be explored. The elaborate technical vocabulary of semiology is aimed at clarifying the different ways in which signifiers and signifieds are attached to (and detached from) each other. The first stage of a semiological analysis, then, is to identify the basic building blocks of an image: its signs. Bal and Bryson (1991: 193–4) point out that it is often quite difficult to differentiate between visual signs, because often there are no clear boundaries between different parts of an image. However, once certain elements of an image have been at least tentatively identified as its signs, their meanings can be explored.

Gillian Dyer's book *Advertising as Communication* (1982) points out that the photographs of many adverts depend on signs of humans which symbolize particular qualities to their audience. These qualities – these signifieds – are shifted in the ad from the human signifiers and onto the product the ad is trying to sell. Here is Judith Williamson analysing an advert for the Halifax Building Society (see Figure 5.1), which offers mortgages for house purchase. Her focus is the way hands are signs.

> The ring ... stand[s] for marriage, and in [the] picture the strong male hand stands for 'Promise, Confidence, and Security'. The pictures are clichéd illustrations of three words. But the point of the ad is to undermine the 'Confidence and Security' offered by the man ... The cliché of masculine security and promise is exposed, to show the need for the Halifax. Yet simultaneously, the image of the ad, the hand and the ring etc., undermined in its literal sense of marriage-as-security, is used in all its clichédness to represent the promise, security and confidence offered in reparation by the Halifax ... In other words, Security, signified by the hand, becomes a signifier, in its possible absence, of the need for Halifax; it is then returned to its original status of signified through the conduit of the product. (Williamson 1978: 34)

Dyer (1982: 96–104) has a useful checklist for exploring what signs of humans might symbolize:

Figure 5.1

Halifax
advertisement,
1978 (Williamson
1978: 34)

- *representations of bodies:*
  - *age.* What is the age of the figures in the photograph meant to convey? Innocence? Wisdom? Senility?
  - *gender.* Adverts very often rely on stereotyped images of masculinity and femininity. Men are active and rational, women are passive and emotional; men go out into the world, women are more associated with the domestic.
  - *race.* Again, adverts often depend on stereotypes. To what extent does an advert do this? Or does it normalize whiteness by making it invisible (see Dyer 1997)?
  - *hair.* Women's hair is often used to signify seductive beauty or narcissism.
  - *body.* Which bodies are fat (and therefore often represented as undesirable and unattractive) and which are thin? Are we shown whole

bodies, or does the photo show only parts of bodies (women's bodies are often treated in this way in cosmetic ads)?

- o *size*. Adverts often indicate what is more important by making it big.
- o *looks*. Again, adverts often trade on conventional notions of male and female beauty. Susan Bordo's book *Unbearable Weight* (1993) is an excellent discussion of, among other things, how adverts picture bodies in ways that depend on cultural constructions of race, gender and beauty.

- *representations of manner*:

  - o *expression*. Who is shown as happy, haughty, sad and so on? What facial and other expressions are used to convey this?
  - o *eye contact*. Who is looking at whom (including you) and how? Are those looks submissive, coy, confrontational?
  - o *pose*. Who is standing and who is prone?

- *representations of activity*:

  - o *touch*. Who is touching what, with what effects?
  - o *body movement*. Who is active and who passive?
  - o *positional communication*. What is the spatial arrangement of the figures? Who is positioned as superior and who inferior? Who is intimate with whom and how? Hodge and Kress (1988: 52–63) have a useful discussion of positional communication.

- *props and settings*:

  - o *props*. Objects in adverts can be used in a way unique to a particular advert, but many ads rely on objects that have particular cultural significance. For example, spectacles often connote intelligence, golden light indicates tranquillity, and so on.
  - o *settings*. Settings range from the apparently 'normal' to the supposedly 'exotic', and can also seem to be fantasies. What effects does its setting have on an advert?

Dyer's list provides a good way of specifiying in some detail how a visual image of humans produces certain signifieds. However, this kind of interpretation clearly requires the kind of extensive knowledge of images of culturally specific social difference and social relations.

focus

Look at the adverts reproduced in Figures 5.2, 5.3 and 5.4. What do the various human figures signify?

3.2 ways of describing signs

There is some debate about how useful Saussure's legacy is to semiology beyond this fundamental understanding of the structure of signs. Bal and Bryson (1991) and Hodge and Kress (1988) both argue that Saussure had rather a static notion of how signs work and was uninterested in how meanings change and are changed in use. Other writers wonder whether a theory based on language can deal with the particularities of the visual. Iversen, for example, suggests that the relation between signifier and signified is different in many visual images from that in written or spoken signs:

> Linguistic signs are arbitrary in the sense that there is no relation between the sound of a word and its meaning other than convention, a 'contract' or rule. It is clear that visual signs are not arbitrary, but 'motivated' – there is some rationale for the choice of signifier. The word 'dog' and a picture of one do not signify in the same way, so it is safe to assumed that a theory of semiotics based on linguistics will fall far short of offering a complete account of visual signification. (Iversen 1986: 85; see also Armstrong 1996; Hall 1980: 132)

Both Bal and Bryson (1991) and Iversen (1986), therefore, while acknowledging the importance of Saussure's discussion of the sign, prefer to turn to the work of the American philosopher Charles Sanders Pierce (see also Wollen 1970: 120). This is because 'Pierce's richer typology of signs enables us to consider how different modes of signification work, while Saussure's model can only tell us how systems of arbitrary signs operate' (Iversen 1986: 85).

Pierce suggested that there were three kinds of signs, differentiated by the way in which the relation between the signifier and signified is understood:

- **icon**. In iconic signs, the signifier represents the signified by apparently having a likeness to it. This type of sign is often very important in visual images, especially photographic ones. Thus a photograph of a baby is an iconic sign of that baby. Diagrams are also iconic signs, since they show the relations between the parts of their object.   **icon**
- **index**. In indexical signs, there is an inherent relationship between the signified and signifier. 'Inherent' is often culturally specific, so a current example familiar to Western readers might be the way that a schematic picture of a baby soother is often used to denote a room in public places where there are baby-changing facilities.   **index**
- **symbol**. Symbolic signs have a conventionalized but clearly arbitrary relation between signifier and signified. Thus pictures of babies are often used to represent notions of 'the future', as in a postcard produced by the Italian communist newspaper *Il Manifesto* (see Figure 5.2). This shows a sleeping baby with a raised fist, and the text 'la rivoluzione non russa' ('the revolution isn't snoring/sleeping' but also 'not the Russian revolution').   **symbol**

La rivoluzione non russa.

il manifesto

Figure 5.2
advertisement for the Italian newspaper Il Manifesto, c. *1994*

Since signs work in relation to other signs, it might also be useful to distinguish between two further kinds of signs, paradigmatic and syntagmatic. **syntagmatic** **Syntagmatic** signs gain their meaning from the signs that surround them in a still image, or come before or after them in sequence in a moving image. Syntagmatic signs are often very important for semiologies of film, since film is a sequence of signs. Thus certain signs in a film may gain extra meaning because they have occurred in a previous scene (for a discussion of semiology in relation to film specifically, see Monaco 2000: 151–225). **paradigmatic** **Paradigmatic** signs gain their meaning from a contrast with all other possible signs; thus the baby in the postcard is a paradigmatic sign because we understand that sign as a baby by deciding that it is not a toddler, an adolescent or an adult.

Signs are complex and can be doing several things at once; so you may have to describe the same sign using several of the terms discussed in this section.

focus

Study the adverts reproduced here (Figures 5.3 and 5.4), using the terms introduced so far in this section.

(Continued)

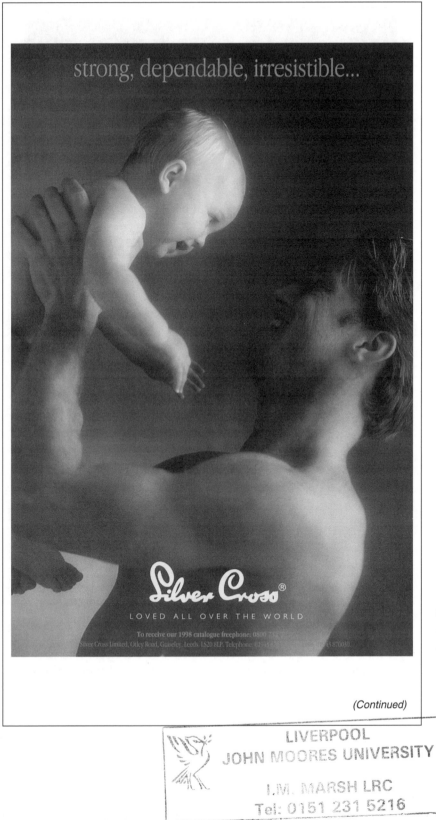

Figure 5.3
*Silver Cross
advertisement,
1998*

(Continued)

What are the photographs' signs? What do each of the photographs' signs signify? In doing this, are they indexical, iconic, or symbolic? Are there syntagmatic signs? What about the text? What signifieds does it evoke? Given the signifieds attached to the visual signifiers, what qualities are viewers of these ads meant to associate with the product?

There are other ways of describing signs. Signs can be distinguished depending on how symbolic they are. Signs can be **denotive**, that is, describing something: a baby, a soother. Roland Barthes (1977) suggests that signs that work at the denotive level are fairly easy to decode. We can look at a picture of a baby and see that it is a baby and not a toddler or an adult, for example. A related term is **diegesis**. Diegesis is the sum of the denotive meanings of an image. My description of the postcard reproduced as Figure 5.1 as showing 'a sleeping baby with a raised fist, and the text "la rivoluzione non russa" is a diegesis of that image. The term is often used in film studies to offer a relatively straightforward account of a film, before a more complex analysis begins. However, although denotive signs at one level may be easy to understand, at another they may have so many potential meanings that a viewer may be confused. A postcard showing a baby, for example, could be a birth announcement, or an advert for baby cream or cot blankets, or a cute card. In the case of the postcard discussed here, the text provides what Barthes (1977: 38–41) called **anchorage**. It allows the reader to choose between what could be a confusing number of possible denotive meanings of a postcard showing a baby. Text in adverts often works as anchorage. In other media, however, (television is an example) the text is much more important in relation to the image; they are complementary, and in this case Barthes (1977: 38–41) described the written or spoken text as having a **relay-function**.

But signs can also be **connotive**. Connotive signs carry a range of higher-level meanings. For example, that postcard uses a picture of a baby as a connotive sign, because that baby connotes the future when the revolution will happen. Connotive signs themselves can be divided into two kinds:

- **metonymic**. This kind of sign is something associated with something else, that then represents that something else. Thus in the postcard example, babies are associated with notions of the future, and the baby is thus a metonymic sign.
- **synecdochal**. This sign is either a part of something standing in for a whole, or a whole representing a part. Thus the city of Paris is often represented by a picture of one part of it, the Eiffel Tower: the image of the tower is a synecdochal sign of Paris as a whole.

Again, it is important to stress that any one sign may be working in one or more of these ways.

Thus, semiology offers a detailed vocabulary for specifying what particular signs are doing.

Marginal glossary terms: denotive; diegesis; anchorage; relay-function; connotive; metonymic; synecdochal

focus

At this point, it is appropriate to mention an interpretative debate among semiologists over the status of signs in photographic images. It is relevant, first, because it has implications for interpreting (some sorts of) photographic images; it suggests that the vocabulary developed in this section may not fully address the impact of photographic imagery on its viewers. Secondly, it is relevant because it parallels the debate in visual culture studies mentioned in section 4.2 of Chapter 1, which is that too much analysis refuses to engage with the 'awe at the power of a ... visual experience' (Holly in Cheetham et al. 2005: 88).

Photography is often thought of as picturing reality, as section 4.1 of Chapter 1 noted. Unlike any other visual technology, there is a sense in which the camera is an instrument that records what was in front of its lens when the shutter snapped; and although photographic images can be framed and filtered and cropped, and can subsequently be manipulated in all sorts of ways and put to all sorts of uses, they nevertheless always retain a visual trace of what was there when the picture was made. Paradoxically, the writer who has made this claim most persuasively – and most movingly – is Roland Barthes, who has also contributed hugely to semiological studies. In his book *Camera Lucida*, which is prompted by Barthes's search for a photograph of his mother, Barthes suggests that:

> It is as if the Photograph always carries its referent with itself, both affected by the same amorous or funereal immobility, at the very heart of the moving world; they are glued together, limb by limb, like the condemned man and the corpse in certain tortures. (Barthes 1982: 5–6)

The referent is there in photographic images in ways it is not in other sorts of visual imagery, Barthes argues. And as a result, he suggests that photographs can be interpreted in two ways. First, there is the level of the **studium**, which is a culturally informed reading of the image, one that interprets the signs of the photographs. But he says that some photographs produce a different response, which is a second kind of reading, by containing what he called a **punctum**. A punctum is unintentional and ungeneralizable; it is a sensitive point in an image which pricks, bruises, disturbs a particular viewer out of their usual viewing habits. And he went so far as to suggest that 'while the *studium*

studium

punctum

(Continued)

is ultimately always coded, the *punctum* is not' (Barthes 1982: 51). That is, there are points in some photographs that escape signifiers and shock the viewer with their 'intractable reality' (Barthes 1982: 119).

Other semiologists disagree with Barthes's claim that parts of some photographs are beyond signification (see for example Hall 1980: 131–2). They argue that photographs are always understood through the meanings that are articulated through them and that no photograph can escape that process even partially. John Tagg (1988), for example, insists that the signifieds of photographic signs always have signifiers, and section 1 of Chapter 8 will return to his argument. Even in iconic signs, where the signifier represents the signified by having a likeness to it, these semiologists insist that that likeness is culturally established, not inherent. As Iversen (1986: 92) says, iconic signs have 'a reception as a reflection of the real'. That is, they are seen like that; they are not actually like that.

Photography thus raises some specific questions in relation to semiology, and these have methodological implications. Is the analytical language of signs adequate to the task of elucidating the impact of photographs? Or is some notion necessary, like the *punctum*, or the 'feel' of an image, or its 'expressive content', which lies beyond the field of its meaning?

3.3 signs in relation to each other

To reiterate a point already made in passing, the distinction between signifier and signified can help us understand the structure of advertisements. Goldman (1992) and Williamson (1978) argue that adverts work by transferring (or trying to transfer) visual and textual signifieds onto their product. Thus the signs in an ad's image and writing usually signify notions of taste, luxury, health, happiness and so on, and adverts attempt to shift the signifiers from the signs in the image and text to their own product. This section explores this process of meaning transference in advertising images more fully.

One of the most productive aspects of Williamson's (1978) analysis of images is precisely the way she shows how adverts work by shifting signifieds from one signifier to another. Indeed, she suggests that this is crucial to how adverts work. The signifieds attached to certain signs in ads get transferred to other signifiers. This process is at work in both adverts in Figures 5.3 and 5.4.

objective correlates

Williamson suggests that the transfers are often made so persuasively that certain objects become the **objective correlates** of certain qualities: certain objects become taken for granted as having certain qualities. Thus by the 1990s it seems quite comprehensible to have a muscled, naked, young-ish man represented as 'strong, dependable, irresistible'. That image can be the objective correlate of strength, dependability and irresistibility, and ads can transfer those qualities from a sign of a man to, in this case, the brand name of a pram and pushchair company.

Williamson (1978: 20–4) discusses some of the formal mechanisms used by adverts that facilitate this transfer of meaning between objects, humans and qualities in an image. She suggests that the spatial composition of the advert is important: what is put next to what, how certain elements are framed. Goldman (1992) concurs, and he notes that most adverts have the same basic visual structure (Goldman 1992: 39–40). First, they have a photographic image; secondly, they have what Goldman (1992: 61–84) calls a

mortise

mortise, which is an image of the product framed in some way; thirdly, they have text in the form of headlines, captions and copy; and finally, they use graphic framing devices to make certain visual links between these components. (However, as Goldman [1992: 70] himself notes, the mortise box may not literally appear in the advert; and indeed, in Figure 5.3 the product is not pictured at all.) Williamson (1978) suggests that one of the most subtle ways in which signifieds are transferred by images is in their use of colour. The use of similar colours in different signs in an advert works to connect those signs and to effect a transfer of their signifieds. These transfers can be between the product and an object, the product and the world, the product and a person, or the whole world might be retinted in the product's colours (as in the adverts for the *Financial Times* newspaper. The paper is printed on pink paper, and its adverts use black and the same pink photography. With their slogan 'No *FT*, no comment', these ads suggest the world is unknowable, or certainly unsayable, without looking through the pink filter of the *FT*'s journalism.)

The transfers of meaning within an image – which operate between and within both text and image – can be very complex. Goldman (1992: 77) suggests that one way to begin to unravel that complexity is to map the transfers. He offers an example of this technique in which he reduces an advert to its basic spatial organization by sketching its compositional structure (see section 3.3 of Chapter 3 for another example of this technique). As Figure 5.5 shows, he then labels the signs in the ad and draws arrows between them to show a transferred signified.

He suggests this is rather a schematic and crude way to represent a process as complex and fluid as the advert's meaning-making, and in this he is correct. But it is also a useful way to begin to think carefully about the relationships between signs in an advert.

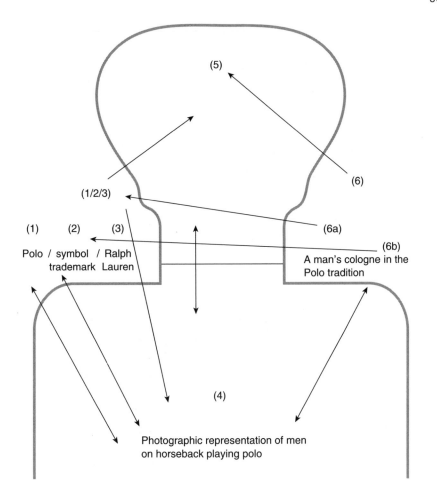

(5)

(6)

(1/2/3)

(1)   (2)   (3)

(6a)

(6b)

Polo / symbol / Ralph
trademark Lauren

A man's cologne in the
Polo tradition

Figure 5.5
*diagram of
the spatial
organization
of an advert's
signs (Goldman
1992: 77)*

(4)

Photographic representation of men
on horseback playing polo

focus

How do the adverts in Figures 5.3 and 5.4 work to transfer signifieds
between signifiers? Try mapping these exchanges of meaning using
Goldman's suggestions: sketch the structure of the adverts, label each
sign and draw links to show the transfers of meaning between signs.

Williamson (1978) also shows how the relationships between the signs in
different adverts have meaningful effects. Her example is two perfume ads,
one for Chanel and one for Babe (Williamson 1978: 25, 26). Figure 5.6 reproduces
them.

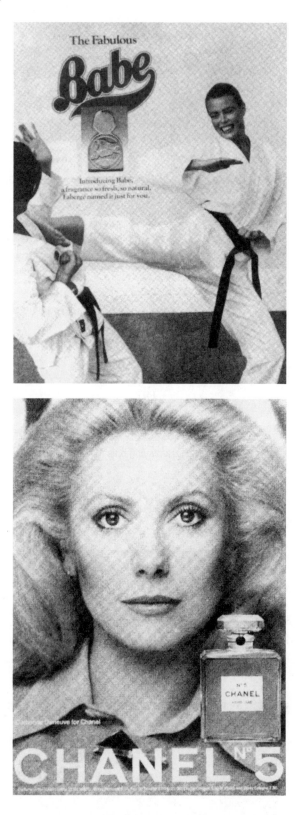

Figure 5.6

Chanel
and Babe
advertisements,
1978 (Williamson
1978: 25, 26)

Williamson quickly notes how the signifieds attached to the two women are transferred within the adverts from the women to the perfumes they are advertising. Thus Chanel is given connotations of French chic and sophistication by the juxtaposition of Catherine Deneuve's face and the bottle, while Babe is made energetic and young by the leaping figure of Margaux Hemingway. But Williamson also argues that the meanings generated by the adverts depend not only on these slippages within each advert. They also depend on the contrast between the two adverts. Thus the quiet sophistication of Chanel is constructed through Deneuve and in opposition to Babe/Hemingway, whereas Babe's youth is constructed through Hemingway and in opposition to Chanel/Deneuve. As Williamson notes, this must be the case, not only because signs work in relation to each other, but also because of the ideological purpose of advertising. As she points out, actually (scientifically), there's very little difference between the products that advertisers aim to sell, so advertisers have to create difference. Thus two bottles of perfume are sold not only in terms of what they apparently are (sophisticated or youthful) but also in terms of what they apparently are not (youthful or sophisticated).

---

focus

Williamson (1978: 29) uses this diagram to represent her analysis of the Chanel and Babe adverts.

Figure 5.7

analysis of Channel and Babe advertisements (Williamson 1978: 29)

$$\begin{array}{ccc} \text{C.D.} & (\neq) & \text{M.H.} \\ \| & & \| \\ \text{No. 5} & (\neq) & \text{Babe} \end{array}$$

Semiological studies often use diagrams to represent structures of meaning spatially: diagrams like Williamson's here, or Goldman's mapping technique. Barthes (1973) notes that this spatialization is only a metaphor: in other words, a metonymic sign. Compare this to Pierce's definition of diagrams as iconic.

In relation to the connections between adverts, Williamson's argument has some methodological implications which she does not spell out. It suggests that in order to analyse one image, or a few, it is necessary to look at the images they are constructed in contrast to, or in relation to. But how are these other images to be identified? Williamson offers no guidance on this point, other than implying that, since adverts have to create difference between basically the same products, it is to other ads for the same sort of product that the semiologist should look. Hence her example comparing two perfume adverts. However, there are a number of other issues to bear in mind. First, Goldman (1992: 44), whose book uses only perfume ads in order to make its arguments, points out that the 1970s was an era of 'celebrity ads', in which famous people were frequently used to promote products. In this sense, the Chanel and Babe ads are actually quite similar. So the criteria of 'similarity' and 'difference' in the relations between ads may need to be carefully considered. Secondly, the self-referentiality of much contemporary advertising might mean that comparing adverts selling similar products may be too restrictive to pick up on an ad's resonances. Thirdly, the meanings of adverts may also be established less in relation to other (dis)similar ads and more in relation to whatever other texts and images surround them in their place of display. This is a consideration ignored by all the semiologists of advertising whose work this chapter has so far cited. But Mieke Bal (1996: 117–28) offers an interesting interpretation of a visual image which argues that the context of its display is crucial to the meanings it accrues to its viewers (and more particularly to her as its viewer: an example of her reflexivity). Her example is a painting by Caravaggio hanging in the Berlin–Dahlem Art Gallery, and she suggests that both the surrounding paintings and the captions on the wall of the gallery, as well as the knowledges and feelings she brings to the painting, affect what it means to her.

If images gain meanings not only from their own signs then, but also from their relation with the signs of other images, it is necessary to consider what sort of relation to other images is most important for the images you are considering. Is it a relation based on 'content'? Or on a shared location of display? Or on explicit cross-referencing? Reaching this decision will help to clarify what other images you need to examine in relation to the ones of your case study. Even so, you will need to develop a broad knowledge of other images in order to be able to identify those that are in a relevant relation to the ones that constitute your case study.

3.4 signs and codes, referent systems and mythologies

Section 3.2 noted that certain sorts of signs – indexical, symbolic and connotive especially – refer to wider systems of meaning. These 'wider systems' can be characterized in a number of ways. They have been called 'codes' by Stuart Hall (1980), 'referent systems' by Williamson (1978) and 'mythologies' by Barthes (1973). Each of these terms means something rather different, and each has somewhat different methodological implications.

code   A **code** is a set of conventionalized ways of making meaning that are specific to particular groups of people. In the context of making television news programmes, for example, Stuart Hall (1980: 136) comments on what he calls the 'professional code' that is mobilized in the work of producers, editors, lighting and camera technicians, newscasters and so on. This professional code guides such things as 'the particular choice of presentational occasions and formats, the selection of personnel, the choice of images, the staging of debates'. It has a 'techno-practical nature' according to Hall because it operates with 'such apparently neutral-technical questions as visual quality, news and presentational values, televisual quality, 'professionalism' and so on' (Hall 1980: 136). The makers of adverts have their professional codes too, which results in the frequent occurrence visual structure described by Goldman (1992) as photographic image, text, mortise and graphics (see also Dyer 1982: 135; Myers 1983). Adverts depend on other sorts of codes too. Crucially, they depend on the codes held by the particular group of consumers their makers want to sell their product to (hence the use of focus groups by advertising agencies to find out what those codes are). Thus the Chanel ad analysed by Williamson (1978) depends for its effectiveness on its audience 'knowing' that Catherine Deneuve is beautiful, stylish and chic; she has to be already *encoded* as such for the advert to be able to transfer those signifiers from her to the perfume. An audience unfamiliar with Deneuve would not be able to make sense of this advert.

Codes can be researched in a number of ways. Goldman (1992), for example, seems to use a very informal (and implicit) kind of content analysis of the adverts to reach his fourfold characterization of advertising's visual code. Leiss, Kline and Jhally (1986), on the other hand, use content analysis explicitly to examine the visual structure of adverts. They also interview the producers of adverts to explore what codes they deploy in the production process. Similarly, Catherine Lutz and Jane Collins (1993), in their study of the photographs used in *National Geographic*, which was examined in the previous chapter, supplemented their content analysis with interviews with the editors, writers and photographers at the magazine, in order to explore the codes they mobilized to make the publication look the way it does.

As Hall (1980) makes clear, codes allow the semiologist access to the wider ideologies at work in a society. 'At the connotive level, we must refer, *through* the codes, to the orders of social life, of economic and political power and of ideology', because codes 'contract relations for the sign with the wider universe of ideologies in a society' (Hall 1980: 134). Thus Deneuve/Chanel are encoded as beautiful and glamorous, and that code is a particular expression of the ideology that all women should be beautiful and glamorous for men. Hall (1980) describes such ideologies as 'metacodes' or **dominant codes**. Williamson (1978), on the other hand, describes something similar as **referent systems**. Williamson (1978) says that there are three major referent systems on which the signs of adverts depend: Nature, Magic and Time. Referent systems, like dominant codes, are knowledges which pre-exist advertising and which structure not only adverts but many other cultural and social forms too. Thus

dominant codes
referent systems

of the referent system of Nature she says, 'Nature is the primary referent of a culture' (Williamson 1978: 103). However, Williamson characterizes referent systems in a more rigid way than Hall does dominant codes. Following the work of the structuralist anthropologist Claude Lévi-Strauss, Williamson argues that referent systems are organized in binary terms. Hodge and Kress (1988: 30) refer to this structure as 'an abstract elemental binary principle, with infinite particular forms produced by this principle applied repeatedly to the material basis of the code'. Thus Nature, says Williamson (1978: 103–37) is in adverts represented in only two ways: it is either 'raw' or 'cooked' (that is, transformed by culture). Many adverts suggest that their products improve nature and picture this with images of 'cooked' nature. Many ads use images of 'science' to suggest that their products can order, investigate or overcome nature (again, in Williamson's terms, cooking it). And many ads use images of 'raw' nature to confer apparently natural qualities onto their products, such as perfectibility, danger and obviousness. Thus Nature is for Williamson a referent system that underlies many of the particular signs and codes of adverts.

Using Willamson's notion of referent systems depends on a broader understanding of culture more generally that is more likely to come from social theory than from empirical investigation. Indeed, Leiss, Kline and Jhally (1986: 165) find Williamson's referent systems just too huge to shed much light on adverts specifically. They imply that analyses of ads would be better based on some sort of 'middling level' structures of meaning, like 'fashion' or 'domesticity'. I suggest that this is what the notion of codes is useful for: referent systems can be accessed through codes, which themselves inform signs.

mythology   Barthes's notion of **mythology** is different again. Barthes (1973: 117) says that 'myth is not defined by the object of its message, but by the way in which it utters this message: there are formal limits to myth, there are no "substantial" ones'. That is, whereas Williamson's referent systems are substantive – her discussion of Nature, for example, is about how Nature is pictured in adverts – Barthes instead argues that mythology is defined by its form, not its content. Myth, he suggested, is a 'second-order semiological system' (1973: 123). By this he meant that myth builds upon denotive signs. Denotive signs consist of a signifier and a signified but they are fairly easy to understand, and Barthes suggests this is the first order semiological system. The denotive sign, however, becomes a signifier at the second, or mythological, level of meaning. At this second level of meaning, this signifier is then accompanied by its own signified. And these second level signifieds and signifiers then form second level signs. In order to avoid confusion, Barthes adopted a clear terminology for these different elements of signs. He called the sign at the first level, meaning; when it is referred to as the signifier of a mythical sign, he called it form. The signified is the concept. And the second level of sign – at the level of myth – he called signification.

'In meaning', Barthes (1973: 127) writes, 'the meaning is already complete, it postulates a kind of knowledge, a past, a memory, a comparative order of facts, ideas, decisions.' Barthes elaborates what he means by this through an example. 'I am at the barber's, and a copy of *Paris-Match* is offered to me. On the cover, a young Negro in a French uniform is saluting, with his eyes uplifted, probably fixed on the fold of the tricolour' (Barthes 1973: 125). This is the meaning of the image (at the denotive level). He suggests that the image contains a kind of richness at this level (remember Barthes's claim that the photograph carries its referent with it in ways other forms of visual imagery do not); the black boy 'appears as a rich, fully experience, spontaneous, *indisputable* image' (Barthes 1973: 128, emphasis in original). When this meaning becomes form, however, this richness is almost lost. 'When it becomes form, the meaning leaves contingency behind; it empties itself, it becomes impoverished, history evaporates' (Barthes 1973: 127). The meaning is put at a distance, and what fills the gap is signification. In this case, signification produces the notion that 'France is a great Empire, that all her sons, without any colour discrimination, faithfully serve under her flag, and that there is no better answer to the detractors of an alleged colonialism than the zeal shown by this Negro in serving his so-called oppressors' (Barthes 1973: 125). The contingency and the history of the meaning becomes remote, and instead a myth inserts itself as a non-historical truth. Myth makes us forget that things were and are made; instead, it naturalizes the way things are. Myth is thus a form of ideology. French imperialism is the drive behind this myth, says Barthes, and this image presents it as natural. But the myth is believable precisely because form does not entirely replace meaning. 'The meaning will be for the form like an instantaneous reserve of history, a tamed richness, which it is possible to call and dismiss in a sort of rapid alternation' (Barthes 1973: 127); the meaning both hides and sustains the form.

As with dominant codes and referent systems, then, the interpretation of mythologies requires a broad understanding of a culture's dynamics.

3.5 slippery signs

This section has explored various ways of understanding how signs make what kinds of meanings. Not all these approaches are completely compatible with each other. However, they do share certain characteristics. Above all, they emphasize the relationality of signs: what one sign means depends on its relations with others. As Bal and Bryson (1991: 177) note, this makes the analysis of signs difficult because it is hard to know where to break into that relationality: 'meaning [arises] exactly from the movement from one sign or signifier to the next, in a *perpetuum mobile* where there could be found neither a starting point for semiosis, nor a concluding moment in which semiosis terminated and the meaning of signs fully "arrived".' In semiology there is no stable point that can provide an entrance into the meaning-making process; all meanings are relational not only within the image but also in relation to other images and to broader dominant codes, referent systems and mythologies. Any point of entry will be artificial and arbitrary, then. But, providing this is borne in mind, this section has suggested a number of steps through which, faced with an image, a semiological analysis might be initiated. In summary, these are:

- decide what the signs are;
- decide what they signify 'in themselves';
- think about how they relate to other signs 'in themselves' (here the vocabulary of section 3.2 is useful, and making a diagram of the movement of signifieds between the signifiers of an image may also help);
- then explore their connections (and the connections of the connections) to wider systems of meaning, from codes to ideologies;
- and then return to the signs via their codes to explore the precise articulation of ideology and mythology.

4 on audiences and interpretations

The meanings of signs are, therefore, extraordinarily complex. This complexity means that their meanings are multiple, and this multiplicity is referred to **polysemy** as **polysemy**. A sign is polysemic when it has more than one meaning. How is it then that Williamson (1978), for example, can speak of an advert as having a powerful meaning that positions its viewers in a specific imaginary social place? Is polysemy limited in some way? Williamson argues it is. This section explores how semiology argues that most images most of the time **preferred meaning** produce what Hall calls the **preferred meaning**.

> Any ... sign is potentially transformable into more than one connotive configuration. Polysemy, however, must not be confused with pluralism ... Any society/culture tends, with varying degrees of closure, to impose its classifications of the social and cultural and political world. These constitute a *dominant cultural order*, though it is neither univocal nor uncontested ... The different areas of social life appeared to be mapped out into discursive domains, hierarchically organised into dominant or preferred meanings. (Hall 1980: 134, emphasis in original)

preferred These preferred meanings (or ideologies) become **preferred reading** when they **reading** are interpreted by audiences in ways that retain 'the institutional/political/ideological order imprinted on them' (Hall 1980: 134).

There are two ways in which semiologists explain the production of preferred readings. The first of these focuses on the visual and textual relation between an image and its viewer, and the second emphasizes the social modalities of the reception of an image.

4.1 the decoder of advertisements

In its discussion of advertising, this chapter has so far argued that the fundamental process through which adverts make meaning is by transferring signifieds between signs. But this elides a crucial part of Williamson's (1978) arguments. Adverts do not effect this transfer by themselves. The source of the movement of signifieds is not the ad itself, says Williamson, but the viewer of the ad. It is the viewer that makes sense of the advert, not the advert itself. Indeed, without a viewer to decode the advert, the ad would be, literally, meaningless. 'All signs depend for their signifying process on the existence of specific, concrete receivers, people *for* whom and in whose systems of belief, they have a meaning' (Williamson 1978: 40). It is in this sense that Bal and Bryson argue that semiology is centrally concerned with the reception of images by audiences; 'semiotic analysis of visual art does not set out in the first place to produce interpretations of works of art, but rather to investigate how works of art are intelligible to those who view them, the processes by which viewers make sense of what they see' (Bal and Bryson 1991: 184).

Williamson (1978) elaborates this argument in a way that has particular methodological implications. Unlike some other semiologists, she pays little attention to possible disjunctures between the systems of beliefs that viewers bring to adverts and what is encoded in the adverts. (Perhaps her estimation of the fundamental importance of referent systems to all forms of cultural expression is responsible for this uninterest in conflicts of meaning.) Instead, she develops an analysis of how adverts encourage their viewers to produce preferred readings. That is, *Decoding Advertisements* analyses the success of ideology. Williamson (1978) argues that ads invite their viewers to create meaning. But in that process of making meaning, the viewer is also made in specific, ideological ways.

> We [the advertiser viewer] must enter the space between the signifier and signified, between what means and what it means. This space is that of the individual as subject: he or she is not a simple receiver but a creator of meaning. But the receiver is only a creator of meaning because he/she *has been called upon to be so*. As an advertisement speaks to us, we simultaneously create that speech (it means *to us*), and are created by it *as its creators* (it assumes that it means to us). (Williamson 1978: 41, emphasis in original)

Thus, she continues, adverts 'invite us "freely" to create ourselves in accordance with the way in which they have already created us' (Williamson 1978: 42). This sense of creative freedom is the most subtle form of adverts' ideology, says Williamson, because it deceives us into thinking that we can choose our social position through what we consume. That apparent choice is deceptive, says Williamson, not only because actual social position is determined by the class structure of capitalist societies and not by consumption, but also because adverts depend on codes and referent systems which precisely delimit our interpretive powers.

Williamson (1978) elaborates this argument by exploring the stages of a viewer's encounter with an ad. First, she says, the viewer creates the meaning of a product by making links between signs. Then, the viewer gives meaning to him or herself from the product; we believe we will become strong and dependable (though perhaps not irresistible – prams are not usually encoded as seduction devices) by buying a Silver Cross product. Third, we become cre-

appellation ated by the ad, in a process Williamson calls, after Althusser, **appellation**. The advert hails us, 'hey you', often quite directly, and thus incorporates us into its signifying world:

> Every ad assumes a particular spectator; it projects out into the space in front of it an imaginary person composed in terms of the relationship between the elements in the ad. You move into this space as you look at the ad, and in doing so 'become' the spectator, you feel that the 'hey you' *'really did'* apply to you in particular. (Williamson 1978: 50–1)

Williamson suggests a number of ways in which adverts pull a spectator into their signifying effects:

- the *spatial organization* of an image offers a particular position to its spectators. For example, Chapter 1 explored how a photograph by Robert Doisneau projects out into the space in front of it a spectator composed in terms of the relationship between the elements of the photograph.
- ads contain or imply *visual absences* that the viewer is invited to fill. For example, the ad in Figure 5.3 does not show the products Silver Cross makes; it involves us by making us fill it in.
- the *written text* draws us in.
- many adverts rely on textual and visual *puns* or puzzles, that make us stop and look at them in order to work out 'what's going on'. Ads can show incongruity, or use no words at all, again to attract our attention and involvement.
- *calligraphy*. This is when the product is transformed into a word. The word then becomes a referent of a real object, the product.

Thus Williamson focuses on the compositional modality of the adverts themselves in her understanding of how they produce preferred meanings.

Finally, she suggests that we create ourselves in the advertisement itself. At this point in her argument she turns to certain ideas from psychoanalysis – including the imaginary – in order to explore the dynamics of precisely how we imagine adverts mirror our self. These arguments will be explored in the following chapter.

4.2 making meaning socially

As the previous section noted, Judith Williamson (1978) explores the ways in which adverts work to produce their viewers in particular ways.

Even though she says it is the viewers doing the work, nonetheless her argument implies that adverts are themselves powerful in the sense that they produce certain kinds of ways of seeing through their visual and verbal organization and connotations. Other semiologists have paid more attention to other ways in which the polysemy of signs is limited, however. In particular, some prefer 'to interrogate which social and political pressures do check the actual dissemination' of meanings (Bal and Bryson 1991: 193).

Perhaps the most sustained attempt to do this – or at least to assert its importance – is the book by Robert Hodge and Gunther Kress (1988) called *Social Semiotics*. They suggest that what they call 'mainstream semiotics' stresses 'system and product' (which is certainly true of Williamson's work, for example), whereas they prefer to emphasize 'speakers and writers or other participants in semiotic activity as connecting and inter*acting* in a variety of ways in concrete social contexts' (Hodge and Kress 1988: 1; see also Jewitt and Oyama 2001). To do that, they refer to 'a second level of messages which regulates the functioning of ideological complexes' which they term the **logonomic system** (Hodge and Kress 1988: 4).

logonomic system

> A logonomic system is a set of rules prescribing the conditions for production and reception of meanings; which specify who can claim to initiate (produce, communicate) or know (receive, understand) meanings about what topics under what circumstances and with what modalities (how, when, why). Logonomic systems prescribe social semiotic behaviours at points of production and reception, so that we can distinguish between *production regimes* (rules constraining production) and *reception regimes* (rules constraining reception). A logonomic system is itself a set of messages, part of an ideological complex but serving to make it unambiguous in practice ... The logonomic rules are specifically taught and policed by concrete social agents (parents, teachers, employers) coercing concrete individuals in specific situations by processes which are in principle open to study and analysis ... Logonomic systems cannot be invisible or obscure, or they would not work. (Hodge and Kress 1988: 4)

production regimes
reception regimes

This seems to me to be a crucial addition to the analytical lexicon of semiology, since, as Chapter 1 insisted, these sorts of social modalities are fundamental to the interpretation of visual images.

Let us briefly consider its implications for thinking about how adverts are interpreted (their reception regime; the discussion of professional codes in section 2.3 very briefly touched on their production regime). Perhaps one of the most important rules constraining the reception of adverts in their original places of display (that is, in magazines or on television or in a cinema or on a billboard, for example, not in a gallery or in an academic text where different reception regimes apply; see Hodge and Kress [1988: 68] for a useful discussion of the importance of the setting of a visual image to its interpretation) is that they are not to be taken too seriously. They are fun, entertainment, they are the gaps in the TV programme when you nip to the kitchen to make a drink. But they are not meant to deal with serious issues. Now of course semiologists would argue that adverts do indeed deal with serious issues: they engage with some of the most important issues, indeed, with questions of social difference and social hierarchy. But part of their power is precisely that they are not seen like that. Their reception regime suggests that they are pretty superficial things. This explains much of the controversy surrounding the advertising campaigns produced in the early 1990s by the clothing company Benetton (Back and Quaade 1993; Ramamurthy 1997: 188–96). Their ads showing a man dying from AIDS-related illness, or a bombed car in an Italian street, caused outrage because these images challenged the reception regime of advertising. They were clearly asking their viewers to engage with 'big' issues – death, violence – and this violated the regime's rule that adverts do not do that. The ensuing efforts by other advertising agencies, by magazines and the rest of the media (that relies on advertising income) to re-establish the reception regime by branding these images immoral or obscene reasserted once more the apparent harmlessness of non-controversial advertising.

Hodge and Kress (1988) also explore the way signs are mobilized by social groups as markers of their difference from others; they call these **metasigns** metasigns. These are the kind of signs that the advertisers of products that are aimed at very specific audiences might try to encode into their adverts, with the aim of appellating that group through the advert and thus encouraging them to buy it.

Finally Hodge and Kress (1988) persistently make the point that all social identity is constructed through ideologies of social difference. They thus insist that different social groups (however defined) encode the world in very different ways and may thus interpret visual images in very different ways. Their example is an advert for cigarettes that has been covered with grafitti by an anti-smoking organization. Bal and Bryson (1991) make the same point in their discussion of visual art. They suggest that there is probably always resistance to dominant scopic regimes, which might 'range from polite parody to outright defacement, from the clandestine inversion of existing rules of viewing to the invention of wholly new sets of rules, from subtle violations of propriety to blank refusal to play the game' – quite apart from the private languages of looking that are evoked, for example, by Barthes's notion of the *punctum* (Bal and Bryson 1991: 187). However, there are very few semiological studies that pursue the diversity of interpretive practices, and the next section explores this and some other limitations of semiological approaches to visual images. Chapter 9 will return to the question of researching audiences' interpretations.

5 semiology: an assessment

by some about the appropriateness of using
images, it seems that semiology can nonetheless
of thinking about visual meaning. Semiology
images, and its reliance on case studies, and its
ogy, create careful and precise accounts of how
ages are made. Moreover, semiology is centrally
ion of social difference through signs. Its focus
plexes and dominant codes, and its recognition
that it cannot avoid considering the social effects

circumstances and according to a finite number
onal, yet not unalterable rules ... The selection of
ination leads to specific interpretive behaviour.
framed, and any semiotic view that is to be
deal with this framing, precisely on the grounds
ny of meaning and the subsequent possibility of
here is no way around considerations of power,
emy. (Bal and Bryson 1991: 208)

sentence indicates, semiology can also imply the
of signs to reflect on their own meaning-making
does an interpretation of a visual image claim?
knowledged in that interpretation? Is the process
or denied?
t semiology fulfils all the criteria for a critical
in Chapter 1. It takes images seriously, provid-
nderstanding exactly how a particular image is
ocial conditions and effects of images, both in
nay have its own effects and how the logonomic
and reception. And it is able to acknowledge
ves working with signs, codes and referent sys-
in nothing more, though certainly nothing less,
rs of meaning in which a particular image par-
n reflexivity.
has some methodological drawbacks. First, its
gs of individual images raise questions about the
bility of its analyses. This is a doubt Leiss, Kline
about Williamson's work. They are unclear
on chose the adverts she works with; are they
general? And would someone else using those

same adverts have come to the same conclusions about them? Williamson would presumably respond that these questions are not important since she was using the ads to construct a general theory that could critique how adverts work; she was not trying to offer empirical generalizations about what they are. And certainly her book's illustrations are there to forward her argument about particular processes of meaning-making, not to exemplify particular types of adverts.

Another criticism often faced by semiology is its elaborate theoretical terminology. Ball and Smith (1992), Wells (1992) and Leiss, Kline and Jhally (1986: 165) all voice concern that semiology tends to invent new terminology for its own sake, and from my experience of writing this chapter I tend to agree. Often these terms are useful; they have particular meanings that are clearly defined, and refer to processes that are not easily described otherwise (this latter point is crucial). These sorts of neologisms are thus worth persevering with, no matter how clumsy their use might feel initially. However, sometimes new terms are confusing or unnecessary, and sometimes they are used to give a veneer of sophistication to something that is actually not particularly interesting. As Leiss, Kline and Jhally (1986: 165) remark, this can lead to an obscurantist text that does 'little more than state the obvious in a complex and often pretentious manner'. This sort of use of jargon should be avoided. If a simpler term will do, use the simpler term.

The use of a somewhat elaborate terminology leads to another issue that needs some thought when semiology is deployed as a method: reflexivity. I have commented, mostly in relation to the work of Mieke Bal, that semiology is capable of acknowledging its own interpretive practices. I would term such an acknowledgement reflexive. However, there is also a strong anti-reflexive strain in certain sorts of semiology, particularly those that claim to delve beneath surface appearances to reveal the true meaning of images. Thus Goldman (1992: 36), at the end of his first chapter which argues that adverts envehicle three key aspects of commodity form, says that 'the triumph of the commodity form is that we do not recognise its presence at all'. This statement immediately invites the question, 'who is this "we"?' It clearly excludes Goldman, since he has just spent 36 pages describing the commodity form in detail. So does 'we' refer to the rest of us poor dupes who don't know our Marx (and Goldman) well enough? What makes Goldman so insightful? How can he see these ads differently to recognize their commodification of product and viewer? Goldman positions himself here as simply the one who sees and knows. He doesn't even clarify his methodology as a way of grounding his claims. This kind of non-reflexivity, I think, cannot be part of a critical visual methodology.

Finally, there is another omission in much semiological work, which is the empirical exploration of polysemy and logonomic systems. Semiology is very ready to admit to polysemy and to the contestation as well as to the transfer and circulation of meaning in theory, but there are very few semiological studies that really get to grips with diverse ways of seeing. Don Slater (1983) has addressed this absence and suggests that it is not a coincidence: semiology is simply not concerned with the social practices, institutions and relations within which visual images are produced and interpreted. He blames this on the structuralist tradition within which much semiology was situated when he was writing, which, he says 'takes as assumed, as given, precisely what needs to be explained: the relations and practices within which discourses are formed and operated' (Slater 1983: 258). This is certainly the case with Williamson's work. She does not explain how she decided that there were only three referent systems underpinning adverts, for example, nor how she decided that Nature, Magic and Time were the three. It seems that this was a theoretical decision that then informed her reading of the adverts. Nor does she pay any attention to the social institutions producing adverts, nor does she consider how different audiences might react to adverts differently or even simply not 'get' them (Myers 1983; Wells 1992). For the advert reproduced as Figure 5.3 to work, for example, you need to know that Silver Cross is a company that makes prams and pushchairs. If you don't – and I imagine lots of readers of this book might not, although most readers of the magazine where it originally appeared probably would – the ad simply does not make its intended connections. Williamson (1978) does not talk about ads that fail like that; her focus on 'the image itself' produces what Slater (1983: 258) calls a 'radically internal analysis of signification' which cannot address these sorts of issues. This is perhaps the most telling criticism of semiology (and one that Bryson and Bal (1991), for example, writing fifteen years after Williamson, are keen to dispel).

summary

- *associated with:*
  Semiology, in its various forms, has been extremely influential across the whole range of disciplines currently interested in visual culture. Its approach has therefore been applied to many sorts of visual materials. Given its theoretical provenance, it is used as a form of critique of those materials.

- *sites and modalities:*
  Semiology focuses on the site of the image and its compositional and social modalities.

- *key terms:*
  The *sign* is the key term of semiology; the *referent* is what a sign refers to in the real world. The transfer of a sign's signifieds is structured through *codes*, which in turn give *onto dominant codes*. Codes and dominant codes encourage *preferred readings* of images by viewers.

- *strengths and weaknesses for a critical visual methodology:*
  This method provides a precise and rich vocabulary for understanding how the structure of images produces cultural meaning. It permits reflexivity. It does not, however, demand reflexivity; its terminology can be difficult to understand, and it remains uninterested in how different viewers interpret images differently.

Further reading

Roland Barthes's *Mythologies* (1973) remains one of the best exemplifications of semiology; it consists mostly of short essays each looking at elements of postwar French culture, but the last section on 'Myth Today' is a more analytical account of his approach. Mieke Bal and Norman Bryson's essay in *Art Bulletin* (1991) is a good introduction to semiology's more recent themes.

6
psychoanalysis
visual culture, visual pleasure, visual disruption

key example feminist psychoanalytic criticism of three films directed by Alfred Hitchcock: *Rebecca,* released in 1940, *Rear Window* (1954) and *Vertigo* (1958).

1 psychoanalysis and visuality: an introduction

Psychoanalysis consists of a range of theories that deal most centrally with human subjectivity, sexuality and the unconscious. Many of its key concepts were developed, and often then revised, by Sigmund Freud (1856–1939). Later writers have then taken his ideas and reworked them, so psychoanalysis is now a very large and diverse body of work. This chapter cannot hope to cover all aspects of psychoanalysis; even more than other chapters in this book, this will be a very selective account. One element of its selectivity is that it will focus on those parts of psychoanalysis that address the visual. However, the visual is actually very important to psychoanalysis. Freud suggested that **scopophilia** – pleasure in looking – was one of the basic drives with which all (sighted) children are born, and the visual is especially important in the work of the psychoanalyst Jacques Lacan. Lacan, building on various claims of Freud, argues that certain moments of seeing, and particular visualities, are central to how subjectivities and sexualities are formed. For this reason, his work has become quite prominent in some approaches to visual culture.

    Another aspect of this chapter's selective approach to psychoanalysis is its focus on a number of feminist authors who are using psychoanalysis, often in its Lacanian guise, to understand how the visual is imbricated in the production of sexual difference. These writers work with various kinds of psychoanalysis to produce readings of paintings and photographs, but most often of films. They pay close attention to these visual images, and they are centrally concerned with their social effects: the ways they produce particular spectating positions that are differentially sexualized and empowered. In this

scopophilia

way their use of psychoanalysis conforms to the first two criteria for a critical visual methodology that the first chapter of this book outlined. As for the third criterion – reflexivity – the assumptions made by psychoanalysis about subjectivity raise some interesting questions in relation to reflexivity, and this chapter will explore these in section 8.

Psychoanalysis often takes the form of a therapeutic practice, with an individual talking to their analyst over a long period of time, hoping to find rest from some sort of psychic pain or blockage. However, the psychoanalytic skills brought to bear on the analysis of an individual are not those used in relation to visual culture. Psychoanalysis is not used to analyse the personality of the person producing a particular image, although this can be done; Freud himself wrote an essay on Leonardo da Vinci, for example. Those writers using psychoanalysis, like so many others currently addressing issues of visual culture, are not interested in the producer of images as an individual. Instead, psychoanalytic concepts are used to interpret aspects of visual images and in particular their effects on spectators. Psychoanalysis does not have a strict code of methodological conduct like content analysis, nor does it operate on the 'tool-box' model as the previous chapter suggested semiology does. Rather, psychoanalytic critics often work with just one or two psychoanalytic concepts, exploring their articulation – or rearticulation – through a particular image.

This close theoretical and empirical focus has consequences in relation to an important point raised in the introductory comments to this book and rather underplayed by the methods discussed in previous chapters: that there is no absolute right or wrong way to interpret a visual image. Different psychoanalytic concepts brought to bear on the same image can produce very different interpretations of that image. The case study discussed by this chapter makes the possibility of different interpretations of the same image clear: it is an examination of diverse feminist viewings of some of the films of Alfred Hitchcock. After beginning his film-making in Britain, Hitchcock moved to Hollywood in the late 1930s and then directed many films which, as Tania Modleski (1988) observes, continue to fascinate their audiences – audiences that include feminist critics, some of whom have claimed the films for feminism while others have rejected them as irredeemably misogynist. Three films in particular have been the focus of feminist debate: *Rebecca* (1940), *Rear Window* (1954) and *Vertigo* (1958), and this chapter will focus on them too.

Film has proved particularly amenable to psychoanalytic interpretation, and from the mid-1970s through the 1980s the journal *Screen* carried many essays exploring particular films in relation to psychoanalytic ideas. Cinema is an especially powerful visual medium because a film can create a total world for its audience. Films manipulate the visual, the spatial and the temporal and, as Laura Mulvey (1989: 25) says, by 'playing on the tension between film as controlling the dimension of time (editing, narrative) and film as controlling the dimension of space (changes in distance, editing), cinematic codes create a gaze, a world and an object'. In particular, film is a powerful means of structuring looking, both the looks between the film's protagonists but also the looks between its protagonists and its spectators. Since psycho-analysis in its Freudian and Lacanian forms argues that visuality is central to subjectivity, it follows that film can address our sense of self very powerfully – and that psychoanalysis can offer some powerful readings of films.

Feminist psychoanalytic film critics have of course been particularly con-cerned to see how films visualize masculinity and femininity in ways that dis-empower women, and how that visualization then positions the audience in gendered terms. However, for reasons the next section will explain, the rela-tionship between feminism and psychoanalysis is an uneasy one, and this has meant that psychoanalytic terms have not always been used by feminist film critics in strict accordance with their definitions by Freud or Lacan. Moreover, as Mieke Bal and Norman Bryson (1991: 210) suggest, if looked at atten-tively, images may well suggest modifications or resistances to some of the assumptions of psychoanalysis; they assume that 'the relationship between the [visual] work and psychoanalysis is an interaction ... conducted among three subjects: the psychoanalytic theorist, the work, and the critic' (Bal and Bryson 1991: 196). Thus feminist writers, among others, have also modified some psychoanalytic terms in order to see seeing differently. For there are issues that psychoanalysis is not concerned to address but that certain images may insist upon, and this chapter will conclude by exploring these absences in psychoanalytic theory.

To expand on these comments, this chapter will:

- examine some of the founding assumptions of psychoanalysis's under-standing of subjectivity, sexuality and the unconscious;
- focus on psychoanalytic arguments about how sexual difference is articu-lated visually;
- explore a number of different feminist psychoanalytic methods of inter-preting visual representations of sexual difference;
- address the issues psychoanalysis raises for methodological reflexivity;
- assess the strengths and weaknesses of psychoanalytic approaches to visual images.

2 a longer introduction to psychoanalysis and visuality: subjectivity, sexuality and the unconscious

To say that psychoanalysis deals with subjectivity, sexuality and the uncon-scious provides a starting point for introducing the ways that psychoanalysis contributes to discussions about the visual. These three terms have implications for how psychoanalysis conceptualizes both the viewer of an image and the image itself, and these two sites – that of the *image itself* and its *audiencing* – are the two sites of meaning production that psychoanalysis examines. Discussion here will begin with their implications for understanding the audience of an image.

subjectivity   To begin with, the use of the term **subjectivity** to refer to a viewer's characteristics – rather than, say, identity – has a number of consequences for psychoanalytic approaches. First, 'subjectivity' entails the acknowledgement that individuals are indeed *subjective*: that we make sense of our selves and our worlds through a whole range of complex and often non-rational ways of understanding. We feel, we dream, we fantasize, we take pleasure and are repulsed, we can be ambivalent and contradictory, panic-stricken and in love; and we can react to things in ways that feel beyond words. Psychoanalysis addresses these sorts of emotional states (and indeed would argue that rationality too is often secretly dependent on these other non-rational states of mind). In relation to the visual, this means psychoanalysis often focuses on the emotional effects of visual images, on the way that the impact of an image may be 'immediate and powerful even when its precise meaning remains, as it were, vague, suspended – numinous' (Hall 1999: 311).

But the notion of subjectivity in this context has further implications. In particular – and this is what distinguishes psychoanalytic approaches from others that engage with the emotional – psychoanalysis argues that understanding emotional reactions to, let's say, visual images requires the recognition that not all of those reactions are working at a wholly conscious level.

unconscious Some reactions may be coming from the **unconscious**. Freud's elaboration of the unconscious is sometimes seen as the founding moment of psychoanalysis. Put simply, the unconscious is created when a very young child's drives and instincts start to be disciplined by cultural rules and values. The child is forced to repress the culturally forbidden aspects of those drives and instincts, and their repression produces the unconscious. The unconscious is thus a forbidden zone in two senses. It is forbidden because the conscious mind cannot access it. And it is forbidden because it is full of outlawed drives and energies and logics. But Freud insisted that it nevertheless has its effects on our conscious selves. Sometimes the boundary between the conscious and the unconscious leaks and the unconscious finds indirect expression in things like gestures, slips of the tongue (which the speaker does not notice), dreams and so on. Thus because of the unconscious, subjectivity, in psychoanalytic terms, is never fully conscious, coherent or complete. We can never fully know ourselves, according to psychoanalysis, because the unconscious remains beyond self-consciousness; and our conscious selves are always likely to be infiltrated by excursions from the unconscious. As Jacqueline Rose (1986: 3) says, 'the unconscious is the only defence against a language frozen into pure, fixed or institutionalised meaning, and … in its capacity to unsettle the subject, is a break against the intolerable limits of common sense'. Psychoanalysis does not therefore concur with the modernist notion that to see is to know; indeed, Lacan (1977: 93) has commented that 'in this matter of the visible, everything is a trap'. Instead, the notion of the unconscious focuses attention on the uncertainties of subjectivity and on the uncertainties of seeing; psychoanalysis is especially interested in visual confusions, blindspots and mistakes.

There are two more implications of this particular understanding of subjectivity that need to be addressed before this chapter explores some of the more detailed methodological implications of psychoanalysis. As well as focusing on the subjective and the unconscious, psychoanalysis emphasizes that subjectivity is also always *subject to* certain disciplines. This should be clear from the previous discussion of the unconscious: the unconscious is formed by the disciplines of a culture, by its particular pattern of interdicts and permissions. Subjectivity is thus culturally as well as psychically constructed, and this process of subjection continues throughout our lives. We are made as subjects through disciplines, taboos and prohibitions. And in the sorts of psychoanalysis influenced by Lacan, visuality is one of those disciplines. We learn to see in particular ways, and this is a process that is reiterated every time we look. Thus visualities and visual images are given a kind of agency by psychoanalysis, because our immersion in a certain kind of visuality and our encounters with certain kinds of visual images tutor us into particular kinds of subjectivity. Thus psychoanalytic approaches, while centrally concerned with the psychic processes of subjectivity and visuality, also address the *social modality* of these processes by considering their cultural constitution. (However, as section 8 of this chapter will explore, not all critics are happy with the way in which psychoanalysis deals with cultural processes.)

Psychoanalysis, then, has a dual emphasis: on the one hand, it examines the constant disciplining of subjectivity; on the other hand, it stresses the instabilities of the unconscious which always threaten those disciplines with disruption. Finally then, and concomitant with this, psychoanalytic approaches also emphasize that subjectivity is always *in process*. Never fully achieved, subjectivity must constantly be reiterated through its engagements with various structures of meaning, including visual images. As Griselda Pollock (1992: 10) says, 'visual representation is analysed ... in terms of its continuing necessity as a site for the perpetual cultural process of shaping and working the subject, conceptualized as precarious and unfixed'.

As a consequence of this particular theorization of subjectivity, psychoanalysis understands the process of audiencing in a specific way. The viewer of an image is understood as bringing a certain subjectivity to bear on an image. But, as the previous two paragraphs have also been suggesting, that subjectivity is imbricated in the images it sees. It is formed through specific visualities, and these visualities are constructed through repeated encounters with images that invite specific ways of seeing. Psychoanalysis is therefore also concerned with the effects of visual images on spectators and pays careful attention to images themselves, especially their *compositional modality*. Stuart Hall summarizes this understanding of the relation between image and audience thus:

> The articulation between viewer and viewed is ... conceptualized in this body of work ... as an internal relation. Indeed, the two points in the circuit of articulation privileged here – the viewer and viewed – are seen as mutually constitutive. The subject is, in part, formed subjectively through what and how it 'sees', how its 'field of vision' is constructed. In the same way, what is seen – the image and its meaning – is understood not as eternally fixed, but relative to and implicated in the positions and schemas of interpretation which are brought to bear upon it. Visual discourses already have possible positions of interpretation (from which they 'make sense') embedded in them, and the subjects bring their own subjective desires and capacities to the 'text' which enable them to take up positions of identification in relation to its meaning. (Hall 1999: 310)

This understanding of the mutual constitution of visual images and spectators often encourages psychoanalytic accounts to take the form of case studies of particular visual images and the precise ways in which they subject the spectator. Even longer studies of a particular genre of films, for example, tend to depend on careful viewings of individual movies in order to develop an argument in relation to the genre as a whole.

In their emphasis on the image itself in its compositional modality as a site of meaning production, psychoanalytic approaches are similar to the previous three methods already discussed in this book. The differences between psychoanalysis, compositional interpretation and content analysis, however, should already be clear. Unlike compositional interpretation, psychoanalysis has an explicit interpretive framework. Content analysis, meanwhile, assumes the rational, scientific researcher who can be fully explicit about their methods; Lutz and Collins (1993: 89) in their study of *National Geographic* magazine, remember, advocated content analysis precisely as a means of 'protection against an unconscious search through the magazine for only those which confirm one's initial sense of what the photos say or do'. Psychoanalysis suggests that such a fully rational procedure (and researcher) is an impossible fantasy. Semiology, on the other hand, does have some connection to psychoanalysis. Indeed, Bal and Bryson (1991), in their discussion of semiology, suggest that psychoanalysis is simply a particular type of semiology; they suggest that it offers a way of interpreting the signs of an image in relation, not to particular referent systems, dominant codes or mythologies, but rather in relation to the unconscious and its dynamics. And Judith Williamson (1978: 60–70) uses Lacan's notion of the imaginary to explain how she thinks adverts do produce preferred readings, and in particular how they offer us idealized images of ourselves (the imaginary will be discussed in section 3.2). One area where psychoanalysis and semiology do differ, though, is the specific things that a psychoanalytic approach picks out.

According to Bal and Bryson (1991: 197), psychoanalysis is 'a searchlight theory, allowing specific features [of an image] to be illuminated, sometimes explained but primarily read, by means of psychoanalytic concepts'. Again, the key concepts in psychoanalytic accounts of the compositional modality of an image are concepts that offer particular understandings of subjectivity, sexuality and the unconscious. Images are interpreted in terms of their subjective effects; and one of the subjections that psychoanalysis has most to say about is that of **sexuality**. Psychoanalysis is centrally concerned with the process through which sexual difference is established and (often precariously) maintained. Freud elaborated what he termed the **castration complex** to explain the differentiation of babies into boys and girls. Freud assumes that all humans begin life in an undifferentiated relationship with their mother. He locates the break from the mother and the beginning of subjectivity with the intervention of the father. (Heterosexual) masculinity is constituted by the boy-child feeling threatened by the father with castration if he does not give up his closeness to the mother (a threat made effective by the sight of the mother's genitalia as apparently lacking); (heterosexual) femininity, in ways less convincingly theorized by Freud, is produced by girl-children seeing themselves as lacking – as already castrated – and transferring their attachment from the mother to the father. (More will be said about the castration complex in section 3.1.) It is this disciplining process, resolved by the oedipus complex, that represses the child's profound drives and desires and thus produces the unconscious.

sexuality

castration complex

The psychoanalytic discussion of sexuality is extremely complicated and often hotly debated. Many feminists reject psychoanalysis outright because they see Freud's account as naturalizing the inferiority of girls or women by affirming them as lacking on biological grounds. Many gay and lesbian theorists reject psychoanalysis on the grounds that it assumes that heterosexuality established through the castration complex is the norm and that homosexuality is a deviation from it. And many black feminists reject psychoanalysis as a colonizing theory that simply erases race as an analytical and political category (see for example Iginla 1992). However, many feminists and theorists of homosexualities and 'race' continue to struggle with psychoanalysis for all its difficulties because they see it as the only productive theory of sexuality that can speak of its complexity, its disciplines and its disruptions. In one of the first sustained explorations of the usefulness of Freudian psychoanalysis for feminism, Juliet Mitchell (1974: xv), for example, insisted that 'psychoanalysis is not a recommendation *for* a patriarchal society, but an analysis *of* one'. And that is the spirit in which this chapter will approach psychoanalysis too: as offering some helpful tools for analysing aspects of the intersection of subjectivity and visuality.

3 watching movies with Laura Mulvey

One of the first – and still one of the most important – essays of psychoanalytic feminist film criticism is called 'Visual Pleasure and Narrative Cinema', and was published by Laura Mulvey in *Screen* in 1975 (Mulvey 1989: 14–26). By 'narrative cinema', Mulvey means mainstream Hollywood cinema. She cites a number of examples and pays some attention to two films directed by Alfred Hitchcock, *Vertigo* (1958) and *Rear Window* (1954).

visual pleasure   The use of the term **visual pleasure** in Mulvey's title immediately suggests that she is concerned with the subjective effect of narrative cinema. This is a subjectivity culturally constructed though: 'this paper intends to use psychoanalysis to discover where and how the fascination of film is reinforced by pre-existing patterns of fascination already at work within the individual subject and the social formations that have moulded him' (Mulvey 1989: 14). Thus Mulvey is exploring the mutual constitution of the psychic and the social. As a feminist, though, Mulvey assumes that the most important of the social formations shaping the subject is patriarchy. She is thus concerned with the disciplining of subjectivity into a particular form of sexual difference. Mulvey is also exploring the mutual constitution of the movie and spectator. She does that by examining the visual, spatial and temporal construction of narrative cinema, and seeing how that effects both the representation of men and women in the movies and the gendering of the spectator. Thus Mulvey's essay addresses many of the key themes of feminist psychoanalytic film criticism. It does so by drawing on two psychoanalytic concepts – the castration complex and the mirror stage – in order to understand the visual articulation of subjectivity, sexual difference and the unconscious in particular ways.

3.1 the castration complex and visual pleasure

Mulvey's account depends on the notion of the castration complex, so, although section 2 briefly outlined Freud's discussion, it is pertinent to say a little more about that complex now. The previous section noted that Freud's account of the castration complex makes the assumption that all humans begin life in an undifferentiated relationship with their mother. However, this is only the first, and least problematic, of a number of assumptions in Freud's argument. Another, and much more problematic, is that all babies feel that to have a penis is normal. Thus when the father intervenes to break up the closeness of that primary relationship, the threat of castration feels real; the baby is threatened with the loss of something important. This notion that the penis is not simply a piece of anatomy but also something meaningful is emphasized **phallus**   by the concept of the **phallus**. Reference to the phallus rather than the penis is meant to indicate 'not that anatomical difference *is* sexual difference … but that anatomical difference comes to *figure* sexual difference, that is, it becomes the sole representative of what that difference is allowed to be' (Rose 1986: 66). In the castration complex, the father asserts that the mother is 'his' and the threat that forces the boy to give up his closeness to his mother (in exchange for himself becoming a man and having 'his own' other woman in the future) is that he sees his mother as not having a penis. And here a third assumption in Freud's account comes into play: that when the boy sees his mother's genitalia, he sees them not simply as different from his, but as lacking. This assumption only works, however, if what Freud is talking about here is not simply vision, but visuality. The boy-child must already be seeing through a visuality that asserts that the masculine position is to look, the feminine is to be looked at, and that the feminine is to be seen as lacking.

Mulvey argues precisely that visuality is structured in this gendered way. She claims that 'in a world ordered by sexual imbalance, pleasure in looking has been split between active/male and passive/female. The determining male gaze projects its fantasy onto the female figure, which is styled accordingly' (Mulvey 1989: 19). Thus sexual difference is understood relationally: visions of femininity depend on the vision of masculinity, and vice versa. As well as this active/male and passive/female distinction, Mulvey argues that the castration complex has implications for images of women in this patriarchal visuality. She says that 'the representation of the female form ... in the last resort ... speaks castration and nothing else' (Mulvey 1989: 14). Thus Mulvey suggests that women cannot be represented in the movies on their own terms, but only in patriarchal terms, as castrated not-men. The analytical importance given to the (missing) phallus in this sort of account often leads to the use of the term **phallocentrism** rather than patriarchy to describe the way cultural meaning is structured around masculine terms. Thus Mulvey's use of Freud's formulation of the castration complex mobilizes not only a set of ideas about sexual difference in relation to subjectivity, but also in relation to visuality.

phallocentrism

focus

The art historian Linda Nochlin (1989: 138 and 142) offers an example of this gendered visuality, reproduced here as Figure 6.1.

Above is a late nineteenth century soft porn postcard showing a woman offering some fruit to the spectator; she is clearly offering herself for 'picking' too. Below, Nochlin has constructed an apparently equivalent image with a man offering fruit/himself. Nochlin's point, though, is that of course these are not equivalent images because the visuality that constructs women as objects to be seen does not allow the spectator to make sense of a man being shown in the same terms; the photo of the man is therefore a joke, laughable. Hence we can see that the dominant form of visuality tutors us into finding only women suitable objects for sexual display.

(Continued)

Figure 6.1
[above] nineteenth century soft porn postcard, [below] Nochlin's construction of an equivalent image (Nochlin 1989: 138, 142)

(Continued)

To what extent might this claim be challenged by more recent ways of visualizing masculinity? Nochlin wrote her essay in 1972. Since then, it has become much more common to use men in advertising apparently as 'sex objects'. Look at the adverts in some recent glossy magazines and consider the ways you, as the reader, are invited to look at the male and female bodies used there. Are both sexualized? How? Are they sexualized in the same way?

Now, it would seem that the sight of women as castrated not-men in the movies would not be very appealing to the movie-goer, and Mulvey has already asserted the pleasurability of the cinema. She resolves this paradox by arguing that cinematic visual pleasure stems precisely from its assuaging of the fear of castration – for men (the role of the female spectator is somewhat problematic in her account, a point to which I will return). 'In the highly developed Hollywood cinema … the alienated subject, torn in his imaginary memory by a sense of loss, by the terror of potential lack in fantasy, came near to finding a glimpse of satisfaction: through its formal beauty and its play on his own formative obsessions' (Mulvey 1989: 16). She argues that this is achieved in narrative cinema in two ways (Mulvey 1989: 21–2). Both these ways involve structuring how the spectator sees images of women in narrative cinema.

The first way she describes as **voyeurism**. Voyeurism is a way of seeing that is active; it distances and objectifies what is looked at. It is controlling and even sadistic, says Mulvey. It is a look that is only given to men by films (whether as characters in the film or as the film's audience). It deals with castration anxiety by investigating the woman and then punishing or saving her. Mulvey notes this is typical of how the women in the film noir genre are represented: as threatening but ultimately guilty and weak. The particular ways in which voyeurism is produced by the spatial and visual organization of a film are various, and some of the tools of compositional interpretation are useful here to describe them (see Chapter 3). What Mulvey looks for is how that relationality between masculinity and femininity is constructed. Particular filmic techniques can include:

voyeurism

- *putting distance between the male and female protagonists of a movie.* In Hitchcock's film *Vertigo*, for example, retired policeman Scottie becomes obsessed with the beautiful woman he has been asked to follow, and the first part of the film shows him trailing her, always keeping his distance to remain hidden from her. In *Rear Window*, photo-journalist Jeffries is immobilized with a broken leg and becomes fascinated with what he sees going on in the apartment opposite his; Mulvey says that his erotic interest in his girlfriend is rekindled only when she enters that other apartment and Jeffries sees her over there, away from him.

- *putting distance between the female protagonist of a movie and the movie audience*. In both *Vertigo* and *Rear Window*, the camera often occupies the position of the hero. Thus the audience sees what he sees, and the women in the film (Madeleine/Judy in *Vertigo* and Lisa in *Rear Window*) are distanced from the audience just as they are distanced from him.

The second way that the image of the castrated woman is disavowed by narrative cinema, according to Mulvey, is **fetishistic scopophilia**. This is when the female figure is represented simply as a beautiful object of display (her objectification shows how voyeurism and this kind of fetishism can overlap). Again, this is a mode of representation directed both at the hero of the film and at the male spectator: she is on display for both of them. Her beauty is so overwhelming, often pictured in huge close-ups, so perfect, that the threat of castration is assuaged as she is turned into a reassuring object in an intimate relation to the spectator. Drawing on Mulvey's work, Mary Ann Doane (1982: 76) says that 'the woman's beauty, her very desirability, becomes a function of certain practices of imaging – framing, lighting, camera movement, angle. She is thus ... more closely associated with the surface of the image than its illusory depths.' Again, the particular ways in which fetishism is produced by the spatial and visual organization of a film are various. They can include:

- *framing*. The obvious framing device is the use of close-up shots, that exclude everything from the viewer's gaze except the body, or parts of the body (often the face) of the female star.
- *lighting*. Doane (1991) describes the way lighting was used in many of Greta Garbo's films to make her face luminous, and so to convey a sense of her almost ethereal, fascinating beauty.
- *camera movement*. Modleski traces the various ways in which the camera shows Madeleine/Judy for the first time in *Vertigo*:

> The camera itself takes over the enunciation ... it first shows Scottie sitting at a bar and then detaches itself from his searching gaze to conduct its own search for the woman through the restaurant. Finally it comes to rest in a long shot of a woman seated ... at a table, with her back to the camera. Romantic music emerges slowly on the soundtrack, and the camera moves slightly forward. It cuts back to Scottie looking and to a point of view shot of Madeleine, who gets up from her chair and walks into a closeup shot of her profile. Only much later will we be able to see her entire face and only at that time will we get to hear her speak. (Modleski 1988: 91)

This camera movement establishes Madeleine, says Modleski (1988: 92) as the 'mute, only half-seen object of man's romantic quest'.

Mulvey also notes that the fetishism and voyeurism through which women are represented in narrative cinema often works to halt the narrative flow of the film; women are represented as passive spectacle.

focus

If you can, watch the opening half an hour of *Vertigo*. How does it invite voyeuristic and fetishistic ways of seeing? If you can't get to see that film, then think about the same question the next time you watch a mainstream Hollywood film. If you're not watching it in a cinema, think about whether the seductive power of film is reduced when it's being shown on a tv screen.

3.2 the mirror stage and visual pleasure

The other major psychoanalytic concept used by Mulvey in 'Visual Pleasure and Narrative Cinema' is the mirror stage. The idea of the mirror stage was developed by Lacan and it is one of the ways in which his work has impacted on some accounts of visual culture.

According to Lacan, babies go through the **mirror stage** when they rec- **mirror stage** ognize an image in a mirror as their self. However, as with the baby's 'recognition' of their mother's castration, this other recognition happens through a particular visuality, and also through a particular construction of spatiality. On the one hand, the mirror image and the body it apparently simply reflects are seen by the baby as complete and whole. This is fascinating and seductive, for the baby's own bodily co-ordination is still incomplete. As Malcolm Bowie (1991: 23) says, 'the child's attention is seized ... by the firm spatial relationships between its real body and its specular body and between body and setting in the specular image'. Thus the child sees a coherent body in a coherent, three-dimensional space. As well as giving the baby a certain pleasing sense of his or her own bodily image and space, this vision also allows the identification of other objects in that space. This is the founding moment therefore of the **Imaginary**, which is the field of interrelations between subject **Imaginary** and other people or objects. On the other hand, the mirror image also involves a misrecognition, since the baby knows that the image is not actually its self. The mirror image involves a certain alienation from what is seen: 'identification of an object world is ... grounded in the moment when the child's image was alienated from itself as an imaginary object and sent back to it the message of its own subjecthood' (Rose 1986: 173). Thus the mirror stage involves both identification with an image, and alienation from it: both recognition and misrecognition.

Lacan suggests that the dynamics of the mirror stage continue to structure subjectivity, and that they explain the importance of the visual to our sense of self. (Judith Williamson's (1978) use of the term 'Imaginary' in her account of the power of advertisements to produce a sense of their spectator's self implicitly references Lacan's argument.) But clearly these dynamics are complex, and the contradiction between identifying with the mirror image and being alienated from it is one of those moments of visual uncertainty that psychoanalytic accounts tend to emphasize.

Mulvey uses the mirror stage to explore the representation of male figures in narrative cinema, and the ways in which the audience is positioned by that representation. The male movie star, the hero of the film's narrative, occupies that coherent space seen during the mirror stage. 'The active male figure ... demands a three-dimensional space corresponding to that of the mirror recognition, in which the alienated subject internalized his own representation of his imaginary existence'; he is 'free to command the stage, a stage of spatial illusion in which he articulates the look and creates the action' (Mulvey 1989: 20). Thus the male hero of the movie occupies a space of depth (compared to the surficiality of representations of women), in which he actively looks. The masculine figure is not therefore himself subject to looking, according to Mulvey. He also propels the narrative; he is active, unlike the passive figure of woman. Ways that a film's spaces and gazes produce this effect include:

- *deep focus*. A deep focus emphasizes the apparent depth of the scene being shown by the film, and allows the hero to move through a space that is extensive. Even in *Rear Window*, a film in which the hero is immobilized by a broken leg, Modleski (1988: 79) suggests that the deep focus given to his view from his apartment window constructs that view as 'an image of wholeness and plenitude' over which his gaze can roam freely.
- *camera movements determined by male hero.*

Mulvey argues that the spectator identifies with the movie hero because he embodies the spectator/subject's mirror stage self-image:

> A male movie star's glamorous characteristics are ... those of the more perfect, more complete, more powerful ideal ego conceived in the original moment of recognition in front of the mirror. The character in the story can make things happen and control events better than the subject/spectator, just as the image in the mirror was more in control of motor co-ordination (Mulvey, 1989: 20)

This identification is encouraged by the way the cameras assume the male protagonist's position when picturing the film's narrative. This can involve:

- *camera position*. The camera literally is in the same position as the male protagonist is shown to be, so the audience sees (apparently) exactly what he sees. For example, in the first scene of *Vertigo*, Scottie is trying to overcome his vertigo by slowly climbing up a small stepladder next to a window; we see him look out and down from the window and the next shot is of the view downwards, which rapidly zooms forward/down and then back again to show what Scottie's vertigo looks like to him.

- *points of view*. Reverse shots often establish which character's view the camera is showing. In *Vertigo*, the camera persistently shows the spectator what Scottie sees during his surveillance of the mysterious woman he is following. Moreover, the audience never sees what she sees as she sees it: we are only given a good look when Scottie goes to look at it too.

Mulvey thus uses two central psychoanalytic concepts – the castration complex and the mirror stage – to explore the way in which narrative cinema produces 'woman as image, man as bearer of the look' (Mulvey 1989: 19). Her use of both these concepts assumes a phallocentric scopic regime in which woman can only figure passively as a castrated man, and men appear as active and powerful, controlling the visual, the spatial and the temporal. This, she says, is 'the way the unconscious of patriarchal society has structured film form' (Mulvey 1989: 14). Mulvey suggests that Hitchcock's movies explore this unconscious. In her brief discussion of *Vertigo* and *Rear Window*, she notes that their heroes are voyeurs of one kind or another. In both films, Mulvey says,

> The power to subject another person to the will sadistically or to the gaze voyeuristically is turned onto the woman as the object of both. Power is backed by a certainty of legal right and the established guilt of the woman (evoking castration, psychoanalytically speaking). True perversion is barely concealed under a shallow mask of ideological correctness – the man is on the right side of the law, the woman on the wrong. Hitchcock's skilful use of identification processes and liberal use of subjective camera from the point of view of the male protagonist draw the spectators deeply into his position, making them share his uneasy gaze. The spectator is absorbed into a voyeuristic situation within the screen scene and diegesis, which parodies his own in the cinema. (Mulvey 1989: 23)

3.3 Mulvey's searchlight

Mulvey focuses on certain aspects of the cinematic image – its spatial organization, the scale of what it shows, its orchestration of looks both between the actors on the screen and between the audience and the screen, and in particular the gendering of who sees and who is seen in certain ways – in order to characterize a way of cinematic seeing that is both gendered and gendering. The pleasure of these ways of seeing for the audience is then also understood in a particular way, as a denial of the threat of castration.

Mulvey's essay has been enormously influential on feminist film theory and feminist theory more widely. Indeed, notions of a voyeuristic **male gaze**   **male gaze** remain extensive in feminist work, and are often used without reference to the specifically psychoanalytic ideas through which Mulvey formulated her arguments. But Mulvey's arguments, though polemical, are nuanced. She suggests that voyeurism and fetishism have quite particular visual, temporal and spatial articulations. These conceptual details are important to remember when utilizing psychoanalytic arguments. Psychoanalysis in many ways depends on the details of an image for its interpretive insight; and it is necessary to be similarly attentive to the detail of psychoanalytic concepts.

Mulvey's arguments are not without their problems, however. She seems to assume that not only can women only be seen as castrated, but that women can only see themselves like that too. This is because she assumes that all the members of a cinema audience, whether male or female, are positioned in the same way in relation to the figures on the screen and that all see them in the same way; the implication is that all of a film's spectators are made to be fetishistic and voyeuristic by the visual and spatial structure of the film. In that sense, Mulvey's argument positions all cinema spectators as male. But is she too quick to suggest that women represent castration and nothing else? Or can women be represented differently? Can women also see actively? Moreover, are all men only voyeurs and fetishists when they look at women? Are other ways of seeing possible, less powerful, less pleasurable too perhaps? And what about men who want to look at men, and women who want to look at women, pleasurably?

None of these questions can be addressed in Mulvey's framework. She assumes a powerful, patriarchal and heterosexual narrative cinema, and places her hopes for critique and change in avant-garde cinematic practices that refuse the visual and spatial organization of Hollywood's narrative cinema. However, other feminist critics have been less willing to give up on what are, after all, hugely popular cultural practices like mainstream Hollywood film. They have looked for other psychoanalytic ways of seeing films, and have brought other theoretical terms to bear on them.

4 from the fetish to the masquerade: other representations of femininity

There are many ways in which psychoanalysis can be used to explore ways of seeing. Many feminists, not surprisingly, have been particularly concerned to see images of femininity that do not 'speak castration and nothing else', for example. Indeed, the notion that femininity can only be represented as lacking – as castrated – has been contested by many feminists, who have turned to other psychoanalytic notions to see femininity in other ways.

Elisabeth Bronfen (1992: 43), for example, has noted that 'one of the theoretical problems inherent in Freud's definition is how the castration complex can be applied to both sexes when for the girl there appears to be no threat in losing something she never possessed'. This does not appear to be a problem for Mulvey, for example, but other feminists have tried to rework the castration complex in order to displace its implication that women can only be represented as castrated. Bronfen (1992), for example, suggests that what Freud explored through the castration complex was the universal process of leaving the primary carer, and anatomical parts other than the penis/phallus might symbolize that process: the navel, for example. Through such strategies, images of women may not necessarily represent 'castration and nothing else'.

One possibility that has been pursued in relation to visual images is to suggest that if women are indeed often represented as smooth surfaces on display for a male gaze, fetishisation might not be the only way to interpret that representation. Perhaps that smooth surface does not hide something horrible, does not conceal a castrated body. Perhaps it hides something else. Or perhaps it is simply that, a surface, that hides nothing: a **masquerade**. This **masquerade** latter possibility was most famously proposed by the psychoanalyst Joan Riviere in an essay first published in 1929 (Riviere 1986). Riviere's essay took off from her analysis of an academic woman who, after her articulate and professional presentations of her work to her peers, would feel compelled to flirt with the men in her audience. Riviere suggested that this woman saw her success in terms of being successful in a man's world and therefore in a sense, for the duration of her performances, becoming a man. This though she knew her mostly male audiences would find very threatening (the only thing more threatening than a castrated woman being a non-castrated one), so after her lectures she would conform to their expectations of female behaviour, and flirt and be charming and non-confrontational. From this Riviere concluded:

> Womanliness could therefore be assumed and worn as a mask, both to hide the possession of masculinity and to avert the reprisals expected if she was found to possess it – much as a thief will turn out his pockets and ask to be searched to prove that he has not stolen the goods. The reader may now ask how I define womanliness or where I draw the line between genuine womanliness and the 'masquerade'. My suggestion is not, however, that there is any such difference; whether radical or superficial, they are the same thing. (Riviere 1986: 38)

Riviere is suggesting that since femininity is not natural but constructed – through processes such as the castration complex but also, we might add, through things like watching movies – there are ways of thinking about femininity as just that, a construction. Femininity can be seen as a mask, a masquerade, performed by mimicking what being a woman is meant to be about. Femininity might be thought of as 'a decorative layer which conceals a non-identity' (Doane 1982: 81). Luce Irigaray has taken this argument even further to suggest that masquerade – or what she calls mimesis – might even be an evasion, in part at least, of those disciplines of femininity. She suggests that 'if women are such good mimics, it is because they are not simply resorbed in this function. *They also remain elsewhere*' (Irigaray 1985: 76).

What are the methodological implications of these arguments about masquerade? Doane (1982) raises the possibility (although she is not herself persuaded by it) that masquerade might provide a way of thinking about how women see themselves and each other that does not depend on the way of seeing outlined by Mulvey. Other critics are more confident that here may be traces of a manipulation of the position of femininity, or its parody, in visual images like films, marked by strategies such as:

- *excess.* The film performances of Marlene Dietrich have been characterized as so excessively feminine that the audience is 'watching a woman demonstrate the representation of a woman's body' (Bovenschen cited in Doane 1982: 82).
- *construction.* A film may show moments when the female body is quite literally donning the mask of femininity: make-up, hairstyle, dress, comportment. An example from a Hitchcock film could be a scene in his 1940 movie *Rebecca*. The heroine of this film (who is never named) is shown at first as a gauche and nervous young woman whose qualities are characterized only by what she cannot do. Thinking that she has lost the love of her husband Maxim (whose first, dead wife was called Rebecca), she attempts to win it back by dressing for a fancy dress ball in the costume of one of his ancestors whose painting hangs in their grand house, and she is thus shown as constructing herself as glamorous.
- *repetition.* In film, repetition may take narrative or visual form. The heroine of *Rebecca* is shown using visual repetition as a means of becoming glamorously attractive too, since her masquerade is a copy of an already existing image of glamour.

Or there may be traces of the 'elsewhere' mentioned by Irigaray: hints at spaces other than those constructed through objectifying distance or fetishizing intimacy.

- *distorted spaces.*
- *points of view impossible in coherent space.*
- *(in)visible absences.* Modleski (1988) persuasively argues that in *Rebecca*, although the character Rebecca is dead, her presence continues to haunt the film in ways that refuse the usual representations of femininity. In particular, her disruptive sexuality is marked by traces of her own masquerades: her clothing, her unfaithfulness to her husband while appearing to be the perfect wife, the way the housekeeper evokes Rebecca's thoughts and actions in the film. Finally, in what Modleski (1988: 53) calls 'one of the film's most extraordinary moments the camera pointedly dynamizes Rebecca's absence. When Maxim tells the heroine about what happened on the night of Rebecca's death ('She got up, came towards me,' etc.), the

camera follows Rebecca's movements in a lengthy tracking shot'. This is a flaunting of lack, not its hiding, and it suggests that the representation of femininity need not represent absence in the phallocentric way that Mulvey suggests.

focus

Some feminists have criticized the notion of masquerade, suggesting that it is naïve to think that constructions of femininity can escape the disciplines of cultural representation. Judith Butler (1990), for example, has chastised Irigaray in these terms, and even Modleski (1988: 53) in her discussion of *Rebecca* has to admit that 'in the film's narrative, Rebecca is subjected to a brutal devaluation and punishment'.

Watch *Vertigo* if you can. The central female figure – Madeleine/Judy – might be seen as exemplifying femininity as masquerade since Madeleine is apparently copying a dead ancestor, 'Madeleine' is being impersonated by Judy, and Scottie forces 'Judy' to dress up as Madeleine again. The movie thus has a narrative and scenes that show the construction of femininity. But does the movie suggest that in being able to make these transformations Madeleine/Judy is occupying an 'elsewhere' beyond phallocentric visions of femininity? Are there other visual or spatial suggestions in the film that this is the case? Or are those transformation scenes embedded in a filmic organisation of the visual and spatial that captures Madeleine/Judy in Scottie's terms?

Mary Ann Doane's (1987) discussion of *Rebecca* raises a similar question in relation to the liberating possibilities of disorientating spaces. She describes the incoherent domestic spaces of a cycle of post-war Hollywood movies not as elements of subversive masquerades of femininity, but as representing a paranoia deeply threatening to the film's female protagonists. Thus in *Rebecca*, the bedroom of Rebecca has been kept as it was before her death by the housekeeper, and when the heroine finally gathers the courage to enter it, it is a strange and disorienting space. Everything is slightly too large for the heroine (implying she is childlike), curtains blow oddly, the housekeeper appears from nowhere and forces the heroine to touch Rebecca's clothes, to sit at her dressing table, to let the housekeeper brush her hair as she brushed Rebecca's.

(Continued)

Figure 6.2 *still from Hitchcock's* Rebecca

The room disorientates the heroine, and what goes on there threatens to replace her own subjectivity with that of Rebecca. Thus, as Doane (1987) notes, this particular distorted space is hardly a subversive space for articulating the heroine's subjectivity. However, Modleski (1988) prefers to emphasize that it is a space in which Rebecca remains powerful, even if the heroine does not. Section 7 returns to the different ways they interpret *Rebecca*.

Clearly the interpretation of masquerade and incoherent spaces needs to take many other aspects of a film into account before an account of their effects can be persuasive.

Notions of masquerade have been employed to disrupt the apparent hegemony of the male gaze as characterized by Mulvey, then. However, they disrupt by offering a supplement to that gaze. That is, they do not fundamentally challenge Mulvey's characterisation of that gaze; they simply suggest that that might not be the full story.

5 from the voyeuristic gaze to the Lacanian Gaze: other ways of seeing

The 'male gaze', then, has become a staple of certain feminist critiques of patriarchal visuality; even those feminist strategies that are more critical of

Figure 6.3 *still from Hitchcock's* Vertigo

Mulvey's reliance on Freud's theorization of the castration complex have tended to take that gaze for granted, even as they search for other ways of seeing. But did Mulvey's polemic exaggerate the power of that gaze? There are hints, even in her original essay, that the voyeuristic and fetishistic gaze produced its own difficulties. After all, the 'hero' of *Vertigo* goes nearly mad in his obsession with the woman he follows. Did Mulvey underestimate the inherent difficulties of masculine looking, then? Other feminists have chosen psychoanalytic materials other than castration, voyeurism and fetishism to work with, precisely in order to theorize a visuality that, while dominant, is not all-powerful. If women are not necessarily castrated not-men, then neither are all men necessarily voyeuristic fetishists.

The psychoanalytic term used to develop this possibility is Lacan's version of the **Gaze**. As Joan Copjec (1989) insists, the Lacanian Gaze is not the **Gaze** same as the 'male gaze' initially theorized by Mulvey and then popularized in many feminist discussions. The most important difference is that the Gaze is striated by inherent failure. Lacan elaborated his notion of the Gaze sometime after his exploration of the mirror stage (for a detailed exegesis, see Silverman 1992: 145–53). In this later work, he is less interested in how the subject sees and more interested in how the subject is seen. The Gaze thus supplements his earlier account of the mirror stage. The Gaze is a form of visuality that pre-exists the individual subject; it is a visuality into which subjects are born. Like the visuality that subjects adopt as their own, though, the Gaze is culturally constituted.

> Between the subject and the world is inserted the entire sum of discourses that make up visuality, that cultural construct, and make visuality different from vision, the notion of unmediated visual experience. Between the retina and the world is inserted a *screen* of signs, consisting of all the multiple discourses of vision built into the social arena ... when I learn to see socially, that is, when I begin to articulate my retinal experience with the codes of recognition that come to me from my social milieu(s), I am inserted into systems of visual discourse that saw the world before I did, and will go on seeing after I see no longer. (Bryson 1988: 91–2)

Following this assertion, there are three ways in which this Gaze fails to offer visual mastery. The first is suggested by Bryson. Since the Gaze 'will go on seeing after I see no longer', Bryson says that it 'casts a shadow of *death*' (Bryson 1988: 92, emphasis in original). It reminds us of our own mortality. Secondly, the Gaze cannot offer visual mastery because it is diffuse, evanescent and irridescent, says Lacan. Indeed, given the way it predates and will outlast the subject, in a sense it looks at the subject rather than the subject looking at or through it. 'In the scopic field, the gaze is outside, I am looked at, that is to say, I am a picture ... What determines me, at the most profound level, in the visible, is the gaze that is outside' (Lacan 1977: 106). The consequence of the externality of the Gaze is that when 'I solicit a look, what is profoundly unsatisfying and always missing is that – *You never look at me from the place which I see you*' (Lacan 1977: 103, emphasis in orginal). Finally, the Gaze fails precisely because it is structured through a screen of signs. Signs, as semiology notes, are substitutes for their referents. As representations, they are different from that to which they refer. For Lacan, the child's entry into culture – into the signs that constitute language, visuality and what he called the **Symbolic** – is a traumatic separation from intimacy with referents. (Lacan's term for a world of referents before the Symbolic was the Real.) Indeed, Lacan reworked Freud's account of the castration complex to suggest that what that complex deals with is not perceptions of anatomical difference but rather the entry into the Symbolic and the substitution of

Symbolic

Figure 6.4
Hans Holbein, The
Ambassadors, *1533*

signs for referents which all babies, boys and girls, go through. Hence the
Gaze, as part of the Symbolic, is also marked by the lack inherent in that
substitution.

Lacan uses a painting to emphasize the lack that haunts the Gaze: *The
Ambassadors*, painted at the court of Henry VIII in London in 1533 by Hans
Holbein (Figure 6.4).

The painting shows two men in luxurious dress, surrounded by the
instruments of scientific knowledge and artistic expression: they are shown as
powerful, socially, artistically and scientifically. But in front of them, at their
feet, is a strange oval shape, incomprehensible in terms of the coherent, per-
spectively represented space of the rest of the painting. This oval only makes
visual sense if the spectator stands to one side of the painting, when it then
appears as a skull. It is a reminder of death, a popular device in seventeenth
century paintings that otherwise celebrated the richness of life. However, its
disruption of the coherent space of the ambassadors and the spectator is a

reminder for Lacan (1977: 88) of 'the subject as annihilated', not only by death, but by the lack that structures the (visual) Symbolic.

This definition of the Gaze has some profound implications for Mulvey's argument about sexual difference in the field of vision. As Kaja Silverman (1992: 151) for one notes, 'since the gaze always emerges for us within the field of vision, and since we ourselves are always being photographed by it even as we look, all binarizations of spectator and spectacle mystify the scopic relations in which we are held'. Hence, since the Gaze looks at everyone, men as well as women are turned into spectacles through it; and since its status as a screen of signs means it is never a complete vision, neither women nor men can attain visual mastery through it.

For feminists like Silverman, this is a much more satisfactory formulation of the dominant scopic regime than Mulvey's analysis of the male gaze. It breaks down the binary distinction between 'woman as image, man as bearer of the look', to suggest that man may be image too and that both men and women may look, but neither and never all-powerfully. For Silverman (1996: 2), this opens the door to what she calls 'an ethics of the field of vision' that might 'make it possible for us to idealize, and, so, to identify with bodies we would otherwise repudiate'. In other words, the Gaze allows a greater range of ways of seeing to become possible, some of which may work against the cultural construction of some visualized identities as inferior.

Some of the methodological implications of working with the Gaze also become evident in Silverman's work, especially her 1992 book *Male Subjectivity at the Margins*. Here, she explores what she calls 'deviant masculinities' – those that do not conform to the dominant fiction of phallic masculinity – 'some of which do indeed say "no" to power' (Silverman 1992: 2). For Silverman, these are masculinities which embrace those qualities that the dominant fiction ascribes to femininity. She thus provides some methodological pointers. She is interested in representations of masculinity that:

- *acknowledge and embrace castration.* Silverman's (1992: 52–121) own example of a film which explores 'the castrations through which the male subject is constituted' (Silverman 1992: 52) is a 1946 film directed by William Wyler called *The Best Years of Our Lives*. It traces the return home of three soldiers at the end of the Second World War, and according to Silverman (1992: 67), 'male lack is so fully displayed in that film that even four decades after its original release it remains profoundly disturbing, and at times almost unwatchable'. As just one instance, she notes the way in which the aircraftman who has lost both hands eventually shows his amputated arms to his girlfriend, unable to look at her as he does so. His bodily loss is paralleled by his loss of vision, and it is the female subject who can see this. Modleski (1988) argues strongly that Hitchcock's heroes are also much less secure in their masculinity than Mulvey's argument allows. She points to a number of ways in which the films assert the fragility of masculine subjectivity: in Jeffries's broken leg, in his passivity as opposed to his girlfriend's increasing activity in *Rear*

Window, in Scottie's vertigo, in Scottie's obsession with Madeleine which comes close to driving him mad, in his inability to see properly after he thinks he has witnessed her death.

- *are specular*. Silverman (1992) offers another example from *The Best Years of Our Lives*. Another of the soldiers returning home in uniform and medals is greeted by his wife '*as spectacle* – as a glamorous and heroic image ... However, the first time she sees him in civilian clothes she visibly recoils, appalled by his shabby and unfashionable suit' (Silverman 1992: 77; for more general discussions of spectacularized masculinities in film, see Cohan and Hark 1993; Dyer 1982; Neale 1983).

Mobilizing Lacan's notion of the Gaze, then, permits a more complex visuality to be seen than that proposed by Mulvey (1989).

6 from the disciplines of subjection to the possibilities of fantasy

Another tactic adopted by some feminist film theorists to explore a wider range of ways of seeing than that allowed by Mulvey's account is to draw on the psychoanalytic understanding of fantasy. In psychoanalytic work, fantasy is not used in the popular sense of something that is quite distinct from 'reality'. Instead, fantasy is seen as something that partly structures a subject's reality.

Fantasy is located between the conscious and the unconscious; it is where   **fantasy**
the transactions between these two zones occur (Burgin 1992). In fantasy – daydreams, for example – the unconscious is given some sort of temporal, spatial and symbolic form by the conscious. Certain lost objects are dreamt about, and they are given a particular spatial arrangement and placed in a particular narrative. Thus fantasy is often described as a kind of staging. This sense of a fantasy being staged is also appropriate because the subject often feels, in part, that they are looking on at the fantasy: they are its audience. A parallel with cinema is immediately obvious, since cinema too stages objects, times and spaces through particular codes of representation for an audience in ways that depend, according to feminist psychoanalytic critics, on fantasies about sexual difference in particular. Elizabeth Cowie (1990: 150) notes, however, that Mulvey, for example, only allows for one fantasy in cinema: that concerning the masculine fear of castration.

There is another connection too between cinema and fantasy: visual pleasure. Freud suggested that fantasy begins when the infant dreams of lost pleasurable objects, their mother's milk or breast, for example. The pleasure gained from fantasizing about lost objects is called **desire**. Cowie (1990: 149)   **desire**
describes fantasy as 'the mise-en-scène of desire, the putting into a scene, a staging, of desire'. These emphases on the spectator's visual pleasure suggest why fantasy has tended to be used to address questions of spectatorship in cinema. Mary Ann Doane's (1987) book about the so-called 'women's films' made by Hollywood in the 1930s and 1940s is called *The Desire to Desire*.

Like Mulvey though, Doane does not see narrative cinema allowing women to see films, or be seen in them, in terms other than those set by phallocentric visuality. Thus, in relation to these movies, women can only desire desire.

Cowie sees Mulvey's and Doane's reliance on the implications of the castration complex as too restrictive in the way it fixes the spectator into a particular, masculinized viewing position. Cowie (1990) instead turns to the notion of fantasy because she thinks it provides a way of loosening that fixity. In that sense, her aims are the same as those feminists who have deployed the masquerade or the Gaze. All want to suggest that even within a phallocentric cultural form like mainstream Hollywood cinema, there are traces of non-dominant ways of seeing, in both the film and in its audience.

Cowie's (1990) key point about fantasy is that the subject need not only be the audience of a fantasy. The subject may also imagine that they participate in the fantasy as well, and in perhaps more than one role. All fantasies, she says, 'present a varying of subject positions so that the subject takes up more than one position and thus is not fixed' (Cowie 1990: 160). This is because the fantasy consists, not of objects *per se*, but of their interrelations, their staging. Thus 'the subject is present or presented through the very form of organization, composition, of the scene' (Cowie 1990: 160); the subject is positioned through the scenic organization of the fantasy and is therefore part of each object in it. The implications for cinema spectatorship are that audiences may refuse to be positioned in the ways that Mulvey suggested they would be, as men. Instead, men and women in the audience may be positioned while watching a film in ways that correspond to the dynamics of their own fantasies.

Cowie's (1990) essay contains an extended discussion of one of the 'women's films' of the 1940s, *Now Voyager*, directed by Irving Rapper and starring Bette Davis. She begins by noting what sort of fantasies the film addresses, and she detects these fantasies by looking at three aspects of the film:

- *narrative*. Cowie notes how the story of the film contains a number of wishes for rather conventional kinds of success: erotic success and social success in particular. But the film also presents some more prohibited fantasies. Cowie (1990) argue that fantasies very often do just this, because of their borderline location between the conscious and the repressions of the unconscious. The prohibited desires often centre on the relations between parents and children. Thus in *Now Voyager*, the Bette Davis character rejects her own domineering mother as head of the household, and mothers in her turn without a male partner.
- *equivalences between characters*. In a discussion of another film, Cowie (1990) suggests another way in which a film may allow multiple entry points for fantasied identifications with several characters. She notes that both narratively (in terms of what they do, especially in relation to other characters) and visually (in terms of how they are seen), a film may suggest that certain characters are equivalent: two characters may be shown as 'fathers' in relation to a family, for example, even though only one 'really' is. Thus spectators may respond to both characters as 'fathers'.

- *visual substitutions.* If fantasies often articulate repressed desires, they must do so seductively in ways that do not invite rejection, says Cowie. And Hollywood movies can achieve this by making visual substitutions: visual moments that repeat themselves but with a difference. Cowie (1990: 178–9) explains this with an example from *Now Voyager*. Bette Davis's transformation from dowdy daughter to glamorous independent woman (an articulation of both her erotic and social success) is marked by a tilt shot that starts at her legs and ends at her head. The first time, it shows flat shoes, thick stockings, glasses: the second time, beautiful shoes, silk tights, a stunning hat and no glasses. Such visual puns entice the audience into accepting the film's terms, says Cowie.

Cowie's last example is, as she notes, also an example of the masquerade of femininity. But she argues that the subversiveness of the masquerade can only be understood if the fantasies in which it is embedded are also made clear. (Modleski [1986: 129] also notes that the 'elsewhere' central to Irigaray's account of masquerade needs to be specified if its potential for critique is to be fulfilled.) In particular, Cowie (1990: 180) argues that the narrative resolution of *Now Voyager* – in which Bette Davis agrees to mother the daughter of the married man she spent one night with – is a woman's fantasy of having a child without accepting the (rule of) the father. It thus sidesteps the position offered to women in Freud's account of the castration complex.

Cowie's discussion of fantasy clearly remains within psychoanalysis. Fantasy, it is argued, still deals with subjectivity, sexuality and the unconscious, with the dynamics of the child's relation to its early carers and of sexual difference. Teresa de Lauretis (1995: 75) insists on this, and warns against 'the optimistically silly notion of an unbounded mobility of identities for the spectator-subject ... the film's spectator [cannot] pick and choose any or all of the subject-positions inscribed in the film regardless of gender or sexual difference, to say nothing of other kinds of difference'. However, in its engagement with the repressions of the unconscious, fantasy also allows a greater range of interpretive possibilities in relation to films and their audiences.

focus

Watch *Rebecca* if you can.

What are the fantasies of success (and failure) that structure the film?

How are characters made equivalent? For example, in an early scene the heroine describes to Maxim her close relation to her father, and is shown as childlike as she does so: clumsy, gauche, eating runny eggs.

(Continued)

> Does Maxim become equated with her father? And if that is the case,
> is the heroine's struggle to become a 'proper' wife also a struggle to
> overcome Rebecca as some sort of powerful mother? Modleski (1988)
> suggests this is the case.
>
> Are there visual substitutions? What are the implications of both
> Rebecca and the heroine dressing up in the same costume in terms of
> fantasy, and for whom?

7 queer looks

Much psychoanalytic feminist film theory (and certainly that of Mulvey)
assumes that the structure of gendered differences in visuality and representation is heterosexual: that is, that the important structure is that articulated
between masculine and feminine, or male and female. This assumption clearly
produces a number of omissions in Mulvey's account, and these have been
criticised by gay and lesbian critics. Writers adopting Mulvey's analysis are
unlikely to pay much attention to how gay and lesbian characters might be
represented in a film, and nor are they likely to consider the possible ways
that lesbian and gay moviegoers might see certain scenarios or narratives in
particular ways.

Psychoanalysis does have something to say about homosexuality, but
this is often to position lesbian and gay sexuality as in some way perverse or deviant. This means that the psychoanalytic concepts that might
be useful in focusing on the possibility of gay and lesbian desires in the
cinema usually need to be heavily reworked. As Patricia White (1995:
87) says of psychoanalysis, 'lesbianism can not be fully "explained" in its
terms'. However, some of that reworking has been done, and one starting point has been the difficult position of little girls in relation to the
castration complex (a point already made by Bronfen in section 4 of this
chapter).

> Unlike the little boy, who must simply displace his love for the mother to
> other women and thereby consolidate his identification with the father and
> all that he represents, the little girl is asked to change her object from mother
> to father, her disposition from active to passive, and her sexual zone from
> clitoris to vagina, in order to become woman, post-Oedipal and heterosex-
> ual. (White 1995: 86)

Given the elaborateness of this change, it is not surprising that the little
girl might not manage all of it successfully, and might retain her desire for her
mother. Freud certainly thought this could and did occur, although he tended

to see it as a problem in the path towards 'normal' heterosexual womanhood. Silverman (1988) has picked up on this, however, and, far from seeing it as a 'problem', has suggested that elaborating this desire between mother and daughter could provide a way of inserting desire between women into psychoanalytic accounts of sexuality.

This is a controversial suggestion. Teresa de Lauretis (1994) in particular has criticized it for evoking a general feminine subjectivity and thus erasing the specificity of lesbian desire. For her own part, de Lauretis suggests that what defines lesbian desire is a desire for a lost female body which is actually the subject's own lost body image (de Lauretis 1994: 231). Sue Thornham (1997: 128) responds in turn that de Lauretis's concern with the particularity of lesbian desire ends up reasserting a fixed boundary between lesbian and heterosexual women which denies the mobility of desire and fantasy.

These debates are theoretically complex, and this is not the place to attempt their resolution. Their insistence that filmic structures of sexuality, difference and desire are not always heterosexual does, however, offer some further methodological pointers for thinking about visual culture, visual pleasure and visual disruption (and there are parallel debates made by theorists of gay movies and spectators; see for example Dyer 1990). They suggest the need to be alert for narratives, scenes, looks and spaces that do not articulate heterosexual visualities or spatialities.

Modleski (1988) offers an example of this need in her discussion of *Rebecca*. She suggests that there is a strong suggestion in the film that the housekeeper – Mrs Danvers – was sexually attracted to Rebecca. She points to the scene in which Mrs Danvers shows the heroine of *Rebecca* her predecessor's wardrobe and all its beautiful clothes, which Mrs Danvers caresses and strokes. Modleski suggests that this is disruptive of Mulvey's analysis of narrative cinema not only because it is another evocation of the absent Rebecca's powerful and sexual presence, but because that sexuality is shown to be attractive to women as well as to men.

---

focus

Read Modleski's (1988: 43-56) account of *Rebecca*, then Mary Anne Doane's (1987: 123–75) and her later response to Modleski (Doane 1991: 33–43). Both Doane and Modleski have watched the film carefully and both ground their interpretations in psychoanalytic theory. Modleski argues that Hitchcock's films are ambivalent in their representation of femininity. It is because they show femininity as

(Continued)

threatening that they punish their female characters, she says; feminist interpretations, she argues, should therefore focus on that threat. Doane argues that this is an overly optimistic viewing of Hitichcock's oeuvre. She sees the films as fundamentally phallocentric, and insists that, no matter how popular they are, that should not be an excuse for feminists to argue for meanings in them that the films themselves cannot sustain.

Clearly this debate is about more than methodology: it is also about more than abstract theory. It is about the critical effects of different sorts of theory. Modleski demands a kind of viewing of Hitchcock's films that can recover some feminine power for both their characters and their female audiences; Doane argues that these films deny such power and that feminist efforts should be directed at finding new forms of visuality that do give feminine subjectivities power. These are in effect different politics of critique.

8 reflexivity

This chapter has structured its discussion around certain developments in psychoanalytic feminist film criticism since Laura Mulvey's key essay. In many ways, Mulvey's essay has been a point of departure for subsequent critics; they have accepted some of her premises but have sought a less restrictive interpretation of both film and specatorship. However, there is one thing that later writers share with Mulvey, and that is a certain sort of reflexivity.

In the social sciences, reflexivity is claimed to be unnecessary for work that defines itself as scientific. Thus the practitioners of content analysis and semiology – discussed in Chapters 3 and 4 here – do not engage in reflexivity, since both, for different reasons, claim their work is scientific. However, reflexivity is a crucial aspect of work that participates in the so-called cultural turn. There, reflexivity is an attempt to resist the universalizing claims of academic knowledge and to insist that academic knowledge, like all other knowledges, is situated and partial. Reflexivity is thus about the position of the critic, about the effects that position has on the knowledge that the critic produces, about the relation between the critic and the people or materials they deal with, and about the social effects of the critic's work. Frequently now, it is assumed that before the results of a piece of research can be presented, the author must explain how their social position has affected what they found; a kind of autobiography often precedes the research results.

There are a number of ways in which psychoanalytic approaches are incompatible with this autobiographical reflexivity (for a fuller discussion, see

Rose 1997). To begin with, autobiographical reflexivity implies a full understanding of the researcher's self. It implies that self-knowledge is possible (even if the researcher chooses not to reveal all that knowledge in their reflexive moment). But of course psychoanalysis claims that this is an impossible goal. Full self-knowledge is impossible because a central part of our subjectivity – the unconscious – is not accessible to consciousness. Secondly, psychoanalysis's emphasis on the relationality and of subjectivity – the relations between carers and babies, between masculinity and femininity, between movies and their audiences, for example – means that to split an account of 'who I am' from 'what I studied' is also impossible. Who you are depends, in part, on what you study, what you watch, whom you talk to. This split is also impossible to sustain because of the psychoanalytic emphasis on the subject in process. Again, who you are also depends on what you relate to. It is a process of mutual constitution, not one of a pre-existing person impacting on other people or images. Moreover, the psychoanalytic account of visual culture also recognizes that audiences bring their own ways of knowing to the images they encounter, and the same is true of the audiences for academic work. Thus autobiographical reflexivity may over-emphasize the writer at the expense of the critical agency of their audiences.

So none of the critics whose work I have cited offer any sort of autobiographical account before their interpretation of a movie (although Doane [1991: 1–14] offers an interesting discussion of some of the theoretical and institutional relations within which her work is embedded). None starts by saying 'this is who (I think) I am, and this is how that's shaped me as a spectator of this film'. They are, however, theoretically explicit, and, while none offer methodological toolkits, it is usually possible to trace quite clearly the methodological implications of their conceptual tools in their work. Their theoretical starting points make clear the particular way of seeing this work invites. The reader can trace the interpretive implications of the theoretical position adopted. This theoretical explicitness has the effect of positioning their work in some way. The frequent use of case studies also often enhances this sense of the particularity of each psychoanalytic study.

However, the positionality of these critics is more strongly marked in another way. Almost all of them say quite clearly that they are writing with political – that is, feminist – aims in mind. Mulvey (1989: 14), for example, begins by saying that in her essay, 'psychoanalytic theory is ... appropriated here as a political weapon, demonstrating the way in which the unconscious of patriarchal society has structured film form'. Modleski (1988: 121) says her readings are without doubt partial, because she wants to place the evidence in Hitchcock's films of men's guilt in women's hands. And there is Kaja Silverman's (1996) project for an ethics of the field of vision. The reflexivity of this work, then, rests in part on its theoretical explicitness and its reliance on detailed case studies, but mostly on the articulation of its critical aims. It uses its awareness of its status as a particular kind of politics of critique to position itself (as the previous section's discussion of the disagreement between Modleski [1988] and Doane [1987, 1991] implied).

9 psychoanalysis and visuality: an assessment

The three criteria for a critical visual methodology outlined in Chapter 1 of this book would seem to be fufilled by the psychoanalytic work discussed in this chapter. That work pays detailed attention to the images with which it is concerned, often in the form of case studies. It allows visual images to have their own effects, and these effects are seen as both psychic and social. Discussions of sexual difference, for example, work at both the latter levels; they engage with questions of fantasy but also the cultural coding of masculinity and femininity. The effect of visual images on spectators is a central concern of psychoanalytic approaches too. And there is a certain reflexive effect in their work, even if the explicitly reflexive moments are limited to claims of allegiance to feminist goals. However, all of these criteria are dealt with by psychoanalytic writers in quite specific ways, which do have some omissions for which psychoanalysis has been criticized. And there are some issues about which psychoanalytic methods have almost nothing to say.

Psychoanalytic approaches to the way visual images produce social difference through their picturing of subjectivity are very much dominated by studies of sexuality. This is hardly surprising, since sexuality was the main concern of both Freud and Lacan. However, sexuality is not the only axis through which social difference and social power relations are articulated: far from it. And psychoanalytic film theory has been criticized for neglecting issues of class and race. As Jane Gaines (1988) points out, at a certain historical period in the United States, men were lynched for looking at women – black men were hanged for looking at white women. Indeed, Gaines (1988) argues that racialized aspects of subjectivity are not just neglected by psychoanalysis, but actively erased from consideration, particularly in generalizing accounts of the so-called 'male gaze'. Gaines suggests that the erasure of 'race' from psychoanalytic film theory is produced by the white middle-class norms of family relations that psychoanalysis implicitly assumes; and in her discussion of the film *Mahogany* starring Diana Ross, she shows that the only men whose gaze at Ross is sanctioned by the film are white. 'Race', she insists, must therefore intersect with sexual difference in accounts of spectatorship, but Gaines (1988) sees psychoanalyisis as actively unhelpful in this regard. Lola Young (1996), among others, has nevertheless explored the possibility that psychoanalytic ideas may address issues of racialization as well as sexuality. She draws on the work of Frantz Fanon (1986) to make this claim. Doane justifies addressing issues of racialization through psychanalytic concepts thus:

> For Fanon, a psychoanalytic understanding of racism hinges on a close analysis of the realm of sexuality. This is particularly true of black–white relations since blacks are persistently attributed with a hypersexuality. Why is it sexuality forms a major arena for the articulation of racism? From a psychoanalytic point of view, sexuality is the realm where fear and desire find their most intimate connection, where notions of otherness and the exotic/erotic are often conflated. (Doane 1991: 217)

Clearly this remains a contested claim, and theorizing 'race' through psychoanalytic terms is likely to remain as controversial as theorizing gender and sexuality. As for class, there is nothing that I know of in psychoanalytic feminist film criticism that addresses the possible class specificity of certain ways of seeing (but see Pollock [1994] for a psychoanalytic discussion of this in relation to other visual media). These absences clearly weaken the critical potential of psychoanalytic theory.

Moreover, there are some worries that, although psychoanalysis asserts the intersection of the cultural with the psychic, in practice its emphasis is very much on the latter. Evidence of the neglect of the social and cultural in psychoanalytic film theory can be found in two places. The first of these is, paradoxically, in its treatment of the audience. While psychoanalytic film theory argues that the audience is central to its accounts of the effects of films, there has been very little work that tries to explore empirically the workings of specific fantasies, say, for certain spectators constituted by particular mediations of both cultural and psychic dynamics. De Lauretis, for example, is very unusual in her insistence that not all of a fantasy's spectators will get pleasure from it:

> A particular fantasy scenario, regardless of its artistic, formal, or aesthetic excellence as film representation, is not automatically accessible to every spectator; a film may work as fantasy for some spectators, but not for others ... the spectator's own sociopolitical location and psycho-sexual configuration have much to do with whether or not a film can work for her as a scenario of desire, and as what Freud would call a 'visualization' of the subject herself as subject of the fantasy: that is to say, whether the film can engage her spectatorial desire or, literally, whether she can see herself in it. (de Lauretis 1995: 64)

Because this possibility is rarely acknowledged, let alone investigated, the psychoanalytic claim that the film and its audience are mutually constitutive remains one that is asserted rather than demonstrated. And since it is the film that is paid most attention in psychoanalytic accounts, the effect is to suggest that the film positions the audience.

Secondly, the focus in psychoanalytic film theory on the film itself produces a further absence, which is any consideration of the social institutions that produce films and the social contexts in which movies – or any other visual image – are shown (the work of Guiliana Bruno [1993, 2002] is an exception here). As the first chapter here suggested, the spaces in which visual images are displayed usually entail quite specific visual practices. How might the social practices of cinema-going intersect with these arguments about cinematic visualities? How might the effects of a film change between its screening in a cinema and its showing as a video on a home tv screen? I'm thinking here not just of things like the size of the screen and so on – which Mulvey for one does mention as part of the visual pleasure of narrative cinema – but of the ways that people watch differently in different places, and how these social practices are disciplined. Psychoanalysis, like the other methods discussed so far in this book, has nothing to say about these questions either. Thus it is not surprising to find that some psychoanalytic accounts of film spectatorship are turning to other theorists – most notably perhaps to Foucault – to ground their accounts of visuality in social practices and institutions (Mayne 1993 discusses this shift). The next two chapters will turn to Foucault's work for the same end.

summary

- *associated with:*
  Psychoanalysis has most often been used as an approach to interpreting film.

- *sites and modalities:*
  Psychoanalysis is most concerned with the sites of the image and its audiencing. It is particularly concerned with how aspects of the compositional modality of an image offer particular spectating positions to viewers.

- *key terms:*
  Key terms include subjectivity, sexuality, the unconscious, visual pleasure, fantasy and desire.

- *strengths and weaknesses:*
  Like semiology, psychoanalysis offers a rich and nuanced vocabulary for interpreting the visualization of sexualized difference, and for speculating about the complicity of audiences with those visualizations. However, kinds of difference other than sexual difference are neglected, and psychoanalysis cannot address the social practices of the display and audiencing of visual images.

Further reading
Sue Thornham's (1997) *Passionate Detachments: An Introduction to Feminist Film Theory* provides some very useful surveys of the debates within psychoanalytic feminist film criticism.

7
discourse analysis I
text intertextuality and context

key example a wide range of images picturing the East End of London in the 1880s, from maps and fine art paintings to book illustrations and newspaper graphics.

1 discourse and visual culture: an introdction

The previous chapter examined certain psychoanalytic approaches to visual images, and ended with the concerns expressed by some writers that psychoanalysis does not pay enough attention to the social construction of difference. This claim is made on two grounds: first, that psychoanalysis has very little to say about some forms of social difference, such as 'race' and class; and, secondly, that it concentrates on the psychic and visual construction of difference at the expense of considering the social construction and consequences of difference. Very little attention is paid either to the ways of seeing brought to particular images by specific audiences, or to the social institutions and practices through which images are made and displayed.

One writer whose work is often turned to in order to address these absences in psychoanalytic theory is Michel Foucault. For various reasons, Foucault was quite hostile to psychoanalysis, but Foucault's approach does have some compatibilities with that of Freud. Most importantly, perhaps, Foucault's understanding of the subject is in some ways similar to that of psychoanalysis. Like psychoanalytic approaches to the subject, Foucault too considered that human subjects are produced and not simply born. Human subjectivity is constructed through particular processes, he argued, and much of his work consists of detailed historical studies of some of those processes at particular periods in Western history (actually, mostly French history). He wrote books on the emergence of the human sciences in modern Europe, on the development of modern clinical and psychiatric medicine, on the birth of the prison, and on attitudes towards sexuality. In all of these he paid close attention to the ways various practices and institutions defined what it was to be human (and therefore also what it was to be sub-human, abnormal or deviant) in very particular ways. Thus his work has appealed to those writers cited in the previous chapter who are concerned that psychoanalysis, for all its other analytical insights, does not pay enough attention to the social processes through which a range of subjectivities are constituted. Stuart Hall (1996: 7), for example, argues that 'if ideology is effective, it is because it works at *both* the "the rudimentary levels of psychic identity and the drives" *and* at the level of the discursive formation and practices which constitute the social field'. Teresa de Lauretis (1994), too, concludes her Freudian account of 'perverse desire' by emphasizing the need to connect Foucault and Freud; Freud, she says, provides an account of how the social processes described by Foucault are subjectively articulated. And Kaja Silverman (1992), in the opening pages of her study of *Male Subjectivity at the Margins*, also argues that the work of Foucault and Freud needs to be brought together, although she suggests a rather more complicated relation between the psychic and the social than does de Lauretis.

Although many of Foucault's ideas are now broadly disseminated, it is still useful to begin a discussion of the methodological implications of his **discourse**   work by discussing some of his theoretical terms. The notion of **discourse** is central to both Foucault's theoretical arguments and to his methodology. Discourse has a quite specific meaning. It refers to groups of statements which structure the way a thing is thought, and the way we act on the basis of that thinking. In other words, discourse is a particular knowledge about the world which shapes how the world is understood and how things are done in it. Lynda Nead (1988: 4) defines discourse as 'a particular form of language with its own rules and conventions and the institutions within which the discourse is produced and circulated', and she gives medical discourse as an example: 'in this way, it is possible to speak of a medical discourse ... which refers to the special language of medicine, the form of knowledge it produces and the professional institutions and social spaces which it occupies'. Discourse also produces subjects: hence medical discourse produces, among other subject positions, doctors, nurses and patients. Nead suggests that 'art' can also be understood as a discourse, as a specialized form of knowledge. She says that 'the discourse of art in the nineteenth century [consisted of] the concatenation of visual images, the language and structures of criticism, cultural institutions, publics for art and the values and knowledges made possible within and through high culture' (Nead 1988: 4). On this understanding, 'art' becomes not certain kinds of visual images but the knowledges, institutions, subjects and practices which work to define certain images as art and others as not art. Discourses are articulated through all sorts of visual and verbal images and texts, specialized or not, and also through the practices that those languages permit. The diversity of forms through which a discourse can be **intertextuality**   articulated means that **intertextuality** is important to understanding discourse. Intertextuality refers to the way that the meanings of any one discursive image or text depend not only on that one text or image, but also on the meanings carried by other images and texts.

It is possible to think of visuality as a sort of discourse too. A specific visuality will make certain things visible in particular ways, and other things unseeable, for example, and subjects will be produced and act within that field of vision. Some of the arguments made by psychoanalytic feminist film critics and discussed in the previous chapter can be recast in these Foucauldian terms. Thus the visuality that, according to Laura Mulvey (1989: 19) makes 'woman as image, man the bearer of the look', could be described as a visual discourse that has effects on the making of masculinity and femininity, men and women. John Berger (1972: 46) points out some of the implications for everyday practice of that discourse: 'a woman must continually watch herself. She is almost continually accompanied by her own image of herself'. This example is also relevant to another Foucauldian term, that of discursive formation. A **discursive formation** is the way meanings are   **discursive formation** connected together in a particular discourse. Foucault (1972: 37) describes discursive formations as 'systems of dispersion', in that they consist of the relations between parts of a discourse. 'Whenever', he says, 'one can define a regularity (an order, correlations, positions and functionings, transformations), we will say, for the sake of convenience, that we are dealing with a *discursive formation*' (Foucault 1972: 38). Thus, to continue for a moment to translate psychoanalytic work into Foucauldian terms, Mulvey argues that phallocentric visuality has a structure in which images of women depend on particular forms of masculine seeing. This is a relational argument in that masculinity and femininity depend on each other for their characteristics: woman always signifying castration, and man always enacting voyeuristic and fetishistic ways of seeing. That relation – that correlation and those positions – could be described as a discursive formation.

Foucault was quite clear that discourse was a form of discipline, and this leads us to his concern with **power**. Discourse, he says, is powerful, but it is   **power** powerful in a particular way. It is powerful, says Foucault, because it is productive. Discourse disciplines subjects into certain ways of thinking and acting, but this is not simply repressive; it does not impose rules for thought and behaviour on a pre-existing human agent. Instead, human subjects are produced through discourses. Our sense of our self is made through the operation of discourse. So too are objects, relations, places, scenes: discourse produces the world as it understands it. Thus, to translate once more some of the arguments of the previous chapter, it might be said that certain kinds of masculinity are produced through a discursive visuality that is voyeuristic and fetishistic.

An important implication of Foucault's account of power is that power is not something imposed from the top of society down onto its oppressed bottom layers. Power is everywhere, since discourse too is everywhere. And there are many discourses, some of which clearly contest the terms of others. Foucault (1979: 95) claimed that 'where there is power, there is resistance … a multiplicity of points of resistance', and by this he meant that there are many discourses that jostle and compete in their effects. We might define the efforts of feminist film critics like Silverman and de Lauretis, for example, as efforts to develop visual discourses that do not discipline looking in a phallocentric manner, but that produce other (ways of visualizing) masculinities and femininities. But certain discourses are nonetheless dominant, and Foucault was particularly concerned in his own work with the emergence of institutions and technologies that were structured through specific, even if complex and contested, discourses. And he suggested that the dominance of certain discourses occurred not only because they were located in socially powerful institutions – those given coercive powers by the state, for example, such as the police, prisons and workhouses – but also because their discourses claimed absolute truth. The construction of claims to truth lies at the heart of **power/knowledge** the intersection of **power/knowledge**.

> We should admit ... that power produced knowledge (and not simply by encouraging it because it serves power or by applying it because it is useful); that power and knowledge directly imply one another; that there is no power relation without the correlative constitution of a field of knowledge, nor any knowledge that does not presuppose and constitute at the same time power relations. (Foucault 1977: 27)

Foucault insisted that knowledge and power are imbricated one in the other, not only because all knowledge is discursive and all discourse is saturated with power, but because the most powerful discourses, in terms of the productiveness of their social effects, depend on assumptions and claims that their knowledge is true. The particular grounds on which truth is claimed – **regime of truth** and these shift historically – constitute what Foucault called a **regime of truth**. Some historians of photography have argued, for example, that the 'realism' of the photographic image was produced not by new photographic technology, but by the use of photographs in a specific regime of truth, so that photographs were seen as evidence of 'what was really there'. This argument will be examined a little more fully in the next chapter.

Foucault's work is radical in many ways. It has been adopted with enthusiasm by many working in the social sciences and humanities, but has also been greeted with hostility and even derision by others. His controversial status is in small part explained by his methodological programme (which is perhaps spelled out most clearly in *The Archaeology of Knowledge* [1972]; see also Andersen 2003; Kendall and Wickham 1999). Foucault refused the premise which forms the basis of all the analytical methods that this book has examined so far. Content analysis, semiology and psychoanalysis all assume that analysis needs somehow to delve behind the surface appearance of things in order to discover their real meaning. Content analysis seeks out latent meanings that it claims become evident only from systematic quantitative study; semiology searches for the dominant codes or myths or referent systems that underlie the surface appearance of signs; and psychoanalysis looks for signs of the unconscious as they disrupt the conscious making of meaning. This approach to the interpretation of meaning is widespread in the humanities and social sciences, and subtends many other methods apart from these three. Foucault rejected such 'penetrative' models of interpretation at the level of method, but also at the level of explanation, since he also wanted to avoid explanatory accounts of *why* power works in the way it does. He explicitly rejected the Marxist claim that meaning was determined by the system of production, for example; he was always vague about how discourses connected to other, non-discursive processes such as economic change; and while he acknowledged that power has aims and effects, he never explained these by turning to notions of human or institutional agency. Michele Barrett (1991: 131) says that Foucault's notion of causality and dependency was 'polymorphous'. Both methodologically and theoretically, then, he rejected approaches that look behind or underneath things and practices for other processes that would explain them. Instead, as Barrett (1991) makes clear in her account of his work, he focused on the question of *how* power worked. How does it do what it does, how did it do what it did? Certainly his most satisfying works, to me, are his empirical accounts of particular texts and institutions, often focusing on their details, their casual assumptions, their everyday mundane routines, their taken-for-granted architecture, their banalities. It is these detailed descriptions that produce his most startling accounts of how subjects and objects were and are discursively produced.

Elaborating Foucault's method is not easy, however. As Barrett (1991: 127) notes, his methodological statements are rather vague, and Niels Åkerstrøm Andersen (2003: 8) comments that even then, he often did not follow his own prescriptions. More recent discourse analysts can also be rather coy about their methods. Nelson Phillips and Cynthia Hardy (2002: 75) say that methods are 'emergent', for example, while Jonathan Potter (1996: 140) describes discourse analysis as a 'craft skill' and suggests that the only way to learn it is to get on and do it (although in fact these authors do also offer some guidelines; see Phillips and Hardy 2002: 59–81; Potter and Wetherell 1987: 158–76). This vagueness, combined with the huge amount of Foucault's work now available – which include many interviews and pieces of journalism quite apart from his many books and papers – and the fact that, not surprisingly, his ideas changed as his projects shifted, means that his methodological legacy has been complex and diffuse. (And, to complicate matters, there are forms of discourse analysis which owe rather little to Foucault: the influential work of Fairclough [1995] for example.) In exploring work that does owe explicit allegiance to Foucauldian arguments, I will use my own terminology. This chapter and the next one will focus on two methodologies that I will call discourse analysis I and discourse analysis II. Both depend on specifically Foucauldian notions of discourse, but each puts Foucault's arguments to work in rather different ways, with rather different effects.

2 discourse analyis I and discourse analysis II

I have suggested that Foucault's work has produced two somewhat different methodological emphases, which I am calling discourse analysis I and discourse analysis II. I distinguish between them thus:

- *discourse analysis I*. This form of discourse analysis tends to pay rather more attention to the notion of discourse as articulated through various kinds of visual images and verbal texts than it does to the practices entailed by specific discourses. As Rosalind Gill (1996: 141) says, it uses 'discourse' to 'refer to all forms of talk and texts'. It is most concerned with discourse, discursive formations and their productivity.
- *discourse analysis II*. This form of discourse analysis tends to pay more attention to the practices of institutions than it does to the visual images and verbal texts. Its methodology is usually left implicit. It tends to be more explicitly concerned with issues of power, regimes of truth, institutions and technologies.

This distinction is not clear-cut. It is not difficult to find work that examines visual images, verbal texts, institutions and social practices together (see Green [1990] for example). However, in terms of current discussions of methodologies in the social sciences, it does seem to me that there is a case to be made for discussing these two methodological emphases separately, since they do produce rather different kinds of research work. Thus this chapter will examine the first type of discourse analysis, and the next chapter will examine the second. For convenience, whenever this chapter mentions discourse analysis, it is referring to what has just been characterized as discourse analysis I, unless the text specifies otherwise.

This first type of discourse analysis is centrally concerned with language. But, as Fran Tonkiss emphasizes:

> language is viewed as the topic of research ... Rather than gathering accounts or texts so as to gain access to people's views and attitudes, or to find out what happened at a particular event, the discourse analyst is interested in how people use language to construct their accounts of the social world. (Tonkiss 1998: 247–8)

Discourse analysis can also be used to explore how images construct specific views of the social world, in which case, to paraphrase Tonkiss, visuality is viewed as the topic of research, and the discourse analyst is interested in how images construct accounts of the social world. This type of discourse analysis therefore pays careful attention to an *image itself* (as well as other sorts of evidence). Since discourses are seen as socially produced rather than created by individuals, this type of discourse analysis is especially concerned with the *social modality* of the image site. In particular, discourse analysis explores how those specific views or accounts are constructed as real or truthful or natural through particular regimes of truth. As Gill (1996: 143) says, 'all discourse is organized to make itself persuasive', and discourse analysis focuses on those strategies of persuasion. It also pays attention to the more socially constituted forms of discursive power, looking at the social construction of difference and authority, for example. Discourse analysis is thus concerned too with the social production and effects of discourses.

This chapter will explore the usefulness of these methodological foci through a case study of the work of several historians who have examined the discursive construction of the East End of London in the 1880s. These historians work with a variety of images and texts in order to examine the way bourgeois commentators produced an apparently truthful account of this working-class area, and to explore the effects that had on its residents in terms of the various institutional interventions legitimated by that 'truth'. Gareth Stedman Jones (1976: 10–11) points out that in the 1870s and 1880s, most British social thinkers assumed that economic progress would eliminate poverty. The fact that it did not – most blatantly in London's East End, an area with a seasonal and casual labour market and high levels of poverty – was blamed on what were seen as 'the still unregenerate poor: those who had turned their back on progress, or been rejected by it'. Jones continues:

> This group was variously referred to as 'the dangerous class', the casual poor or, most characteristically, 'the residuum' ... In the explanation of the existence of the residuum the subjective psychological defects of individuals bulked even larger than before ... The problem was not structural but moral. The evil to be combated was not poverty but pauperism; pauperism with its attendant vices, drunkenness, improvidence, mendicancy, bad language, filthy habits, gambling, low amusements and ignorance. (Jones 1976: 11)

This particular definition of the problem led to specific strategies to combat it: strategies that aimed to alter the morality of the poor rather than their standard of living.

Discourse analysis thus addresses questions of power/knowledge. Because of this, it also fulfils two of the three criteria for a critical visual methodology that were outlined in the first chapter. As a method, discourse analysis pays careful attention to images, and to their social production and effect. Phillips and Hardy (2002) also claim that discourse analytic methods are inherently reflexive. This is a controversial claim, however. Foucault himself, certainly in his early work, was not at all sympathetic to notions of 'reflexivity' as they are currently constituted in the social sciences. He seemed clearly to separate his own practices as an academic from those of the thinkers he was discussing, and, in another parallel with psychoanalytic approaches, in the introduction to *The Archaeology of Knowledge* he derided autobiographical efforts at reflexivity: 'do not ask me who I am and do not ask me to remain the same: leave it to our bureaucrats and our police to see that our papers are in order' (Foucault 1972: 17). In the section on reflexivity in their book on Foucault, Gavin Kendall and Gary Wickham (1999: 101–9) echo this refusal and say very little about reflexivity as it is currently debated in the social sciences. Phillip and Hardy's assertion that discourse analysis is in fact reflexive depends on their argument that since discourse analysis 'involves a set of assumptions concerning the constructive effects of language' (Phillips and Hardy 2002: 5), any discourse analysis must implicitly constitute itself as constructed from the effects of language, or risk incoherence. Acknowledging its constructed nature is what constitutes discourse analysis's reflexivity, according to Phillips and Hardy. The final section of this chapter will return to their claim.

In order to discuss more fully what discourse analysis entails, and to assess it critically, this chapter will:

- explore more fully the notion of discourse and discursive formation and its implications for finding sources for discourse analysis;
- examine how discourse analysis addresses the discursive construction of truth claims, through both the structure of discourse and its institutional location;
- examine how discourse analysis engages with reflexivity.

3 finding your sources

Doing a discourse analysis assumes that you are concerned with the discursive production of some kind of authoritative account – and perhaps too about how that account was or is contested – and with the social practices both in which that production is embedded and which it itself produces. Discourses are articulated through a huge range of images, texts and practices, however, and any and all of these are legitimate sources for a discourse analysis. When beginning a piece of discourse analysis, then, it is necessary to think carefully about what sorts of sources you need.

3.1 finding your sources: in general

For most sorts of research questions, some key sources will be immediately obvious, either from your own knowledge or from the work of other researchers. In the work of historians looking at the discursive construction of the East End of London in the 1880s, for example, a number of sources recur (Cowling 1989; Curtis 2001; Fishman 1988; Jones 1976; Jones 1989; Keating 1976; Livesy 2004; Nead 1988, 2000; Walkowitz 1992). These are: contemporary newspapers, often London ones rather than national ones; contemporary accounts of visits to the East End by journalists, clerics, philanthropists and others, which often take the form of travel diaries and could be published in pamphlet or book form as well as in newspapers; novels and, less often, poems; and documents produced by various branches of government such as the Census, reports by local Medical Officers of Health, and other sorts of government reports. Many of these written sources are illustrated with figurative images – often engravings – or with maps or cartoons or other visual images. Almost all of these historians also use photographs of the area, some taken by philanthropic institutions and some by journalists, but the provenance of many of these is now hard to trace. It is important to note the seeming eclecticism of these sources. They are not constrained by notions of genre, for example, or technology. Even a study concerned to examine just one sort of visual construction relevant to the production of the East End, such as Nead's (1988) study of 'art', uses a wide range of sources, including paintings, engravings and drawings, but also journalism, parliamentary reports and fictional and non-fictional writing. This eclecticism is demanded by the intertextuality of discourse. As Nicholas Green (1990: 3) says, discourse is 'a coherent pattern of statements across a range of archives and sites'.

In the face of the breadth of source material demanded by discourse analysis, it is useful to begin by thinking about what sources should be selected as the *starting points* for your own research: the sources that are likely to be particularly productive, or particularly interesting, or 'provide theoretically relevant results' (Phillips and Hardy 2002: 66). This may mean you draw on sources that others have often used. Or it may mean that you need to locate and access previously unused materials. Or your key sources may already be to hand; perhaps stumbling across them was what started you off on this research in the first place. However, once the more obvious starting points for a discourse analysis have been established, it is important then to *widen* your 'range of archives and sites'.

Ways of doing this are diverse. Those initial images and texts may well contain references to other images and texts that you can then track down. Reading what other researchers working on the same or similar topics have said about your area of interest will produce other leads. A discourse analysis may also be able to use verbal material; you may want to conduct interviews yourself, or to record naturally occurring talk (see Potter 1996; Potter and Wetherell 1994). And you also need to invest time in the kind of browsing research that leads to serendipitous finds. Some of the most interesting discourse analyses are interesting precisely because they bring together, in convincing ways, material that had previously been seen as quite unrelated.

If this sounds potentially time-consuming – it can be. Indeed, one of the difficulties of the discourse analytic method is knowing where to stop the data collection process. As you begin to find other texts related to the materials you started with, and then more materials related to them in turn, it becomes tricky to know when to stop without making your end points seem arbitrary. Andersen (2003: 13) quotes Foucault's presumably ironic suggestion that 'one ought to read everything, study everything'; but, clearly, reading 'everything' is impossible. What brings the intertextual search to an end, as both Phillips and Hardy (2002: 74) and Tonkiss (1998) note, is the feeling that you have enough material to persuasively explore its intriguing aspects. That is, discourse analysis does not depend on the quantity of material analysed, but its quality. 'What matters', according to Tonkiss (1998: 253), 'is the richness of textual detail, rather than the number of texts analysed.' Thus you may quite legitimately select from all possible sources those that seem particularly interesting to you. As long as you have located some intriguingly complex texts, your discourse analysis can begin.

---

focus

Suppose you are interested in exploring the ways pregnant women are visualized in contemporary Western culture. What might your initial sources be? Where else might you look for visual images and texts that construct the pregnant female body?

This task raises the question of different, possibly competing discourses that participate in that construction. For example, you may not be familiar with the conventional medical discourse of pregnancy, but this is perhaps the most powerful discourse a pregnant woman encounters as she attends her antenatal appointments. How might you access that particular discourse? And what others might challenge or confirm it? How might you access how some pregnant women construct their sense of bodily self, for example? What about advertising? And are adverts showing pregnant women the only relevant ones? Or is the fact that pregnant women are very rarely visualized in what are called 'women's magazines' also relevant? That is, is the invisibility of pregnant women also an interesting issue to investigate?

3.2 finding your sources: iconography

One method that does offer some clearer guidelines about what sorts of sources are relevant to understanding some kinds of visual images is iconography. Iconography is a method developed by the art historian Erwin Panofsky. Chapter 2 suggested that many art historians rely on having a 'good eye' which focuses almost entirely on how an image looks. Panofsky (1957: 26) distanced himself from this kind of eye by insisting that 'iconography is that branch of the history of art which concerns itself with the subject matter or meaning of works of art, as opposed to their form'. The subject matter or meaning was, for Panofsky, to be established by referring to the understandings of the symbols and signs in a painting that its contemporary audiences would have had. Interpreting those understandings requires a grasp of the historically specific intertextuality on which meaning depends.

Panofsky took care to spell out just how he thought this comparison between different visual images and verbal texts should work. Panofsky (1957) divides visual interpretation into three kinds, which he gives various names to:

1 primary	natural	pre-iconographic
2 secondary	conventional	iconographic
3 intrinsic	symbolic	iconological

The example he uses to explain the differences between these three kinds of images is 'when an acquaintance greets me on the street by lifting his hat' (Panofsky 1957: 26). He suggests that recognizing that he has encountered a 'gentleman' with a 'hat' requires some interpretation, but of an 'elementary and easily understandable' sort (p. 26). This is therefore interpretation at the primary or pre-iconographic level. (In methodological terms, this level has some parallels to the close observation demanded by compositional interpretation.) However, 'my realization that the lifting of the hat stands for a greeting belongs in an altogether different realm of interpretation' (p. 27). This different realm addresses images that have a specific symbolic resonance; this is the secondary level of interpretation, of a conventional or iconographic image. The third level of interpretation is brought to bear on visual images in order to explore their general cultural significance. Panofsky suggested that, in the case of his acquaintance with the hat, seeing that image in symbolic or iconological terms would mean interpreting the gesture of lifting the hat as a symptom of that man's whole personality and background. The iconological or intrinsic meaning of an image 'is apprehended by ascertaining those underlying principles which reveal the basic attitude of a nation, a period, a class, a religious or philosophical persuasion – qualified by one personality and condensed into one work' (p. 30).

As an example of Panofsky's method, we can turn to the portrait painted by Jan van Eyck in 1434 for the marriage of Giovanni Arnolfini, a merchant in Bruges, to Giovanna Cenami, and reproduced in Figure 7.1 (for other accounts of this painting, see Bedaux 1986; Hall 1994; Seidel 1993).

Panofsky (1953: 201–3) offers a detailed iconographic interpretation of this image which depends on his knowledge of the iconography at work in early Netherlandish painting more generally. Thus Panofsky insists that, despite its location in 'a comfortably furnished interior', despite all its signs of worldly wealth (the lamp, mirror, jewellery, clothing), and despite its use of oil paint which, in Berger's (1972) analysis, makes the painting as much of

Figure 7.1

Jan van Eyck,
The Amolfini
Wedding Portrait,
1434

a commodity as the objects it depicts, this is a painting that glorifies the
Christian sacrament of marriage. Thus the hand gestures are those of the
Catholic marriage ceremony, and the candle, clearly not needed for light since
the room is bathed in sunlight from the window, represents the all-seeing
Christ. The fruit on the windowledge and chest symbolize the purity of
humankind before the Fall. The statue of St Margaret at the top of the tall
chairback represents childbirth, and the dog symbolizes marital fidelity.
Moreover, the colours used by van Eyck also have symbolic meaning. John
Gage (1993: 142–3) notes that the colours in the portrait have significance in

relation to the ideas of contemporary alchemists about colours and the essential properties of matter. Deep purple and green – the clothes worn by the couple – symbolize fire and water, as does the jewellery hanging next to the mirror in the painting – amber beads and pearls. The painting thus suggest that this is not only a coupling of two people, but a complementary union of two elemental properties which will be harmonious and fertile. Both Panofsky and Gage rely on the notion of intertextuality in order to interpret the meanings this image would have had for its contemporary audiences, although they relate the portrait to different texts: Gage refers to alchemy books while Panofsky compares the portrait to other marriage portraits.

As an intertextual method, iconography is most often applied to Western figurative images and to architecture, usually from the sixteenth to the eighteenth centuries. During that period, compendia of symbols (in the loose sense of the word) were written for both artists and for patrons. These explained the meanings of hundreds of visual motifs, allegories and personifications, and it is these compendia that art historians have consulted to produce iconographic interpretations of specific images. Iconography needs a thorough grounding in historical context to be successful, therefore, and Panofsky argued that actually, in order to understand the possible secondary and intrinsic meanings of an image, two things were necessary. One was a deep familiarity with the texts, both visual and written, that the artist producing a particular piece of work would have had, and this might need to extend beyond those published guides to symbolism just mentioned. The second thing was 'synthetic intuition' (Panofsky 1957: 38), or what other commentators on this method have called common sense. This second quality was important because, while various texts could provide important information and clues about iconographic and iconological meaning, Panofsky (1957) argued that they could never provide full explanations for a particular image, and their relevance thus had to be judged by the critic on the basis of his or her intuition.

There are some aids available for developing this requisite sense of historical context. Roelof van Straten (1994) provides a guide to the compendia of symbols that were used by artists and patrons. Another very helpful publication is the *Encyclopedia of Comparative Iconography* (Roberts 1998). This two-volume work consists of a number of long, illustrated essays on themes such as Crucifixion, Death, Arms Raised, Money, Whiteness, Pregnancy and Hair/Haircutting (to list some almost at random). Each entry explores the iconography of its theme and lists relevant works of art from various periods. It also suggests other useful reading that can direct you to original sources.

As defined by Panofsky, iconography is not a Foucauldian method. Panofsky (1957: 41) suggested that iconological analysis could show how the 'essential tendencies of the human mind' were translated into visual themes and concepts, and this reference to the 'essential tendencies of the human mind' is decidedly non-Foucauldian. As we have seen, Foucault insisted that there could be no 'essential tendencies' because human subjectivity is entirely constructed. Iconography has also been seen as close to more structural kinds of semiology, with Panofsky's primary level of interpretation echoed in the notion of denotive signs, and his secondary level in connotive signs (see also van Leeuwen 2001). However, in their shared concern with intertextuality, there are some parallels between iconography and the sort of discourse analysis under discussion here, and the term 'iconography' is now often used in a loose sense to refer to the kind of approach to images that I am calling discourse analysis I.

A work that might be described as an 'iconography' in this looser sense is Mary Cowling's (1989) study of 'the representation of type and character in Victorian art'. Cowling's work contributes to an account of the discursive construction of the East End of London in the 1880s too, since she points out that the East Ender was shown by Victorian artists as a particular social type. She argues that Victorian audiences assumed that paintings needed to be read – that their meanings required decoding – and that there were two, related, bodies of knowledge, both understood as scientifically true, that were used especially frequently for decoding images of social difference: physiognomy and phrenology.

> In the Victorian age, physiognomy, or the indication of character through the facial features and forms of the head and body, was all but universally believed in. The more specific indication of character through the shape of the skull, expounded as a complete system in the form of phrenology, was also widely subscribed to. Whether the human face was looked at with the eyes of the artist, the writer, or even the scientist, belief in physiognomy characterised contemporary attitudes towards it. (Cowling 1989: 9)

Cowling shows how books like *Physiognomy Made Easy* (c.1880), *Self-Instructor in Phrenology and Physiology* (1886) and *The Study of the Human Face* (1868), among many others, showed faces and heads divided into types that were differentiated in terms of their morality, social position and notions of 'race'. Aspects of heads and faces such as nose profile, forehead slope, chin profile, skull size and lip shape were all presented as clues to the moral standing, social class and 'race' of an individual, and these clues were used too in the work of cartoonists, novelists, scientists and artists. An example of how these shared interpretations of heads and faces were commonplace is given by Cowling (1989: 64–5), and it is also a neat example of her own method. Plate 44 of her book shows a page from the *Self-Instructor in Phrenology and Physiology*. There are two engravings on this page, one of a 'good head' and one of a 'bad head'. Cowling compares these in her plate 45 to a caricature of a 'foreigner' that appeared in the magazine *Punch* in 1862, and in plate 46 to a portrait of J.G. Lockhart, the son-in-law and biographer of Sir Walter

Scott, by William Allen in 1876. The 'soaring brow and delicate features' of the latter (Cowling 1989: 65) are repeated exactly in the *Self-Instructor* as the 'good head', and would have indicated to Victorian audiences that this was a man of high moral probity, high social class and English origin. In contrast, the swarthy and coarse features given to the 'foreigner' by *Punch* recur in the image of the 'bad head'. Cowling argues that Victorian audiences would have made these same connections and interpretations. And it is her method to make them too: to trace the relations between different texts in order to identify the meanings their viewers and readers shared.

Cowling's concern with intertextuality focuses on two particular images, however, one of which is particularly relevent to this discussion since Cowling argues that it contains several images of East Enders. This is a painting by William Powell Frith, exhibited in 1862 and called *The Railway Station* (Cowling 1989: 185–231). It is a huge canvas showing the crowd accompanying a train about to leave, and Cowling remarks that it was seen by contemporaries as an image of, and a commentary on, the modern London crowd. That is, its theme was social relations and social difference, and Frith and his audience both used physiognomy and phrenology to make sense of this painting. Having consulted books of physiognomy and phrenology herself, Cowling is able to offer her own key to the painting which notes the kind of social type each figure would have represented to its Victorian audiences (Cowling 1989: 242–3). Her key includes 'gentleman in reduced circumstances', 'his daughter, off to take up her first position' (as a governess) and 'villianous recruit – vicious type'. Cowling suggests that these latter sorts of images, of the various types from the residuum, would have been seen by contemporary audiences as East Enders. The social differences among Londoners were also understood as geographical differences in this period, and the residuum, certainly by the end of the 1880s, was always located in the East End of the city. Thus images of members of the residuum were also images of East Enders.

Cowling (1989) uses many sorts of texts to make her case for the importance of facial features and head types for understanding Victorian images of social difference, including magazines, anthropology books, novels, paintings and engravings, as well as those books on physiognomy and phrenology. As I have noted, this range of sources is typical of the kind of discourse analysis I am suggesting iconography is related to. Cowling's method is to look for the commonalities, both textual and visual, among these sources, and to establish these by citing the words and images they have in common: thus she quotes extensively from her sources and she also reproduces their images generously (her book has 370 pages of text and 340 plates). This search for recurring themes or visual patterns is also typical of discourse analysis. However, as the rest of this chapter will show, the proponents of discourse analysis also suggest some further methodological tactics for interpreting intertextual meanings.

4 discourse analysis I: the production and rhetorical organization of discourse

Iconography, then, like discourse analysis, depends on intertextuality for its interpretive power. It also depends, though, on what Panofsky called 'common sense', and many discourse analysts also suggest that successful discourse analysis depends less on rigorous procedures and more on other qualities: craft skill, says Potter (1996: 140); scholarship, according to Gill (1996: 144); 'interpretive sensitivities', in Phillips and Hardy's (2002: 75) words. Nonetheless, there have been some efforts to make the procedures of discourse analysis more explicit, especially in the social sciences. This section explores some of those efforts.

In her discussion of discourse analysis, Tonkiss (1998) suggests that those efforts have been directed to two areas. First, there is the analysis of the structure of the discursive statements. Secondly, there is a concern for the social context of those statements: who is saying them, in what circumstances.

4.1 exploring the rhetorical organization of discourse

One theme of discourse analysis is the organization of discourse itself. How, precisely, is a particular discourse structured, and how then does it produce a particular kind of knowledge? In relation to visual images, many studies have been particularly interested in how social difference is constructed, and the previous section briefly discussed one example of this in relation to the East End: Cowling's (1989) study of the intersection between art, physiognomy and phrenology. Another example is Ruth Livesy's (2004) essay on middle-class women who did charity work in London's East End, and how they saw East Enders. Livesy's study is a useful reminder of the complex and often contested nature of discourse, since it begins by remarking that these women disliked physiognomy and phrenology as ways of seeing and understanding people; instead, they drew on a discourse of 'ethical individualism' (Livesy 2004: 46) which focused on individuals' moral character, and especially their capacity for self-control, thrift, duty and foresight. Hence when they looked at East Enders, they didn't look at the shape of their heads or the character of their faces, but rather looked for signs of cleanliness, sobriety and rectitude in their dress and their houses. Livesy (2004) explores the rhetorical organization of their discourse to establish this way of seeing, and indeed this kind of discourse analysis is interested in, for example, how a particular discourse describes things (although the power of discourse means that it produces those things it purports to be describing), in how it constructs blame and responsibility, in how it constructs accountability, in how it categorizes and particularizes (Potter 1996).

The first step in this interpretive process is, as Tonkiss (1998) and Gill (1996) both emphasize, to try to forget all preconceptions you might have about the materials you are working with. Although an important part of your preparation for your analysis might have been to study what discourses other scholars have suggested are relevant to your sources (and Sunderland [2004] recommends this), nonetheless, when you approach your materials, try your best to read them and look at them with *fresh* eyes. As Foucault (1972: 25) says, pre-existing categories 'must be held in suspense. They must not be rejected definitively, of course, but the tranquillity with which they are accepted must be disturbed; we must show that they do not come about by themselves, but are always the result of a construction the rules of which must be known and the justifications of which must be scrutinized'. In this way, the material may offer you insights and leads that you would otherwise have missed. For visual images, it may be that the tools of detailed description offered by compositional interpretation have a role to play here, in making you look very carefully at every element of an image, and at their interrelation. Allow this process of reading and looking to take its time. Try to *immerse* yourself in the materials you are dealing with. Read and re-read the texts; look and look again at the images.

Having familiarized yourself with your materials, some slightly more systematic methods might be useful. One is a version of the coding process described in Chapter 4 in connection with content analysis (Phillips and Hardy [2002] recommend a quite rigorous version of this). Familiarity with the sources will allow you to identify *key themes*, which may be key words, or recurring visual images. (Remember, though, that the most important words and images may not be those that occur most often.) Make a list of these words or images and then go through all your sources, coding the material every time that word or image occurs. Then start to think about connections between and among key words and key images. According to Foucault, the task is to examine:

> relations between statements (even if the author is unaware of them; even if the statements do not have the same author; even if the authors were unaware of each other's existence); relations between groups of statements thus established (even if these groups do not concern the same, or even adjacent fields; even if they do not possess the same formal level; even if they are not the locus of assignable exchanges); relations between statements and groups of statements and events of a quite different kind (technical, economic, political, social). (Foucault 1972: 29)

How are particular words or images given specific meanings? Are there meaningful clusters of words and images? What objects do such clusters produce? What associations are established within such clusters? What connections are there between such clusters (Andersen 2003: 11–12)? Foucault here also suggests the need to consider the broader, non-discursive context of discourse. These sorts of questions address the productivity of discourse in the sense that they focus on its production of meanings and things.

Nead's (1988) discussion of how 'the prostitute' was discursively constructed through recurring images of bodies and places is exemplary here. Nead accumulates a wide range of visual images of this figure, as well as written accounts, and shows how she was understood by pointing to the limited number of key visual terms used to produce her (see also Gilman 1990; Walkowitz 1992). The prostitute worked exchanging sex for money. She was therefore constructed as a particular sort of moral problem in bourgeois discourses of femininity, and was placed in the residuum. She could be seen as irredeemable or redeemable; prostitutes were portrayed as both evil women and as victims of an evil society. However, as Nead notes, both arguments worked to place her outside 'normal' femininity. This outsider status was signified visually in the way she dressed (provocatively) and the way she looked, especially how she looked boldly at men. Since she was morally deviant, however, she was also pictured as paying the price of her sin. In visual and written narratives of prostitution, she was frequently visualized as losing her looks and her glamorous clothes, and simultaneously moving from the bright lights of the music hall to the dark streets of the East End, and, eventually, down into the dark and murky depths of the river Thames. This last location was often pictured as her final resting place: disease or pregnancy would take their toll, and her inevitable end, according to this discourse, was her suicide by drowning. The final stage of this visual narrative was the verdict passed on her by society. This was usually pictured by representatives of that society looking at the prostitute's dead body. These representatives might be the rivermen who find her, the policeman who inspects the corpse, the passers-by who see it, or the doctor who dissects it; and these are shown either as pitying or condemning. Nead thus identifies several key visual themes in images of prostitution: dress, bodily condition, location, looks. She shows how these themes could be given different meanings in different images or texts – the looks at her dead body could be compassionate or grimly satisfied, for example, depending on whether the prostitute was being constructed as evil or as a victim – but the basic elements used to represent her were repeated again and again in a wide variety of contexts.

focus

Look at Figures 7.2 to 7.6, all reproduced from Nead's (1988) study.

Consider each one in relation to the key themes identified by Nead: dress, bodily condition, location, looks. In particular, think about how each of those themes can be represented in different ways. Compare this relative flexibility in identifying themes with the coding process demanded by content analysis. Which do you prefer, and why?

(Continued)

Figure 7.2
Gustave Doré,
illustration to
The Bridge of
Sighs, *1878*
(Nead 1988)

Figure 7.3
W. Gray, 'Lost',
in W. Hayward,
London by
Night c. *1870*
(Nead 1988)

(Continued)

Figure 7.4

W. Gray, 'Found',
in W. Hayward,
London by
Night c. *1870*
(Nead 1988)

Figure 7.5

Hablot K. Browne
(Phiz), 'The
River', in Charles
Dickens, David
Copperfield,
August 1850,
(Nead 1988)

Figure 7.6
*George Frederick
Watts,* Found
Drowned, *1840–50
(Nead 1988)*

Are there other themes that seem to you to be relevant to these
images?

As this coding and interpretation process proceeds, other issues may start
to become important to your interpretation, perhaps issues that had not initially occurred to you. Unlike content analysis, this does not mean that you
have to halt your analytical process and start again with a revised set of categories. Discourse analysis is much more flexible than that. As new questions
occur, prompted by one moment of coding, you can return to your materials
with different codes in a second – or third or fourth or twentieth – moment
of interpretation. While the Foucauldian framework of discourse analysis is
giving you a certain approach to your materials, it is also crucial that you let
the details of your materials guide your investigations.

An important part of that framework is how a particular discourse
works to persuade. How does it produce its *effects of truth*? This is another
aspect of discourse that your analysis must address. Often this entails focusing on claims to truth, or to scientific certainty, or to the natural way of
things. As well as the visual and textual devices used to claim truth, however,
it is useful to look for moments at which dissent from a discourse is acknowledged (even if implicitly) and dealt with. Search for 'the work that is being
done to reconcile conflicting ideas, to cope with contradiction or uncertainty,
or to counter alternatives' (Tonkiss 1998: 255), because this work will highlight processes of persuasion that may otherwise be difficult to detect.

An example of an account of the East End of London that claimed to be
true because scientific was the map of poverty first published by Charles Booth
in 1889. Booth used 34 School Board Visitors (the local officials responsible for
enforcing attendance at school) to survey the income of every household in the

DESCRIPTIVE MAP OF LONDON POVERTY 1889.

North-Eastern sheet, comprising parts of Hackney, Islington, and Holborn; the whole of the City, Shoreditch, Bethnal Green, Whitechapel, St. George's-in-the-East, Stepney, Mile End, and Part of Poplar.

Figure 7.7

Charles

Booth's

descriptive

map of

London

poverty,

from Life and

Labour of the

London Poor,

1889

East End. He then calculated how many people were living in poverty, and mapped their location. The survey was seen as scientific in a number of ways. First, its coverage was more or less complete in terms of the East End's population (456,877 people were included, according to Booth's figures). Secondly, its coverage was seen as complete in terms of its understanding, and here the visual effect of the map was crucial: the map seemed to lay the East End bare to a scientific gaze that penetrated what others described as its darkest recesses. And, thirdly, Booth's survey and the map classified its subjects in ways that were central to contemporary scientific procedures. Booth argued that while over one-third of the residents of the East End were living in poverty, this was mostly due to fecklessness rather than moral depravity; only two per cent of the residuum, he argued, fell into that latter category. This sort of moral classification was central to other Victorian sciences, particularly those that constructed racial differences (and it is no coincidence that many journalists compared going into the East End of London with visits to Africa, as did General Booth's *In Darkest England*, published in 1890; see Keating 1976). Finally, Booth also relied on statistical analyses of his data which gave his arguments scientific authority too; Nead (1988) notes how some arguments about prostitution were also legitimated by statistical claims. Through these various strategies, then, Booth's map was perceived by (most) contemporaries as scientifically true.

focus

Look at the map in Figure 7.8 and compare it to the extract of Booth's map reproduced in Figure 7.7.

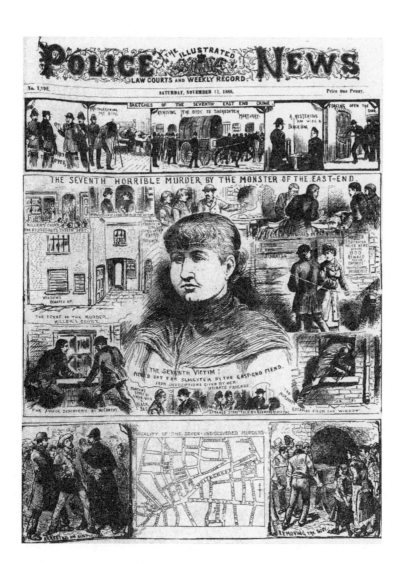

Figure 7.8
front page from Police Illustrated News, *17 November 1888 (Walkowitz 1992)*

The *Police Illustrated News* was a popular newspaper offering sensational crime stories. Does the map carry the same claim to accuracy in both cases? If not, why not?

Another emphasis in discourse analysis is the *complexity and contradictions* internal to discourses. Discursive formations have structures but that does not necessarily imply that they are logical or coherent. Indeed, part of the power of a specific discursive formation may rest precisely on the multiplicity of different arguments that can be produced in its terms. Potter (1996) uses

interpretative repertoire

the term **interpretative repertoire** to address one aspect of this notion of complexity.

> Interpretative repertoires are systematically related sets of terms that are often used with stylistic and grammatical coherence and often organized around one or more central metaphors. They develop historically and make up an important part of the 'common sense' of a culture, although some are specific to institutional domains. (Potter 1996: 131)

Potter notes that interpretative repertoires are something like mini-discourses; they tend to be quite specific to particular social situations. The example he cites is Gilbert and Mulkay's (1984) study of how scientists legitimate their own arguments, and the discovery that they use quite different techniques in their published research papers from those used in informal talk. Here, two interpretative repertoires are deployed in different circumstances, but both are part of a complex discourse of scientific truth. An example of a visual interpretative repertoire is offered by Nead (1988: 128–32). She discusses a watercolour by the Pre-Raphaelite painter Dante Gabriel Rosetti. Called *The Gate of Memory*, it was painted in 1857 and shows a prostitute standing under an archway staring at a group of children playing. It visualizes one of the final verses of a poem by William Bell Scott called 'Maryanne'. But while Scott's poem could describe the degraded body of this woman in some detail, Rosetti's watercolour cannot, says Nead, and this is because 'the prostitute has become the subject of "art" and "art" does not provide space for woman as physically deviant or unpleasurable' (Nead 1988: 132). That is, the Victorian discourse of femininity entailed a number of interpretative repertoires and the repertoire available to artists could only produce certain kinds of images.

An example of the contradictions inherent in discursive formations can be given by placing Jones's (1989) account of the 'cockney' next to other discussions of the construction of East Enders. As we have seen, from the 1880s if not before, the East Ender was constructed as marked, physically and visibly, by moral degeneracy. As Jones (1976), Fishman (1988) and Walkowitz (1992) emphasize, this was a construction that could produce considerable fear among the bourgeois readers of the newspapers, novels, pamphlets and poems through which it was articulated. Walkowitz (1992) and Nead (1988) both emphasize the horror of disease that prostitution might spread, for example (which could involve acknowledging, as it did for campaigners against the Contagious Diseases Act of 1860s, that it was actually men who spread disease, and often bourgeois men visiting working-class prostitutes at that; a good example of the complexity of discourses). Jones (1976) and Fishman (1988) stress the middle-class fear of social unrest that a residuum with no stake in society might create. Hence, through the 1880s and beyond, as a counter to these fears, other images of the East Ender developed. The orderly dock strike of 1889, for example, was seen as evidence that the majority of the poor were decent at heart, and not likely to revolt, and Jones (1989) traces the elaboration of the 'cockney' as the acceptable face of the East End. The cockney was constructed as good-hearted, chirpy, with a resigned sense of humour and a particular style of dress, often a bit flash; they look out for their neighbour and, especially, are stoical under conditions of social hardship. Jones argues that the effect of this discourse was to counter imaginatively what was perceived as the threat to society posed by the residuum, by constructing the cockney as different but lovable. Jones (1989) suggests that this vision of the cockney was expressed most unambiguously in music hall songs at the turn of the century, but he also notes that much of the literature at that period 'veered incoherently' between this cockney and the other vision of the residuum East Ender. Thus Jones's work stresses the contradictions within the discursive construction of the East End, through a careful reading of a wide range of materials.

Finally, discourse analysis also involves reading for what is not seen or said. Absences can be as productive as explicit naming; *invisibility* can have just as powerful effects as visibility. Thus Jones (1989) ends his essay on the construction of the 'cockney' by noting that the cockney was always imagined as white, despite the constant presence of large black communities in the East End. The 'cockney' therefore erased racialized difference by making whiteness the taken-for-granted 'race' of the East Ender. As Jones (1989) also notes, however, this erasure did not last beyond the so-called race riots in Notting Hill in the west end of London in 1958. After that, 'race' could not be made invisible so easily, and the cockney fades as a meaningful cultural category.

Discourse analysis thus depends on reading with great care for *detail*. It assumes that the efficacy of discourse often resides in the assumptions it makes about what is true, real or natural, in the contradictions that allow it interpretive flexibility, and in what is not said, and none of these is accessible to superficial reading or viewing. Hence Gill's (1996: 144) emphasis on the scholarship entailed in discourse analysis: 'the analysis of discourse and rhetoric requires the careful reading and interpretation of texts, rigorous scholarship rather than adherence to formal procedures'.

To summarize the strategies for the intepretation of the rhetorical organization of discourse outlined in this section, then, they include:

- looking at your sources with fresh eyes;
- immersing yourself in your sources;

- identifying key themes in your sources;
- examining their effects of truth;
- paying attention to their complexity and contradictions;
- looking for the invisible as well as the visible;
- paying attention to details.

4.2 exploring the social production of discourse

As Gill (1996: 142) notes, 'all discourse is occasioned'. All discourse takes place in specific social circumstances, and the authors discussed in this chapter draw two methodological implications for their sort of discourse analysis from this.

The previous section looked at some rhetorical strategies that could visually or verbally assert the truth of a particular discursive claim. However, this is not the only way that certain discourses can become more dominant than others: the *institutional location* of a discourse is also crucial. Foucault, for all his reluctance to ascribe unidirectional causality, insisted on the need to locate the social site from which particular statements are made, and to position the speaker of a statement in terms of their social authority (Foucault 1972: 50–2). Thus a statement coming from a source endowed with authority (and just how that authority is established may be an important issue to address) is likely to be more productive than one coming from a marginalized social position. The work of the historians examined in this chapter demonstrates this point in a rather paradoxical way. For they are forced to rely almost entirely on the images and words of the socially and institutionally powerful in their discussions of the discursive construction of the East End, simply because they are the only visions and words that are now available. The powerful had the resources to make their discourses substantial through books and pictures, and these were the materials then put into libraries and archives. It is therefore extraordinarily difficult now to pick up traces of the discourses about the East End articulated by those who lived there in the 1880s, for example, although Fishman (1988) suggests that some contemporary novelists were the faithful recorders of what they heard there. Thus the social location of a discourse's production is important to consider in relation to its effects.

The second way in which the social context of discourse production matters is in terms of the *audience* assumed by images and texts. The explanation given for the same event may be quite different if the audience for that explanation is different. Or the visual images of the same scene or event may be quite different, in terms of their technology or genre or in other ways, for different audiences. The visual images that surrounded the Jack the Ripper murders in the East End in 1888 are a case in point. Popular newspapers, for example, used sketches and maps to show readers the location of the murders and the victims' faces, as Figure 7.8 demonstrates. This was a kind of realism that might be seen as the visual equivalent of the sensationalistic journalism pioneered in the same decade (Curtis 2001; Walkowitz 1992). Other images were used for other audiences, though. Sander Gilman (1990), in his essay on the Ripper murders, notes that police photographs of the victims' mutilated bodies were used by the criminologist Alexandre Lacassagne in his 1889 book on sadism. The apparent veracity of photographs was thought necessary for a scientific text; but only an audience of scientists, too, was considered capable of seeing such images in an objective, scientific way. Notions about audience can thus affect the type of image used.

---

focus

Consider all the figures reproduced in this chapter. How might you go about finding the social locations of their production and reception? What does 'social location' mean in this sense? Does it mean class, gender, 'race', sexuality and so on? How might an institution be ascribed those characteristics?

Thus discourse analysis also entails paying attention to certain aspects of the social context of discourse production. The authors cited in this chapter – Gill, Tonkiss, Potter and Wetherell – tend to focus on the rhetorical organization of a discourse's texts and images and on the impact on those texts and images of the social location of their production. This emphasis neglects to explore the social practices and effects of discourse, however, and this indicates the tendency of this sort of discourse analysis to focus more on texts and images than social institutions.

5 discourse analysis I and reflexivity

The introduction to this chapter noted that Foucault himself was not sympathetic to certain kinds of reflexivity, particularly those that depended on descriptions of subject positions; for him, such descriptions were the work of the police. However, as Phillips and Hardy (2002) pointed out, from a Foucauldian perspective the social sciences are just as discursive as any other form of knowledge production, and in producing a piece of research you too are participating in their discursive formation. The social sciences are the descendants of those human sciences the truth claims of which Foucault analysed in detail. If you are writing a discourse analysis, then, the arguments about discourse, power and truth/knowledge must surely be just as pertinent to your work as to the materials you are analysing. Doing a discourse analysis thus demands some sort of critical reflection on your own research practice. For, as Tonkiss (1998: 259) says, 'the discourse analyst seeks to open up statements to challenge, interrogate taken-for-granted meanings, and disturb easy claims to objectivity in the texts they are reading. It would therefore be inconsistent to contend that the analyst's own discourse was itself wholly objective, factual or generally true.' Discourse analysts have a number of ways of addressing this issue.

The first is to think carefully about the rhetorical organization of a discourse analysis. How should it be written? Since discourse analyses cannot argue that they are the only, true analysis of the materials discussed, discourse analysis aims to be persuasive rather than truthful, and this entails 'a certain modesty in our analytic claims' (Tonkiss 1998: 260). According to Phillips and Hardy (2002: 83–5), any discourse analysis should acknowledge that its language is constructing an interpretation rather than revealing the truth. Different voices, texts and images should pervade the analysis, they continue (Phillips and Hardy 2002: 85); you should acknowledge that you have made choices in what you discuss, emphasizing some materials at the expense of others; you should open up your own work to other readings and interpretations, and be aware how your work engages with that of others.

This modesty is what discourse analysis substitutes for more conventional notions of reflexivity. Clearly, conventional, autobiographical versions of reflexivity are difficult in Foucauldian accounts, for they depend on a notion of human agency that constructs the author as an autonomous individual who then encounters a part of the world in their research. Just as this autobiographical form of reflexivity is inconsistent with psychoanalytic approaches to visual methods, it is equally incompatible with the Foucauldian notion of a subject constituted through the discourses in which they are saturated. Another example of a more modest, Foucauldian approach is Kendall and Wickham's (1999: 101–9) move, in their discussion of reflexivity in relation to Foucauldian methods, towards discussing whether non-human objects or animals should be given the same status as knowledge producers as their human researchers. Their answer is yes. In the visual field perhaps an equivalent move would be to recognize the power of visual images which in some way limits that of the researcher. W.J.T. Mitchell (1996) has addressed this issue in an essay called 'What do pictures *really* want?'. Although reprimanded by Hal Foster (1996) for a kind of commodity fetishism – and this strategy is also vulnerable to the charge of hiding, under a cloak of respecting pictures, simply the critic's own version of what pictures want – Mitchell suggests that the power of images always exceeds our ability to interpret them. He is perhaps articulating a further form of reflexivity that makes sense for Foucauldian discourse analyses. There must be others, but all would share that mark of modesty mentioned by Tonkiss.

However, a complication to this discursive reflexivity arises when the productive context (rather than the rhetorical organization) of the analysis is considered. For being 'persuasive' or 'modest' depends on the interpretative context in which the discourse analysis is produced. And that context is the social sciences. Thus discourse analysis can end up with a rather conventional list of things to consider when writing up your work. Here are the sorts of things mentioned by Potter (1996: 138–9), Gill (1996: 147) and Tonkiss (1998: 258–60):

- using detailed textual or visual evidence to support your analysis;
- using textual or visual details to support your analysis;
- the coherence the study gives to the discourse examined;
- the coherence of the analysis itself;
- the coherence of the study in relation to previous related research;
- the examination of cases that run counter to the discursive norm established by the analysis, in order to affirm the disruption caused by such deviations.

Clearly, these criteria are unobjectionable in relation to the conventions of the social sciences. However, let us ask a Foucauldian question of them: what are the effects of these criteria? What do they produce? Well, they aim to produce a certain sort of text: one that locates the plausibility of the discourse analysis in the text alone. The effect of this is to erase (again, we might say) the institutional context in which a discourse analysis is produced. So perhaps another, reflexive strategy to mark the modesty of discourse analysis would be to note explicitly that the institution and its audience are the co-authors of the analysis, and to recognize the claims to interpretative authority that that co-authorship entails.

6 discourse analysis I: an assessment

In terms of the critical visual methodology described in Chapter 1, the type of discourse analysis discussed in this chapter has clear strengths. It pays careful attention to images themselves, and to the web of intertextuality in which any individual image is embedded. It is centrally concerned with the production of social difference through visual imagery. It addresses questions of power as they are articulated through visual images themselves. And although reflexivity is a tricky issue for discourse analysis, there are ways in which the authority of the discourse analysis can be both marked (by acknowledging its context of production) and perhaps undermined (by rhetorical strategies of modesty).

There are also some difficulties in the method, however. One of these is knowing where to stop in making intertextual connections, and another related to this is in grounding those connections empirically. Gilman's (1990) essay on Jack the Ripper illustrates the dangers (to me at least) of making so many connections that some start to seem rather tenuous. In order to understand why the murderer was seen by many as Jewish, Gilman cites a huge range of contemporary sources, including London newspapers, Wedekind's play and Berg's opera *Lulu*, Freud and Fliess, Hogarth, medical texts, Bram Stoker's novel *Dracula*, Hood's poetry, paintings, engravings and posters, Hahnemann (the founder of homeopathy), 'Jack's' notes, criminologists Lombroso and Lacassagne, contemporary pornography, *Daniel Deronda*, contemporary tracts, and Proust and Zola. The breadth of scholarship is extraordinary, but I begin to wonder how many of those sources could be said to have produced, even indirectly, the London newspapers' and police's description of the Ripper as Jewish? Some, of course, perhaps many. Maybe all. But Gilman's analysis does not attempt to trace such connections in any grounded way; instead, they are related in his work simply through the category of 'discourse'. Discourse as a result seems to become a free-floating web of meanings unconnected to any social practices. The practical problem posed by this sort of discourse analysis, then – where to stop making intertextual connections – can also be an analytical one – how to make the intertextual connections convincingly productive.

Another problem with discourse analysis, for some critics, is its refusal to ascribe causality. As section 1 of this chapter noted, Foucault's project was in some ways descriptive; he wanted to account for how things happened more than why they happened. This means that discourse analysis too is not always very clear about the relation between discourse and its context. Few guidelines are offered about what that context might be, other than the notions addressed in section 4.2 here about the social location of the producers and audiences of specific images or texts. There is also little attempt to outline what the relations between that context and discourse might be, specifically.

Both these problems are connected to the neglected issue in this form of discourse analysis: the social practices of discourse. As this chapter has noted at several points, this kind of discourse analysis is concerned more with images and texts than with the social institutions that produced, archived, displayed or sold them, and the effects of those practices. The next chapter, however, turns to a form of Foucauldian discourse analysis that does address just this issue.

summary

- *associated with:*
  The interpretation of wide and eclectic ranges of textual materials, both visual and written.

- *sites and modalities:*
  Discourse analysis I is most concerned with the site of the image itself, although reference can be made to the site of production too. It is particularly strong at exploring the effects of the compositional and social modalities of images.

- *key terms:*
  Key terms include discourse, discursive formation, power/knowledge and intertextuality.

- *strengths and weaknesses:*
  Discourse analysis I is very effective at looking carefully at images and interpreting their effects, especially in relation to constructions of social difference. It is less interested, however, in thinking about the practices and institutions through which such constructions are produced, disseminated and experienced.

Further reading

Tonkiss's (1998) chapter is a good general introduction to this form of discourse analysis, while Andersen (2003) offers a detailed and accessible exegesis of Foucault's own methods. Phillips and Hardy's (2002) book is also helpful, and discusses in some depth their discourse analysis of a collection of cartoons. As for Foucault, the secondary literature on him is now huge, but he is a much more accessible writer than many students imagine and I suggest trying *Discipline and Punish* (1977) as an introduction to his work.

8
discourse analysis II
institutions and ways of seeing

key example how museums display images and artefacts, looking particularly at three studies of the American Museum of Natural History in New York.

1 another introduction to discourse and visual culture

The previous chapter began with a brief introduction to the work of Michel Foucault, and suggested that there are two methodologies that have developed from his work. Although these two are related and overlap – most particularly because they share a concern with power/knowledge as it is articulated through discourse – these two methodologies have tended to produce rather different sorts of research. The first type of discourse analysis, discussed in chapter 7, works with visual images and written or spoken texts. Although it is certainly concerned with the social positions of difference and authority that are articulated through images and texts, it tends to focus on the production and rhetorical organization of visual and textual materials.

In contrast, the second form of discourse analysis, which this chapter will explore, often works with similar sorts of materials, but is much more concerned with their production by, and their reiteration of, particular institutions and their practices, and their production of particular human subjects. This difference can be clarified by looking at how two exponents of these two kinds of discourse analysis use the term 'archive'. In her discussion of the first type of discourse analysis, Tonkiss (1998: 252) describes the material that that sort of analysis works with as an 'archive'. While Tonkiss herself puts the term in inverted commas, clearly aware that it carries a certain conceptual baggage, she nevertheless uses it to refer to her collection of data, and then moves on to consider what the data shows about certain discursive formations. However, a different kind of discourse analyst, like Alan Sekula (1986, 1989), would spend some time examining the archive itself as an institution, and unpacking the consequences of its particular practices of classification for the meanings of the things placed within it. Referring to archives of photographs in particular, he argues that:

> archives are not neutral; they embody the power inherent in accumulation, collection and hoarding as well as that power inherent in the command of the lexicon and rules of a language … any photographic archive, no matter how small, appeals indirectly to these institutions for its authority. (Sekula 1986: 155)

No doubt Tonkiss would agree with this comment. However, Sekula is at pains to explore the effects of 'archivalization' on texts and images in a way that Tonkiss is not. Sekula and writers like him make that analytical move because they place their understandings of discourses firmly in relation to the account of institutions given by Foucault. Archives are one sort of institution, in the Foucauldian sense, and this second sort of analysis would not treat them as transparent windows onto source materials in the way that Tonkiss seems to. Archives work in quite particular ways that have effects on what is stored within them, and on those who use them (Rose 2000).

As we have seen, several of Foucault's books examine specific institutions and their disciplines: prisons, hospitals, asylums. For writers concerned with visual matters, perhaps the key text is *Discipline and Punish* (Foucault 1977). Subtitled *The Birth of the Prison*, this is an account of changing penal organization in post-medieval Europe, in which alterations in the organization of visuality (and spatiality) are central. The book begins by quoting a contemporary account of a prolonged torture and execution carried out as a public spectacle in 1757. Foucault then quotes from a prison rulebook written eighty years later which is, as he says, a timetable. Foucault's questions are, how (rather than why) did this change in penal style, from spectacular punishment to institutional routine, take place? And with what effects? Through detailed readings of contemporary texts, *Discipline and Punish* traces this shift. By the mid-nineteenth century:

> the punishment–body relation is not the same as it was in the torture during public executions. The body now serves as an instrument or intermediary: if one intervenes upon it to imprison it, or to make it work, it is in order to deprive the individual of a liberty that is regarded both as a right and as a property. The body, according to this penality, is caught up in a system of constraints and privations, obligations and prohibitions. Physical pain, the pain of the body itself, is no longer the constituent element of the penalty. From being an art of unbearable sensation punishment has become an economy of suspended rights … As a result of this new restraint, a whole army of technicians took over from the executioner, the immediate anatomist of pain: warders, doctors, chaplains, psychiatrists, psychologists, educationalists … (Foucault 1977: 11)

The prison was born. As well as a new institution and a new understanding of punishment, in *Discipline and Punish* Foucault describes the emergence of a new set of professions who defined who needed punishment and who could exercise that punishment, and of a new subjectivity produced for those so punished: what he called the 'docile body'. This was the body subjected to these new penal disciplines, the body which had to conform to its 'constraints and privations, obligations and prohibitions'.

A key point of Foucault's argument is that in this new regime of punishment, these docile bodies in a sense disciplined themselves, and Foucault argues that this was achieved through a certain visuality (for general discussions of the role of visuality in the work of Foucault, see Jay [1993] and Rajchman [1988]). Once defined by the new 'expert' knowledges as in some way deviant, these bodies were placed in an institution that was 'a machine for altering minds' (Foucault 1977: 125). Foucault (1977: 195–228) expands this point, and demonstrates the importance of a visuality to it, by discussing a plan for an institution designed by Jeremy Bentham in 1791. Bentham **panopticon** called this building a **panopticon**, and suggested it could be used as the plan for all sorts of disciplining institutions: prisons, but also hospitals, workhouses, schools, madhouses. The panopticon was a tall tower, surrounded by an annular building. The latter consisted of cells, one for each inmate, with windows so arranged that the occupant was always visible from the tower. The tower was the location of the supervisor but because of the arrangement of its windows, blinds, doors and corridors, the inmates in their cells could never be certain that they were under observation from the tower at any particular moment. Never certain of invisibility, each inmate therefore had to behave 'properly' all the time: thus they disciplined themselves and were produced as docile bodies. 'Hence the major effect of the Panopticon: to induce in the inmate a state of conscious and permanent visibility that assures the automatic functioning of power' (Foucault 1977: 210). This sort of visuality, in which one subject is seen without ever seeing, and the other sees without **surveillance** ever being seen, Foucault called **surveillance**, and he argued that, since it was an efficient means of producing social order, it became a dominant form of visuality throughout modern capitalist societies. Through its operation, says Foucault (1977: 200) (in an echo of Lacan), 'visibility is a trap'.

Foucault suggests that institutions work in two ways: through their apparatus and through their technologies. This is a distinction this chapter will use; however, Foucault was rather inconsistent in his use of these terms, and the distinction made here between them is clearer than that found in his **institutional apparatus** work. An **institutional apparatus** is the forms of power/knowledge that constitute the institutions: for example, architecture, regulations, scientific treatises, philosophical statements, laws, morals, and so on, and the discourse articulated through all these (Hall 1997b: 47). Hence Foucault described Bentham's panopticon as an apparatus: at once an architectural design and a **institutional technologies** moral and philosophical treatise. The **institutional technologies** (sometimes difficult to differentiate from the apparatus) are the practical techniques used to practise that power/knowledge. Technologies are 'diffuse, rarely formulated in continuous, systematic discourse … often made up of bits and pieces … a disparate set of tools and methods' (Foucault 1977: 26). An example might be the design of the windows and blinds in the panopticon.

It has been argued by some historians of photography that photography must be understood as a technology in this Foucauldian sense. John Tagg, for example, writes:

> Photography as such has no identity. Its status as technology varies with the power relations that invest it. Its nature as a practice depends on the institutions and agents which define it and set it to work … Its history has no unity. It is a flickering across a field of institutional spaces. It is this field we must study, not photography as such. (Tagg 1988: 63)

For Tagg, photography is diffuse; it is given coherence only by its use in certain institutional apparatuses. He elaborates this claim by studying photographs as they were used in the nineteenth century by police forces, prisons, orphanages, asylums, local government's medical officers of health, and newspaper journalists and publicists. It is its uses in these institutions that Tagg argues gives photography its status as a unified something rather than a diffuse no one thing, and that coherent something is, according to Tagg, the belief that photographs picture the real. (Hence he is very critical of Barthes's (1982) assertion, discussed in section 3.2 of Chapter 5, that the *punctum* of a photograph is a trace of an uncoded referent.) The apparatus of these various institutions – the police, prisons, orphanages, asylums, local government, the emergent mass media – asserted the truth of their claims to be able to detect, or punish, or cure the criminal, the ill, the orphaned, the mad, the degenerate (in part by relying on the scientific status of the discourses of physiognomy and phrenology, discussed in the previous chapter). Producing a certain regime of truth, these institutions used photography as a crucial technology through which these distinctions were made visible. The related opposite of this, as Sekula (1989) notes, was the detection, celebration and honouring of the moral, the familial and the proper in bourgeois photographic portraiture. Thus the institutional uses of photography make us think photographs are truthful pictures, not photographic techniques themselves. For Tagg, then (and see also Lalvani 1996; Sekula 1989), Foucault's emphasis on institutions and power/knowledge is crucial for understanding the belief that photography pictures the real.

This emphasis on institutional apparatus and technologies gives a different inflection to this second kind of discourse analysis. It shifts attention away from the details of individual images – although both Tagg (1988) and Sekula (1989) describe the general characteristics of particular types of photographs – and towards the processes of their production and use. That is, this type of discourse analysis concentrates most on the sites of *production* and *audiencing*, in their *social modality*. In their discussion of nineteenth century police photography, for example, both Sekula and Tagg pay a good deal of attention to the processes used to classify, file, retrieve and use photographs of those who had been pictured as 'criminal'. They both also argue that photography was only one part of what Sekula (1989: 351) calls 'a bureaucratic-clerical-statistical system of "intelligence"', and he suggests that the filing cabinet was actually a more important piece of institutional technology than the camera. They discuss other technologies – such as phrenology and fingerprinting – that were used alongside photography, and they explore other aspects of institutional apparatuses in their studies too. This means that the sources used in their accounts are as eclectic as those of the discourse analysts discussed in Chapter 7. However, certainly in the case of Tagg and Sekula, their work is held together by an insistence on the power relations articulated through these practices and institutions. Visual images and visualities are for them articulations of institutional power.

This is one aspect of their work that has been criticized. For although both take care to distinguish their Foucauldian understanding of power from those that see power simply as repressive, nonetheless there is very little sense in either of their work of the possibility of visualities other than those of dominant institutions. Lindsay Smith (1998), for example, takes them to task for not looking at a wide enough range of nineteenth century photographic practices, and in particular for neglecting the kinds of domestic photography practised by a number of women in the mid-nineteenth century. These women photographers can be seen as producing images that do not replicate the surveillant gaze of the police mug-shot or the family studio portrait: they thwart that classifying gaze by strategies such as blurred focus, collage and overexposure. Moreover, like their discourse analyst cousins whose work was discussed in the previous chapter, there is very little reflexivity in this second type of discourse-analytical work. Ironically, considering their critique of truth claims, Tagg and Sekula both make very strong claims themselves about the veracity of their accounts. Tagg (1988: 1–2) in particular is quite scathing about Barthes, implying that Barthes's insistence on the uncoded quality of certain photographs was merely an emotional response to his search for a photograph that would remind him of his mother after she had died. 'I need not point out', says Tagg (1988: 2) 'that the existence of a photograph is no guarantee of a corresponding pre-photographic existent.' Tagg here counterposes the self-evident ('I need not point out ...'), which he later expands at great length with the use of much theory, to the emotional need driving Barthes's work: as I read it, Tagg is making an opposition between his masculinized rationality and what he sees as the effeminate emotionalilty of the grieving Barthes. Hardly a self-reflexive strategy, I think.

This chapter though will not focus on the work of Tagg or Sekula and their interest in photographic archives. Rather, it will turn to work that considers two other kinds of institutions that deal with visual objects – the art gallery and the museum – and that have also been subject to Foucauldian critique by writers such as Tony Bennett (1995) and Eilean Hooper-Greenhill (1992) (other important discussions include Starn [2005] and the essays collected by Barker [1999], Greenberg, Ferguson and Nairne [1996], Preziosi and Farago [2004], Sherman and Rogoff [1994] and Vergo [1989]). These accounts explore how visual images and objects are produced in particular ways by institutional apparatuses and technologies (as 'art', for example) and how various subjectivities are also produced, such as the 'curator' and 'the visitor'. However, these are institutions which, while of course not free from the workings of power, are not as obviously coercive as those examined by Tagg and Sekula. Their disciplines are more subtle, and they thus provide a more fruitful ground for exploring the extent to which this second type of discourse analysis can address questions of conflicting discourses and contested ways of seeing. The particular case study will be the American Museum of Natural History in New York (hereafter referred to as the AMNH), as seen by Donna Haraway (1989: 26–58), Ann Reynolds (1995), Timothy Luke (2002) and Mieke Bal (1996: 13–56) (although Bal's account also incorporates a semiological approach). Their accounts will also allow another opportunity to consider the possibility of a reflexive discourse-analytic practice.

The status of the art gallery and museum as institution provides a way of examining the methodology of this second kind of discourse analysis. So, this chapter will:

- examine ways of describing the apparatus of the art gallery and the museum;
- examine ways of describing the technologies of the art gallery and the museum;
- examine how this second kind of discourse analysis argues that these institutions produce and discipline their visitors;
- assess the strengths and weaknesses of this type of discourse analysis of institutions.

2 finding your sources for discourse analysis II

The kinds of sources used for this kind of discourse analysis are as diverse as those deployed by the discourse analysis discussed in Chapter 7. A key Foucauldian account of the emergence of the art gallery and the museum as particular kinds of institutions is Tony Bennett's *The Birth of the Museum* (1995), and he is typical in his use of a wide range of sources. He undertakes a careful reading of the many *written texts* that discussed museums and galleries in the second half of the nineteenth century. These were produced by reformers, philanthropists, civil servants and curators who were all arguing, though often in different ways, for the establishment of galleries and museums that were open to the public. Studies of current discussions about museums and their practices supplement this sort of historical written source with other types of documents available now, such as the annual reports of galleries and museums and their mission statements. *Interviews* with the directors, curators and designers of museums and galleries can also be used in contemporary studies (although Phillips and Hardy [2002: 71] suggest that naturally occurring talk is more valid for discourse analysis than talk produced in the context of a research project). Both historical and contemporary studies often use photographs or other *visual images* of buildings, rooms and displays too, sometimes simply as illustrations to their written accounts, and both also pay attention to the *architecture* of the institution: its design, decorations, inscriptions, layout and so on. Studies of contemporary museums and galleries also often rely on visits to the institution and *observation* of the way people visit and work in them.

In relation to studies of the AMNH, Luke's (2002) study is primarily archival, while both Haraway (1989) and Reynolds (1995), writing historical accounts of particular halls of that museum, use written texts such as the autobiographies of curators, the minutes of museum committee meetings, scientific texts and the museum's annual reports; Haraway (1989) supplements this with an account of what the hall she is interested in looks like to the visitor now: or, at least, what it looks like to Haraway now. Both illustrate their arguments using photographs of museum displays and other images. Bal's (1996) account is a reading of a few halls of the museum based entirely on their layout and the displays on show to the visitor in late 1991. (Her study is also interesting in the way it uses illustrations to make her points, as well as written text.)

---

focus

Visit a gallery or a museum. When we visit a museum or a gallery, it is somehow clear that certain things are 'the objects to be looked at': the paintings, the objects, the items in the shop. This time, spend time looking at other things: the architecture of the building, for example, its floor plan, its warders, its other visitors.

---

3 the apparatus of the gallery and the museum

As Stephen Bann comments, the history of museums can be interpreted:

> *grosso modo* in terms of two conceptually distinct phases. The first, roughly
> speaking up to the end of the eighteenth century, qualifies as a 'prehistory'

in the sense that the collection and display of objects appears to answer no clear principles of ordering by genre, school, and period. The second, which represents an almost irresistible movement towards conformity over the course of the last two centuries, is a history in which the musuem has developed and perfected its own principles of ordering by giving spatial distribution to the concepts of school and period, in particular. (Bann 1998: 231; see also Hooper-Greenhill 1992)

Bennett's (1995) discussion of museums and galleries focuses on the second of these phases, and draws much theoretical inspiration from Foucault's *Discipline and Punish: The Birth of the Prison*. Bennett points out that both prisons and modern museums were born in broadly the same historical period, and he argues that they deployed a similar disciplining surveillance. In making this claim, Bennett interprets his sources using the kinds of methods discussed in the previous chapter. Thus he too looks for *key themes*, for *truth claims*, for *complexity* and for *absences* (see Chapter 7, section 4.1). He pays attention to the diversity of ways in which public museums and galleries were justified by nineteenth century commentators, noting, for example, that they were defended as an antidote to working-class men's drunkenness, as an alternative to working-class disaffection and riot, and as a means to civilize manners and morals. But his overall emphasis is very much on the way this discursive formation produced the museum as a disciplining machine:

> the museum, in providing a new setting for works of culture, also functioned as a technological environment which allowed cultural artefacts to be refashioned in ways that would facilitate their deployment for new purposes as part of governmental programmes aimed at reshaping general norms of social behaviour. (Bennett 1995: 6)

His concern, then, is with the power that saturated the museum and gallery, and he explores that power in terms of those institutions' apparatuses. In particular, he focuses on particular discourses of culture and science that shaped their design and practice, and also produced certain subject positions. Hooper-Greenhill (1992: 176), too, is interested in the way 'new technologies and new subject positions were constituted through the adminstration of [a museum's] newly acquired material'.

Bennett argues that there was a specific discourse of 'culture' which saturated the births of the museum and gallery. Using the sources mentioned in section 2, he argues that the power of museums and galleries had the same aim: both use 'culture' as a tool of social management. He notes that the definition of 'culture' used in the two sorts of institutions is somewhat different and that does produce some differences between them, especially in the sorts of objects they display. In the museum, 'culture' tends to refer to that later nineteenth century understanding of culture as 'a whole way of life', and museums often collect objects that are meant to exemplify the way of life of particular social groups. In the nineteenth century, this often meant that museums collected and displayed the artefacts of colonized peoples, and these peoples were seen as less cultured and more natural than those of the West. (Annie Coombes [1994] discusses nineteenth century displays of African artefacts in European and North American museums in her book *Reinventing Africa*.) Bal's (1996) account of her 1991 visit to the AMNH emphasizes its continued articulation of imperialist, white discourse, noting that halls showing the way of life of certain colonized peoples are entered directly after halls displaying stuffed mammals and birds, thus implying that certain groups are closer to nature than others. Galleries, on the other hand, work with an older definition of 'culture' as that which can ennoble the human spirit, and the objects they display are those defined as Art (see the focus in Chapter 3 section 3.5 for more on this notion of Art). Such objects – usually paintings and sculpture from Western traditions – are then also constituted as 'Art', and as noble and uplifting, by being on display.

Bennett also discusses, more briefly, a specific discourse of science that was part of the museum's apparatus of power. In museums, he notes, objects are always classified according to what are claimed to be 'scientific' or 'objective' principles, whether they be drawn from notions of historical progress, scientific rationality or anthropological analysis.

Bal (1996) remarks that differentiations made by the complex discourse of culture are expressed in the gallery and museum that flank either side of Central Park in New York. On the one side, the AMNH, on the other, the Metropolitan Museum of Art.

> By this very division of the city map, the universal concept of 'humanity' is filled with specific meaning. The division of 'culture' and 'nature' between the East Side and the West Side of Manhattan relegates the large majority of the world's population to the status of static being, assigning to a small portion only the higher status of art producers in history. Where 'nature', in the [AMNH] dioramas, is a backdrop, transfixed in stasis, 'art', presented in the Met as an ineluctable evolution, is endowed with a story. (Bal 1996: 15–16)

In his account of the AMNH, Luke (2002) prefers to focus on the parallels between its collecting practices and those of US corporations, suggesting that the museum's 'searches for fossilised bones mimic the quest of large-scale sweeps by American capital through every remote expanse of the world in search of other organic goods from the Paleozoic era, like coal, oil, gas, or pre-Paleozoic inorganic minerals, like gold, silver, copper, bauxite, or iron' (Luke 2002: 121).

Bennett (1995) also pays much attention to the way the *architecture* of museums and galleries articulated these various discourses of culture, art and science. As well as the distinction between two sorts of building – the museum and the gallery – there are the imposing *facades* and *entrance halls* of many nineteenth century galleries and museums, for example, which were designed to be as inspiring and uplifting as the understanding of culture and science articulated within. Haraway looks at the façade of the Theodore Roosevelt Memorial – the main building of the AMNH – and considers the effects of its design:

> The facade of the memorial … is classical, with four Ionic columns 54 feet high topped by statues of the great explorers Boone, Audubon, Lewis and Clark. The coin-like, bas-relief seals of the United States and of the Liberty Bell are stamped on the front panels. Inscribed across the top are the words TRUTH, KNOWLEDGE, VISION and the dedication to Roosevelt as 'a great leader of the youth of America, in energy and fortitude in the faith of our fathers, in defense of the rights of the people, in the love and conservation of nature and of the best in life and in man'. Youth, paternal solicitude, virile defense of democracy, and intense emotional connection to nature are the unmistakable themes. (Haraway 1989: 27)

The *internal layout* also echoes the discourses of science and culture. In the case of galleries, for example, paintings are hung in groups in separate rooms according to periods and (often national) schools, and this works to naturalize these periods, schools and nations, and also to produce a narrative of development from medieval painting to the present day (Bal's art production in history; see also Bann 1998).

As well as these architectural articulations, Bennett (1995) is especially concerned to examine the *social subjectivities* produced through these discursive apparatuses. The strong emphasis he places on how discourse produces social positions, and the consequences for how museums were designed and policed, distinguishes his study from many of those that rely on the type of discourse analysis examined in Chapter 7. He identifies three subject positions produced by the museum and gallery. First, there were the patrons of these new institutions. Thus he is clear that the emergent 'experts' on museum and gallery policy and patronage were white middle-class men, their social position produced through their claims to 'expertness' as well as through the larger discourses of capitalism, patriarchy and racism. Similarly, Haraway (1989: 54–8), in her discussion of the AMNH as 'institution' in the early twentieth century, carefully explores the intersecting discourses of eugenics, exhibition and conservation that were mobilized to justify the founding of the museum, and also notes those three discursive themes were all 'prescriptions against decadence, the dread disease of imperialist, capitalist, white culture' (Haraway 1989: 55). The museum's funders were precisely representatives of 'imperialist, capitalist, white culture', and thus she too is clear on the coincidence between the discourses of the museum and the wider power relations of society. Richard Bolton (1989) offers a more recent example of the effects of exhibition patronage in his discussion of the sponsorship of an exhibition of Richard Avedon photographs at the Institute of Contemporary Art in Boston by a local department store. Secondly, there were the scientists and curators: the technical experts, if you like, who operationalize those discourses of culture and science in their classifying and displaying practices (section 4.5 will return to these latter practices: Bennett pays them little attention). And thirdly, there are the visitors. The visitor with whom the nineteenth century patrons of museums and galleries were most concerned was produced as the morally weak, probably drunk, working-class man. The contemplation of art and the appreciation of museums' knowledge was constructed discursively by these patrons as involving particular ways of visiting museums and galleries, and Bennett (1995) argues that these ways involved orderly appreciation rather than unruly entertainment. In ways he less-than-convincingly demonstrates, he argues that both sorts of institutions disciplined their visitors into what were seen as civilized ways of behaving. Bennett again pays some attention to the visual and spatial aspects of museums and galleries when making this argument, examining architectural plans and noting the way that surveillance of other visitors was often built into the designs of these institutions; he also reproduces some contemporary photographs of museums and exhibitions taken from positions which he claims again articulate the surveillant quality of these spaces. He thus suggests that museums and galleries worked to regulate social behaviour by producing docile bodies. Reynolds (1995) discusses a hall of the AMNH in the 1950s, and notes how it too assumed, addressed and produced a very specific audience, again one in apparent need of education: city dwellers.

Bennett (1995) also makes a distinction between the construction of the gallery visitor and the museum visitor, though. Galleries, he argues, rely on a notion of Art that always remains implicit:

> in art galleries, [Art] theory, understood as a particular set of explanatory and evaluative categories and principles of classification, mediates the relations between the visitor and the art on display in such a way that, for some but not for others, seeing the art exhibited serves as a means of *seeing through* those artefacts to see an invisible order of significance that they have been arranged to represent. (Bennett 1995: 165)

Following the work of Bourdieu and Darbel (1991), who found that the visitors to art galleries were overwhelmingly bourgeois, he argues that this particular sort of Art theory is understood only by middle-class gallery-goers because only they have been allowed access to the sort of education that considers Art. This is a problematic claim and Bennett himself worries that it is too crude in the class categories it itself uses; nevertheless, Bennett concludes that art galleries remain obscure places to some social groups, and that this is a contradiction at the heart of their institutional apparatus. In contrast, museums often do make their classification systems explicit; Henrietta Lidchi (1997), for example, in her account of an exhibition that opened at the Museum of Mankind in London in 1993 which sought to portray the way of life of the Wahgi people on Papua New Guinea, shows the way the exhibition admitted to its own practices of collection and reconstruction. This admission produced a visitor capable of critique, a possibility Bennett suggests is not available in art galleries. However, the question of how visitors actually do look in museums and galleries is one that neither Reynolds nor Bennett addresses; indeed, Bennett (1995: 11) notes explicitly that he is less interested in the visitors to museums and galleries than in their institutional apparatuses. No reason is given for this absence, and it is an absence that occurs in all the studies of the AMNH. Section 4 of this chapter will return to it.

This section's discussion of the discourses that were part of the institutional apparatus of the museum and gallery has been partial. Bennett (1995) ranges more widely in his book; for example, he explores the role of national government in funding public museums and galleries, and notes that this makes the visitors to museums and galleries citizens instead of, or perhaps as well as, docile bodies, and was therefore a potentially democratizing move. Similarly, writers on the AMNH draw on a range of institutions, practices and sites in order to describe the multiplicity of meanings residing in that institution. Haraway (1989), for example, suggests that in order to understand the dioramas in the Akeley African Hall, it is necessary to understand not only the practices of diorama and taxidermy, but of early twentieth century safaris too, the role played in them by photography, and the wider discourses of nature, culture, patriarchal masculinity, eugenics, conservation and so on that were articulated through them. However, the broad aims of these discussions of the institutional apparatus are I hope clear. In their explorations of institutional apparatuses, these discourse analysts of institutional power/knowledge focus on both discourses about museums and galleries but also on how those discourses are materialized in the forms of architecture and subject positions. Their concern is always with the intersection of power/knowledge and with the production of differentiated subject positions.

4 the technologies of the gallery and museum

Section 1 of this chapter defined institutional technologies as the practical techniques used to articulate particular forms of power/knowledge: 'the techniques of effecting meanings' (Haraway 1989: 35). Foucault described them as diffuse and disparate sets of bits and pieces, and this section will enumerate some of these bits and pieces as they work in museums and galleries. The question posed by this second type of discourse analysis is, again, what the effects of certain technologies are in terms of what they produce; and Bann (1998) insists that this question demands carefully detailed and historically sensitive empirical answers. All of the studies of museum and gallery technologies discussed here focus on the public display areas of the institution in question.

4.1 technologies of display

Section 3 has already touched on some aspects of how images and objects are displayed in museums and galleries, but at the large scale: how buildings are differentiated into museums or galleries, how whole rooms are labelled and how this then classifies objects and paintings in particular ways. This section instead will focus on more small-scale techniques of display. These are usually accessed by researchers through visits to museums or galleries, or through historical documentation.

In museums, several technologies of display are available (Lidchi 1997: 172):

- *display cases*, mounted either on walls or on tables;
- *open display*, with no protective cover;
- *reconstructions*, which are supposedly life-like scenes. (The dioramas discussed by Haraway [1989] and Luke [2002] in the AMNH are a particular sort of reconstruction.);
- *simulacra*: objects made by the museum in order to fill a gap in their collection.

Each of these different display techniques can have rather different effects, and their precise effects very often depend on their intersection with other technologies, especially written text. For example, Lidchi (1997: 173) suggests that reconstructions in museums usually consist of everyday objects put together with some kind of reference to their everyday use. Reconstructions thus depend of the presence of 'real' artefacts in an 'accurate' combination, and this makes their display seem truthful; although, as Lidchi also points out, this effect also depends on the visitor's prior faith in the accuracy of the anthropological knowledge used to make the display. Glass display cases, on the other hand, produce a truth not in relation to the apparent representational accuracy of what is on display, but in relation to the classification system of the museum. When placed in a case, an object is dislocated from the everyday context that reconstructions attempt to evoke, and is instead placed in the classificatory schema of the museum. Again though, given the truth regime of the museum as an institution, the effect on the visitor is of a truth: an analytic one this time rather than a representational one.

All the discussions of the AMNH pay a good deal of attention to the social meanings produced through the 'truthful' display of exhibits in their cases or dioramas. These discussions often focus on the effects of the *spatial organization* of displays: how different objects are placed in relation to one another. Haraway (1989: 30), for example, says that in the dioramas showing stuffed large African mammals against painted backdrops of their natural habitat, 'most groups are made up of only a few animals, usually a large and vigilant male, a female or two, and one baby … The groups are peaceful, composed, illuminated … Each group forms a community structured by a natural division of function … these habitat groups … tell of communities and families, peacefully and hierarchically ordered. Sexual specialization of function – the organic bodily and social sexual division of labour – is unobtrusively ubiquitous, unquestionable, right.' Thus patriarchy is naturalized, she says. Similarly, Bal (1996: 40–2) looks at a glass display case in the AMNH's Hall of African Peoples which, according to its caption, contains objects that show the hybridization of Christianity with indigenous African religions. However, Bal notes that the display is dominated by a large carving in the centre of the case of a Madonna and child: thus 'my overall impression of this exhibit is its emphasis on Christianity' (Bal 1996: 42).

Reynolds's (1995) discussion of the Felix Warburg Man and Nature Hall in the AMNH, which opened in 1951, is an especially detailed exploration of the way of seeing invited by a particular group of displays. The displays in this Hall refuse the apparent reality of the dioramas that Haraway (1989) discusses. Instead, Reynolds shows how they offer a visually and spatially fragmented, and clearly illusionistic, series of views of a landscape that draw the visitor closer in for a detailed look at each of the component parts. The effect, 'through foregrounding the very devices of illusionism', says Reynolds (1995: 99), is to transform 'the visitors' eyes into magnifying glasses, microscopes, or scalpels, which could reveal the invisible workings of a previously familiar but superficially understood natural world'. Hence the spatial organization of these displays still produces a reality effect, but it is a rather different one from those that Haraway (1989) and Bal (1996) explore.

In the case of the gallery, consider how the images are *framed* and *hung*. Paintings are now very often hung in a single row around the walls of a room, inviting you to follow them round, looking at each one in turn. That is, they are hung as individual images. This is a twentieth century practice (Celant 1996; Waterfield 1991); in the nineteenth century it was very common instead for the walls of galleries to be packed almost from floor to ceiling with paintings. This change is associated with increasingly detailed modes of classification and changing notions of Art. The discourse of Art as something to be contemplated for universal truths, which section 3 of this chapter described (see also section 3.5 of Chapter 3), became widespread in the twentieth century, and it changed hanging practices. If paintings are hung side by side, it is possible to contemplate each of them individually as pieces of Art. This also has an effect on the viewer: to encourage that contemplative way of viewing (Duncan 1995). The combination of this kind of hanging with the layout of galleries often heightens this effect. As Jean-Francois Lyotard says of the spectator at an exhibition:

> the visitor is an eye. The way he looks, not only at the works exhibited but
> also at the place where the exhibition takes place, is supposedly governed
> by the principles of 'legitimate construction' established in the *quattro-
> cento*: the geometry of the domination over perceptual space. (Lyotard
> 1996: 167)

Thus it could be argued that both the image and the viewer are individualized
through this technology of hanging, and that viewers are produced as contemplative eyes and paintings as objects to be contemplated.

---

focus

What technologies of display are used in the gallery or museum you
visited? Is the list of possibilities provided in this section adequate to
their description? Or are there technologies of display that you want to
consider?

4.2 textual and visual technologies of interpretation

These sorts of display effects always work in conjunction with other technologies, especially written and visual ones. There are a number of textual
technologies to consider, and they can be interpreted using the tools of the
first kind of discourse analysis, described in Chapter 7.

- *labels and captions*. These are a key way in which objects and images are
  produced in particular ways. For example, in a gallery, a painting will
  always have a caption with the name of the artist; it will almost always
  have the date of the painting and its title, and very often the materials
  it was made with. These apparently innocuous pieces of information
  nonetheless work to prioritize certain sorts of information about paintings
  over others. In particular, it makes the artist the most important aspect of
  the painting, in accordance with the notions of Art and Genius examined
  in section 3.5 of Chapter 3: whereas Chapter 1 was at pains to suggest that
  there are many other aspects of an image that are much more important
  than who made it. In a museum, labels have similar effects: they make
  some aspects of the objects on display more important than others. Bal
  (1991: 32) notes that labels and captions at the AMNH almost always
  deploy a rhetoric of realism – 'realism, the description of a world so lifelike
  that omissions are unnoticed, elisions sustained, and repressions invisible' –
  which makes it difficult for visitors to question the kinds of knowledge
  they offer.

focus

Look at the labels and captions in the museum or gallery you're visiting. What might be the effect of taking all the labels and captions away? Take two or three images or objects and invent some new labels for them. What kind of effects are you aiming for in your new text? Bal (1996) also suggests some strategies for undermining the realism of museum labels and captions.

- *panels*. Both galleries and museums often have large display panels of text in their display rooms. These often provide some sort of wider context for the objects or images on display. In the case of the exhibition discussed by Lidchi (1997), the panels were where the exhibition's practices of representation were made explicit. Panels often are more explicitly interpretive than labels and captions.
- *catalogues*. Most larger exhibitions, and many galleries and museums, produce catalogues for sale. These too are part of their technologies of interpretation. Like labels, captions and display panels, though, they convey very particular kinds of knowledge.

Visual technologies can also shape the effects of a museum or gallery. Museums often use photographs as part of display panels or catalogues to show what the use of an object 'really' was, or to assert the authenticity of an object on display by showing a picture of it, or one like it, in its original context of use. Galleries use photographs in display panels much less often, but their catalogues often have them, again usually as apparently documentary images.

All of these visual and textual technologies can be examined using the method of discourse analysis described in Chapter 7. Read them for their key themes, their claims to truth, their complexities and their silences.

4.3 technologies of layout

Section 3 has already touched on aspects of the overall layout of museum and gallery space. Here some of its smaller-scale spatial and visual effects will be explored.

First, there is the *layout* of an individual room. As Kevin Hetherington (1997: 215) says, 'as classifying machines, museums have to deal with heterogeneity through the distribution of effects in space'. Hence the importance of the spatial organization of displays and buildings, but also of rooms. Haraway's (1989) discussion of the Akeley African Hall in the AMNH describes the effect of its spatial organization by means of an analogy:

> The Hall is darkened, lit only from the display cases which line the sides of the spacious room. In the center of the Hall is a group of elephants so lifelike that a moment's fantasy suffices for awakening a premonition of their movement, perhaps an angry charge at one's personal intrusion. The elephants stand like a high altar in the nave of a great cathedral. The impression is strengthened by one's growing consciousness of the dioramas that line both sides of the main Hall and the spacious gallery above. Lit from within, the dioramas contain detailed and lifelike groups of large African mammals – game for the wealthy New York hunters who financed this experience ... each diorama presents itself as a side altar, a stage, an unspoiled garden in nature, a hearth for home and family ... Above all, inviting the visitor to share its revelation, each tells the truth. Each offers a vision. Each is a window into knowledge. (Haraway 1989: 29)

Here, Haraway considers the relation established between elements in the room, and writes to convey the effect of their combination. She emphasizes the coherence of this Hall, both in its spatial organization and in its effects. Hetherington (1997), on the other hand, reminds us that museum and gallery spaces can also be incoherent. Particular objects can disrupt the symmetry or the clarity of the museum or gallery layout, for example.

Rooms can also be *decorated* in particular ways, with particular effects. In galleries of modern art, and also in galleries showing photography as art, the walls are often painted white and any seating is modern and minimal. This practice of display became common after the Second World War, and Duncan (1993) argues that it was encouraged by the insistence of the Museum of Modern Art in New York that that was how its big touring exhibition of postwar abstract expressionist American art should be shown. (Duncan places this exhibition in the context of US attempts to assert its cultural dominance in the Cold War.) The effects of this mode of display are suggested by Brian O'Doherty (1996: 321–2): 'the new god, extensive, homogeneous space, flowed easily into every part of the gallery. All impediments except "art" were removed ... the empty gallery [is] now full of that elastic space we call Mind'. O'Doherty is suggesting that the minimality of the white gallery space again produces the Art work as something to be contemplated separately from any other distractions; and again, it produces the visitor to such galleries as simply an eye unencumbered by considerations other than looking (see also Grunenberg 1999).

focus

By no means all galleries have white walls, and few museums do. In the museum or gallery you visited, what other elements of decoration were important? What about coloured wall coverings, lighting, carpet, screens, other objects? What effects did they produce? If you visited a gallery that had white walls in some of its rooms and not in others, what was the difference between the white and non-white rooms, in terms of their objects on display and the effects created?

4.4 tactile technologies

One of the most important disciplines of museum and gallery spaces for visitors is the almost universal rule that you cannot touch the exhibits. This is enforced in a number of ways: objects are placed in glass cases, ropes are placed in front of paintings, warders watch visitors. Again, the Foucauldian question must be, what kind of subjectivities does this produce? Obviously, it produces a visitor that looks rather than touches (again).

focus

So far, this section has listed a number of 'bits and pieces' that are used in museums and galleries. It has focused on their possible effects in terms of the productivity of their power/knowledge; that is, on how they produce certain knowledges about paintings and objects, and certain subjectivities of visiting and curating.

Does the gallery or museum you have visited use any other technologies to produce particular interpretations of its contents or visitors?

4.5 spaces behind the displays

The rooms in which objects are displayed are of course only some of the spaces through which a museum's or a gallery's power/knowledge works. There are also the *stores* and the *archives*, the *laboratories* and the *libraries*, the *offices* and *service areas*. As Hooper-Greenhill (1992: 7) notes, these spaces are not open to the public (although researchers can often gain access) because they are the spaces in which the museums and galleries produce their knowledges. They are the spaces in which the museum professionals such as curators, restorers, designers and managers work; the spaces in which the classification schemes that structure the public display areas are put into practice. Hence:

> a division [is] drawn ... between knowing subjects, between the producers and consumers of knowledge, between expert and layman ... In the public museum, the producing subject 'works' in the hidden spaces of the museum, while the consuming subject 'works' in the public spaces. Relations within the institution are skewed to privilege the hidden, productive 'work' of the museum, the production of knowledge through the compilation of catalogues, inventories and installations. (Hooper-Greenhill 1992: 190)

Yet very little attention is paid by Foucauldian studies of museums and galleries to these spaces and their particular technologies; indeed Bal (1996: 16) argues that the curators and other museum staff that work in these spaces are 'only a tiny connection in a long chain of subjects' and are therefore not worth studying in any detail. Bann (1998), however, demurs, and I too find this rather an odd omission. While writers like Bal (1996) and Hetherington (1997) are happy to explore the discursive contradictions of museums' and galleries' display spaces, they seem uninterested in the possibly more subversive contradictions at work in the behind-the-scenes practices that operationalize those institutions' regimes of truth. If, as Bann (1998: 239) argues, there are 'internal contradictions built into the development of the modern museum', they too require investigation, and might perhaps be best seen in these hidden spaces.

---

focus

Few of these accounts of museums and galleries deal in any detail with what are now surely two more key spaces which visitors to these institutions encounter: the *shop* and the *café*. Visit the shop and café of your museum or gallery. What sorts of discourses are at work here? What sorts of practices? Are they connected to those of the display spaces? If so, how? If not, how not? Could you use the methods used by the discourse analysts in this chapter to examine the productivities of these spaces?

---

5 the visitor

Sections 3 and 4 have both noted that, according to these Foucauldian accounts of museums and galleries, as well as producing the images and objects in their possession in particular ways, these institutions also produce a certain sort of visitor. This visitor is perhaps above all constituted as an 'eye': someone who sees, and, through seeing, understands in specific ways. Museums do this explicitly, precisely offering their objects to their visitors as a kind of educational spectacle. According to Bennett (1995), things are slightly more complicated in the case of galleries, where the knowledge that produces the 'good eye' is kept invisible in order to maintain the gallery as a space where the middle class can distinguish itself from other social groups by displaying apparently innate 'taste'.

There are, though, more prosaic ways in which visitors to galleries and museums are disciplined. Section 4.4 noted some of these in relation to the prohibition on touching objects and images. There are many other *rules* about what visitors can and cannot do in galleries and museums, and these are enforced by warders. Picknicking and playing music, for example, are forbidden: the effect of this prohibition is to reiterate the 'higher', contemplative or pedagogic, aims of the institution. Other forms of discipline include the *spatial routing* of visitors. Often galleries and museums invite visitors to follow a particular route, either through the layout of rooms or through the provision of floor plans marked with suggested walks; this is very common for very large galleries that expect visitors with little time: routes are suggested which ensure that sort of visitor will see (what are constructed as) the highlights of the collection. Some galleries also give you a clue as to which paintings are especially deserving of this kind of viewing by providing *seating* in front of them. As section 3 of this chapter noted, Bal (1996) pays a lot of attention to the effects of this sort of spatial routing of visitors at the AMNH.

Bennett (1995) argues that there are other, less overt forms of disciplining behaviour in museums and galleries, though. From his historical work, he argues that the contemplation of art and the appreciation of museums' knowledge was expected to involve particular ways of visiting these places, and Bennett (1995) argues that these ways were policed not only by rules and warders but also by other visitors. That is, he reworks Foucault's discussion of the way surveillance makes the operation of power 'automatic' by suggesting that the regulation of social behaviour in these museums is conducted as much by the visitors' knowledge that they are being watched by other visitors, as it is by more obvious forms of discipline.

This emphasis on the productivity of the museum or gallery as an institution in relation to its visitors raises a key question though. Just how effective are these disciplining technologies? Chapter 7 noted that Foucault insisted that wherever there was power, there were counter-struggles, but a common criticism of Foucauldian methods is that they concentrate too much on the disciplining effects of institutions and not enough on the way these disciplines may fail or be disrupted. This is a criticism which can be made of all nearly all the accounts of museums and galleries cited in this chapter. The previous section remarked on their frequent uninterest in exploring the working practices behind-the-scenes in museums and galleries, for example; it seems to be assumed that in those spaces, classifying systems and rhetorics of realism are successfully coherent, even by those writers who question its success in the more public spaces of these institutions. Similarly, few of these studies consider the possibility that visitors may be bringing knowledges and practices to the museum or gallery that are very different from those institutions' knowledges and practices. Bennett (1995: 11) is quite clear that this is not an issue his book is concerned to address:

> My concern in this book is largely with museums, fairs and exhibitions as envisaged in the plans and projections of their advocates, designers, directors and managers. The degree to which such plans and projections were successful in organising and framing the experience of the visitor or, to the contrary, the degree to which such planned effects are evaded, side-stepped or simply not noticed raises different questions which, important though they are, I have not addressed here. (Bennett 1995: 11)

Hooper-Greenhill's (1994) book on *Museums and Their Visitors* focuses on recent attempts by museums and galleries to attract more visitors by increasing the relevance of their displays to potential visitors' lives (and suggests in passing that this involves the decentring of curatorial power), but says little about how visitors respond to their efforts. This neglect parallels the critique made by Smith (1998) of the Foucauldian histories of photography offered by Tagg (1988) and Sekula (1986, 1989). There too, the diversity of engagements with particular fields of power/knowledge is underestimated.

There are a few exceptions to this neglect of visitors as subjects constituted through discourses other than those of the museum or gallery. There are a number of case studies that have focused on exhibitions that have been especially controversial (see for example Lidchi 1997). Several recent exhibitions displaying the artefacts of native peoples, for example, have been heavily criticized for their continued naturalization or exoticization of those peoples, and Elsbeth Court (1999) discusses both this accusation and some artistic and curatorial responses to it in a case study of displays of art by a range of artists from Africa. However, much less attention has been paid to less organized forms of resistance to the museum and gallery's disciplines. One exception to this general neglect is the study by Gordon Fyfe and Max Ross (1996); they interviewed a range of people who visited museums in Stoke-on-Trent in England in order to explore the particularities of their ways of seeing. Their study invites more general questions about the visitors to museums and galleries. Do they critique the particularity of the sort of knowledge about Art offered by a gallery, for example? If so, how? Through their own experience? Through boredom? Through more formalized kinds of understanding, wondering why almost all the artists produced by galleries as great were men, or white? Do visitors touch objects on display, surreptitiously? Do they find routes around museums they shouldn't, or sneak a sandwich while a warder looks the other way? And what are the effects of these possible strategies on the visuality and spatiality of the museum and gallery, and on their paintings and objects? These sorts of questions are not made impossible by this second type of discourse analysis, but they have been pursued only very rarely. Hence none of these studies offers any methodological clues as to how such questions might be answered.

---

focus

This section has noted the consequence of the emphasis in this second kind of discourse analysis on the institution rather than the visitors. What did your visit to a gallery or museum suggest about the power of the institution over its visitors? Did all the visitors you see behave 'properly'? If not, how not? Were there certain groups allowed to behave differently – children, for example? How were any deviations policed, if at all?

---

6 discourse analysis II: an assessment

This second type of discourse analysis follows Foucault in understanding visual images as embedded in the practices of institutions and their exercise of power. It thus pays less attention to visual images and objects themselves than to the institutional apparatus and technologies which surround them and which, according to this approach, produce them as particular kinds of images and objects. This approach is thus centrally concerned with the social production and effects of visual images, and to that extent conforms to one of the criteria set out in Chapter 1 of this book for a critical visual methodology. It offers a methodology that allows detailed consideration of how the effects of dominant power relations work through the details of an institution's practice.

However, this type of discourse analysis pays little attention to the specific ways of seeing invited by an image itself (although it can focus with care on the context of its display). Nor, as sections 4.5 and 5 have noted, has it paid much attention to the way that 'power is exercised from innumerable points, in the interplay of nonegalitarian and mobile relations' (Foucault 1979: 94). Foucault's own arguments do not rule out this latter as a topic of research, but it has not so far been developed by these Foucauldian analysts.

Finally, there is the question of reflexivity. The kind of discourse analysis discussed in this chapter does not spend time on reflexive contemplation. This is no doubt for the same reasons as section 5 of the previous chapter outlined: many of the assumptions underlying the conventional forms of reflexivity in the social sciences are not tenable within a Foucauldian framework. However, unlike the 'certain modesty in our analytic claims' nonetheless advocated by Tonkiss (1998: 260) in her discussion of the first type of discourse analysis, discussed in section 5 of the previous chapter, this second type of discourse analysis tends, if anything, to the immodest. The introduction to this chapter noted as an example of this analytical self-confidence the stinging critique of Barthes made by Tagg (1988). But all the writers on museums and galleries cited in this chapter appear equally confident that the claims they make about the effects of these institutions are correct. Haraway's (1989) essay, for example, makes some highly coloured assertions about the effects of the AMNH's Akeley Hall that give me pause. Here's a taster of her style:

> scene after scene draws the visitor into itself through the eyes of the animals in the tableaux. Each diorama has at least one animal that catches the viewer's gaze and holds it in communion. The animal is vigilant … but ready also to hold forever the gaze of meeting, the moment of truth, the original encounter. The moment seems fragile, the animals about to disappear, the communion about to break; the Hall threatens to dissolve into the chaos of the Age of Man. But it does not. The gaze holds, and the wary animal heals those who will look. (Haraway 1989: 30)

While Haraway here may be attempting, in the Foucauldian manner advocated by Kendall and Wickham (1999: 101–9), to give co-authorship of her encounter with the Akeley Hall to its inanimate objects, she might also be read as offering an account of the effects of the Hall that is somewhat ungrounded in the details of its apparatus or technologies. (This critique has also been made of Luke's [2002] discussion of the AMNH [Rothenberg 2003].) Moreover, I suspect that this sort of writing makes the AMNH a lot more exciting – and powerful – than it is to the vast majority of its visitors.

Hence, this second form of discourse analysis focuses very clearly on the power relations at work in institutions of visual display. However, this focus produces some absences in its methodology too: an uninterest in images themselves, a lack of concern for conflicts and disruptions within institutional practices, a neglect of the practices of viewing brought by visitors to those institutions, and a lack of any form of reflexivity.

summary

- *associated with:*
  Discourse analysis II has most often been used to look at the ways in which various dominant institutions have put images to work.

- *sites and modalities:*
  This type of discourse analysis concentrates most on the sites of production and audiencing, in their social modality.

- *key terms:*
  Key terms include discourse, power/knowledge, surveillance, apparatus and technology.

- *strengths and weaknesses:*
  Discourse analysis II focuses on the articulation of discourses through institutional apparatuses and institutional technologies. It is especially effective at examining the powerful discourses that produce the objects and subject positions associated with various institutions, for example the objects that count as 'art' , the art gallery, and subjects such as patrons, curators and visitors. It is much less interested in the site of the image itself, and also in practice seems uninterested in the complexities and contradictions of discourse. Nor is discourse analysis II concerned with reflexive strategies.

Further reading

A recent collection of essays that showcases a range of critical studies of museums has been edited by Donald Preziosi and Clare Farago, entitled *Grasping the World: The Idea of the Museum* (2004). Henrietta Lidchi (1997) provides a detailed study of a particular museum exhibition that is carefully grounded in the details of the exhibition's apparatus and technologies, and also makes some connections with other methods of looking at museum and gallery spaces, while Mary Anne Staniszewski (1998) discusses the effects of different display practices at the Museum of Modern Art in New York from 1921 to 1970.

9
audience studies
studying how television gets watched

key example how the audiences of different sorts of TV programmes make meaning from those programmes.

1 audience studies: an introduction

The previous six chapters have discussed a range of methods commonly used to interpret visual materials critically. As we have seen, there are significant differences between methods (as well as various emphases within any one approach). These differences are produced by the broader theoretical context in which each method is situated, and the popularity of these contexts has changed over time. As Chapter 3 noted, content analysis was used especially frequently in the postwar period, when positivist epistemologies and quantitative methods were thought to give scientific credibility to social science research. Towards the end of the 1960s, though, this positivist approach came under increasing challenge from a range of structuralist accounts of the social, including some versions of semiology and psychoanalysis. As Chapters 5 and 6 noted, both the study of signs and the study of the unconscious assume that the dynamics of social difference and social relations, as they are played out in cultural representations, could be accounted for by patterned structures not immediately accessible to casual interpretation, because they were caused either by the grammar of signs or by the dynamics of the unconscious. During the 1980s, though, many scholars paid more and more attention to post-structuralist thinkers like Foucault, who refused to locate processes of social differentiation and change in deep causal structures and instead stayed on the surface of things, asking how rather than why. None of these shifts completely replaced other ways of interpreting visual materials, however, and there were very often creative synergies and tensions between them; and in the meanwhile, what I have called 'compositional interpretation' continued to be a useful method used by all sorts of theoretical approaches to the visual.

What all these methods have in common, however, as I have discussed them here, is a relative lack of interest in the site of audiencing. That uninterest takes different forms in relation to different methods. Sometimes, it is inherent in the constitution of the method itself. Compositional interpretation and content analysis, for example, both locate the meaning they recover from visual materials wholly in those materials; these methods simply discount the audience entirely as meaning-makers. Thus, in Catherine Lutz and Jane Collins's (1993) study of the photographs in the magazine *National Geographic*, content analysis was used to explore what the photographs showed, while another method – the group interview – was used to examine how audiences interpreted the photographs. In other methods, or versions of them, the uninterest in audiencing is less predictable. Chapter 5 noted Bal and Bryson's (1991) insistence that semiology is centrally about how audiences interpret the meanings of signs. However, it is only necessary to recall Judith Williamson's (1978) argument that the audiences of adverts are constituted in specific ways by advertising, to see that Bal is unusual among semiologists in emphasizing the meaning-making of images' audiences. Psychoanalytic studies of film, meanwhile, actually pay a lot of attention to the notion of the spectator of a film, as Chapter 6 pointed out. But their initial interest was in how the formal structures of the film position spectators in particular ways, as in Laura Mulvey's (1989) claim that everyone is masculinized when they view Hollywood narrative cinema; and although later studies gave more interpretive agency to the audience, through notions of fantasy, for example (Cowie 1990), no one apparently ever went to any actual audience of any particular film to explore the fantasies of any real spectators. In what was to become a foundational text of audience studies, David Morley (1980) was therefore able to describe both semiology and psychoanalysis as overly **formalist**: that is, they paid too much attention to the formal qualities of the visual image and not enough attention to the ways actual audiences made sense of it. Discourse analyses of the sorts discussed in Chapters 7 and 8, too, it seems to me, have no inherent reason to neglect audiencing; audiences too, they might argue, bring discourses to bear on the visual materials they encounter, and these too could be analysed in order to understand the productive effects of images. But to date, they haven't been, at least in relation to the sorts of visual materials discussed in those two chapters. Audiencing, then, as something involving specific social actors engaging with visual materials in specific contexts, is neglected in all these approaches to visual materials.

formalist

The next two chapters address this omission, and discuss two approaches that focus directly on what I have called the site of audiencing. The next chapter discusses a body of work, mainly based in anthropology, that has a particular take on what I am calling 'audiencing' (although it does not itself use that term): it treats visual images as objects with which people do things. This chapter, meanwhile, looks at the approach to the site of audiencing based in the discipline of cultural studies. It traces its lineage to the work of Stuart Hall quite specifically, and is called 'audience studies'. This book has already touched upon some of Hall's arguments in Chapter 5. There, Hall's work was used to note how visual signs can affirm the dominant ideological or institutional structure of a society by offering audiences what Hall (1980) called the text's 'preferred meaning'. What audience studies do, in essence, is to assess whether and how audiences take up that offer: whether they affirm the dominant order as it is articulated through an image, or whether they resist it in some way. This approach thus immediately has potential as a critical visual methodology, because it is directly concerned with how visual images can produce and reproduce social power relations. This chapter will also discuss audience studies in relation to the other two criteria established in Chapter 1 for a critical visual methodology: that is, taking images seriously, and reflexivity.

Like the distinction made in this book between discourse analysis I and discourse analysis II, the distinction between the two ways of approaching the site of audiencing discussed in this chapter and the next is by no means absolute. There is plenty of cross-over between the two, not least because some versions of audience studies use the same method as all the anthropologists I discuss: ethnography. However, this is not a distinction based on method. Nor is it based on boundaries between disciplines. Just as both these chapters will discuss ethnography, the work of anthropologists like Daniel Miller and Arjun Appadurai, for example, will appear both in the next chapter and be cited by studies examined in this one (for example in Marie Gillespie 1995, 2005a). Instead, the distinction between the two discussions of audiencing here rests on the rather different methodological consequences of their theoretical starting points. Audience studies begin with questions of meaning, and this has different implications from starting with questions of practice, as do the studies examined in the next chapter. Although both starting points are concerned with the relation between images and people, how they theorize that relation, and hence how they go about exploring it, is rather different.

To examine audience studies in more detail, this chapter will:

- elaborate the theoretical context of audience studies based on the work of Stuart Hall;
- discuss the various methods that have been used to explore how audiences decode the meanings of images, looking at studies of TV audiences in particular;
- examine the strengths and weaknesses of this approach as a critical visual methodology.

2 encoding and decoding the meaning of visual images

So, before discussing the methods used by audience studies in any detail, it is important to understand where audience studies are coming from theoretically. In fact, as all reviews of audience studies point out, there are many different sorts of audience studies (see, for example, Alasuutari 1999; Brooker and Jermyn 2003; Livingstone 2005). Audience studies established itself as a specific research field after the Second World War, prompted by both commercial and academic interest in how the audiences for the rapidly expanding mass media – especially radio and television – were reacting to what they heard and saw (McQuail 1997). Most of this work assumed that the mass media contained clear messages, which impacted on their audience. Many researchers acknowledged that various factors affected the degree of impact. To demonstrate this, Sonia Livingstone (2005: 30) discusses a radio broadcast in the USA in 1938 of *The War of the Worlds*, which is a story about Martians invading Earth; the broadcast was presented as if the invasion was actually happening, and thousands of Americans panicked, packing bags and running away. Subsequent research showed that those most likely to have done this, though, were less educated and more religious than those whose scepticism stopped them taking to the road. Thus this early sort of work was well aware that not everyone reacted to the mass media in the same way.

However, this early work in audience studies did assume a linear process through which meaning was transmitted, from the producer to the audience. Exemplifying this linearity, this body of work termed 'producers' the 'senders', and 'audiences' the 'receivers'. And as Livingstone (2005) points out, this sort of assumption remains at the heart of much discussion in the contemporary media of its own effects: witness the worries about the effects of violent videos or computer games on the young children who watch them. However, in an essay available in mimeograph form in the early 1970s but published in 1980, the Marxist critic Stuart Hall offered what was seen at the time as a radically different approach to understanding how audiences engaged with the mass media. Instead of working with a linear model of meaning transmission, Hall (1980) offered a model in which two parallel processes were going on: encoding and decoding.

As section 3.4 of Chapter 5 noted, **encoding** is part of the methodological vocabulary of semiology. A 'code' is a set of conventionalized ways of making meaning that is specific to a particular group of people. The process of encoding, according to Hall (1980), is when a particular code becomes part of the semiotic structure of an image. Chapter 5 mentioned what Hall (1980) called the 'professional code' which patterns how news broadcasts look. The professional code, to remind you, governs things like 'the particular choice of presentational occasions and formats, the selection of personnel, the choice of images, the staging of debates' (Hall 1980: 136). Hall also argued that the mass media usually encode what he called the 'dominant code', which supports the existing political, economic, social and cultural order. In making this argument, Hall was drawing above all on the work of the Marxist theorist Antonio Gramsci, who, living in Fascist Italy in the 1930s, argued that political, economic, social and cultural order was maintained not only by the coercive power of the state – its police and army – but also by the dominant meanings and values of a

encoding

society. This sort of power, maintained by culturally constituted norms, was
hegemony termed **hegemony** by Gramsci. Gramsci also argued that there would be resistance to hegemony, resistance that he called counter-hegemony. As a Marxist-
inspired critical project, then, it was analytically necessary that audience studies
explore both hegemonic values, and chart resistance to them.

Hall thus used semiological tools to understand how social power relations were encoded into the programmes and publications of the mass media.
Crucially for audience studies, however, he also argued in that paper that, as
well as the process of encoding, the mass media were also subject to a process
decoding of **decoding**. Decoding is the central tenet of audience studies. Hall argued
that when people read a newspaper or listened to a radio show or watched a
television programme, they actively decoded their texts, voices, images and
music. Audiences do not just passively absorb the messages contained in the
media, he insisted; rather, they actively make sense of them. And Hall (1980)
argued that they react in three different kinds of ways to the messages in, say,
a TV news broadcast. Hall described these as different sorts of readings:

- *preferred reading*. This is a reading which affirms the hegemonic political,
  economic, social and cultural order, as was noted in section 4 of Chapter 5.
- *oppositional reading*. This is an interpretation of the TV news which
  understands what the news is saying, but challenges the way it affirms the
  dominant order of things. It is counter-hegemonic.
- *negotiated reading*. This kind of reading is a mix of preferred and oppositional reading.

Audiences, then, are constituted in this theory as a discrete site of
meaning-making, as they decode the significance of the mass media that they
encounter in their everyday lives. And they can do this by bringing their own
knowledges and understandings to bear on the products of the media. As
Shaun Moores (1993: 16) says, 'while recognising the text's construction of
subject positions, [this argument] pointed to readers as the possessors of cultural knowledges and competences that have been acquired in previous social
experiences and which are drawn on in the act of interpretation'.

It is important to pause here and reflect on the methodological implications of this model. Although it is often described as a cyclic model (Livingstone
2005; Nightingale 1996), Hall's original diagram is not circular. Instead, as
Livingstone (2005: 32–3) notes, and as her diagram of Hall's argument
implies, what Hall establishes are two different but equally theoretically significant sites of meaning-making: production and audiencing. And what this
encouraged, in what John Tulloch (2000: 6) describes as a 'binary' methodology, were studies that looked at either one or the other of these sites. And
indeed in the 1980s, following Hall's groundbreaking arguments, there were
significant studies of the production of several television drama serials, for
example (discussed in Tulloch 2000). There were also several equally significant and influential studies of audiences, on which the discussion in this

chapter will focus. David Morley (1980) looked at a popular early evening news programme broadcast by the British Broadcasting Corporation called *Nationwide*, while David Buckingham (1987) and Ilen Ang (1985) examined how audiences interpreted the soap operas *East Enders* and *Dallas* respectively. Moreover, this binary methodology also encouraged the use of different methods in relation to its two sites, as we shall see in the work of Morley (1980); semiology was used to decode the preferred meanings of texts and images, while more sociological accounts of audiences were used to interpret their decoding activity (Nightingale 1996).

It's interesting to note that this work was committed to looking at popular cultural forms, but in fact focused mostly on television. No one interested in audiences' reactions to visual images went to art galleries or museums to explore qualitatively the sorts of questions raised by Bourdieu and Darbel's (1991) large-scale quantitative survey of their visitors, for example, and nor did anyone go to cinemas (although John Ellis [1992] raises some interesting questions about how we watch a movie differently depending on whether we see it at a cinema or watch it on television). Indeed, the emphasis on television was such that Moores could comment in the early 1990s that 'audience' in this kind of work had become equivalent to 'the consumers of electronically mediated messages' (Moores 1993: 2).

The dominance of television audiences in work carried out in the 1980s and 1990s can be explained by a development in cultural studies that paralleled its anti-formalist stand. As well as objecting to the formalism of semiology and psychoanalysis, writers like Morley also objected to the kinds of images they tended to study, which were those associated with what have been constructed as the 'higher' art forms. Even Mulvey's (1989) polemic against Hollywood cinema was directed at its classics rather than at its more pedestrian productions that had not stood the test of time. Many audience studies instead wanted to recover and often to celebrate the complex cultural work that surrounded more mundane and popular cultural productions; and much of it wanted to argue that in fact these sorts of productions did indeed deal with complex issues and debates. Some writers – Ang (1985) for example – even declared themselves to be avid fans of supposedly trashy cultural forms like *Dallas*. Ang (1985) actually argued that *Dallas* was less trivial than it seemed to many cultural critics; on the basis of the letters she received, she argued that fans of the series loved it for its emotional realism. They were quite aware that its storylines were improbably melodramatic and on occasion absurd; but they loved it because it showed that relationships were difficult and that happiness was very hard to find. For all its schlock, then, Ang suggested *Dallas* did nonetheless address some important emotional issues; and that, most importantly, it was necessary to listen to the views of its audiences to understand that.

Let's turn to these studies now to see how they did indeed listen to audiences.

3 researching the site of audiencing

Early studies of audiences used different sorts of interviews to explore how audiences reacted to TV programmes. Subsequently, other methods have been advocated, especially ethnography. This section will look at both these methods.

3.1 using interviews to explore decoding

In order to explore the 'cultural knowledges and competences' through which audience members decoded mass media products, many early studies of audiencing turned to interviews with audience members. Interviews are not used in this body of work to discover what people 'actually watch'; other methods are available for that, for example asking people to keep a diary of their viewing. Instead, interviews are used to explore the sense people make of television. Morley (1992: 181) advocates the interview method, for example, 'not simply for the access it gives the research to the respondents' conscious opinions and statements but also for the access that it gives to the linguistic terms and categories ... through which respondents construct their words and their own understandings of their activities'. It should also be noted, though, that other researchers have used other methods to gain access to audience interpretations. In her study of how viewers of the American soap opera *Dallas* understood the programme, for example, Ang placed a small ad in a women's magazine asking people to write to her about why they liked or disliked watching it, saying that she would use their responses in her dissertation. She received 42 replies and used these in her book *Watching Dallas* (Ang 1985).

There is, of course, a huge literature on doing and interpreting interviews, and this chapter cannot hope to do justice to the details of that particular research method in general. In relation to audience studies in particular, though, there have been three sorts of interviews used by researchers interested in how people interpret TV programmes. All are usually unstructured and open-ended discussions of watching television (and its associated technologies like videos).

The first sort of interview is the *one-to-one interview*, conducted by the researcher with one interviewee. This is the sort of interview used by Ann Gray (1992) in her study of how women used video cassette recorders (VCRs) in their homes. The second sort of interview is the *group interview*. This has usually involved working with groups that are already constituted. Morley (1980), for example, found his groups by going into classes that were already established at various institutions of higher education, and Buckingham (1987) found his by working with groups of friends established at schools and youth clubs. The third type of interview that has been used is also a kind of group interview: the *family interview*, in which most or all of the members of a family are interviewed together in their home. Clearly these three types do not exhaust the possibilities of interviewing. Group interviews can be carried out with groups brought together especially for the research project, for example, though this is often time-consuming to organize and it can be difficult to find an appropriate venue. Another possibility, implied by Morley's (1986: 174) comment that the young children in a family often get bored in family interviews, is to interview the younger and older members of a family separately. And finally, it would also be feasible, given the resources, to combine different interview methods, for example interviewing each family member separately either before or after the family interview. Again, Morley (1986: 174) implies this might be useful in his comment on the impact of family dynamics on what a researcher is told in an interview. A dominant family member may impose his or her views in a group interview in ways that one-to-one interviews with other family members would reveal.

These sorts of interviews are tape recorded, transcribed and then analysed. Recording a group interview requires a high-quality tape recorder; transcribing group interviews is also notoriously even more difficult and time-consuming than transcribing one-to-one interviews. The analysis of the interviews is also complex and time-consuming. It is possible to use the procedures of discourse analysis I discussed in Chapter 6. There are also more formalized methods for interpreting interview transcripts, for example the grounded theory approach of Strauss and Corbin (1999), or the rigorous coding procedures advocated by writers like Miles and Hubermann (1994) or Dey (1993). There is no space here to detail these different possibilities, and they are discussed at length in many textbooks on qualitative methods; instead, the following discussion will concentrate on some other methodological issues.

First, more needs to be said about interview methods and especially about the logics underlying the recruitment of interviewees. The early work in cultural studies that was concerned with audiences made some assumptions – later to be problematized – about why it was that different audiences decoded TV programmes in different ways. The argument was that it was the socio-economic position of the audience member that shaped their reaction to the preferred meaning of a TV show. Morley (1980) was clear that that position did not determine the decoding process, and he stated explicitly that other things might affect it, in particular the audience member's involvement in different cultural frameworks such as a particular youth culture or membership of 'racial minorities' (Morley 1980: 23). However, Morley did argue that these sorts of social positionings could explain why certain groups reacted in certain ways to the same programme. He recruited his groups accordingly. While he was happy to mix the gendered and racialized composition of his groups, he never mixed the class composition, and thus he found his groups through different higher education institutions with different student bodies. There were groups of mainly white working-class young men found through an apprenticeship course at Birmingham Polytechnic, for example, and groups of mainly white middle-class men found at a bank's training college; he also found mainly black groups through further education classes, and a group of shop stewards through a Trade Union Congress training college. He screened two *Nationwide* programmes for these groups in their established group setting, and then held the group interview. Similarly, in her study of VCR use Gray (1992) assumed that gender was an important analytical category which might well explain video use and therefore chose only to interview women; she did though try also to interview both working-class and middle-class women. Thus theoretical arguments about what structures the diversity of audience reactions are used to inform the choice of interviewees.

One difference between Gray (1992) and Morley (1980) though, is that Gray chose to use one-to-one interviews while Morley preferred group interviews. Morley (1980: 33) explains his preference for group interviews by suggesting that one-to-one interviews imply that people are 'social atoms', while group interviews allow for the dynamics of social interaction to become evident. Two points could be made here. One is that Gray's (1992) study is very far from assuming that the women she spoke to are social atoms; indeed the whole point of her interviews was to understand the women's video use as a consequence of their role in their family. Although she does not state it explicitly, I imagine she chose to interview women on their own in part because she wanted to access the specificity of individual women's experiences. However, her desire to examine women's views might also have led her to choose one-to-one interviews instead of family interviews in order to avoid the difficulty that Morley does not mention in his 1980 study, which is the issue of family dynamics. Much feminist research on domestic labour has found that in households where men and women co-habit, men tend to over-estimate their contribution to that labour and, moreover, that their version of events often prevails in interviews in which both the man and the woman are present. Gray's own work on VCRs (confirmed by Morley's [1986] own later work on television use in families) suggests that, generally, it is the adult man of the household who controls its use when he is present. This may have been a difficult issue to explore in depth in family interviews – men may have underestimated their control in order not to appear selfish – and thus Gray's choice of one-to-one interviews seems justified as a way of accessing women's views. Indeed, although Morley argues that one of the strengths of group interviews is to make the dynamics of social interaction evident, he does not acknowledge what an extraordinarily complex process making sense of those dynamics is. Nor does he mention the potential difficulties an interviewer might have in facilitating an open discussion in a group with complex dynamics; Buckingham (1991) gives some examples of complicated group interactions in his account of group interviewing children about television. Group interviews are very challenging, both to do and to understand.

Once the interviews have been completed, the interpretation begins. Moores (1993: 18) describes this process as finding 'significant clusters' of meaning and then 'charting the lines that join these clusters with the social and discursive positionings of readers'. For Morley (1980: 34), these significant clusters emerged from a close study of the working vocabulary and speech forms of his interviewees. He established from these what he called their 'lexical repertoires', then looked for patterns of argument and evidence, and finally tried to ascertain the ideologies underlying all of these. His conclusion identified two sorts of decodings of the *Nationwide* programmes, which he did relate to two socio-economic groups. The first was a decoding that broadly accepted the preferred meanings of *Nationwide*, and this was produced by the middle-class members of Morley's groups (as well as many of the young apprentices). The second was an oppositional reading, produced by working-class members of his groups but with important differences among them. Thus the shop stewards produced a politically informed 'radical rank-and-file perspective' while the black further education students offered an 'alienated "critique of silence"' (Morley 1980: 137). Thus Morley could insist that class position alone did not determine the processes of decoding: so too did the cultural constitution of racialized and politicized identities, for example.

In presenting his work, Morley (1980, 1986), like Gray (1992), uses large amounts of transcript in order to allow his readers to make their own assessments of his interpretations. Indeed, in his 1980 study Morley (1980: 163) admitted that he was unhappy with aspects of his methodology and felt that it needed further development. His later study of *Family Television* (1986) did take his work in new directions. In that work he chose to use family interviews. This was because he was increasingly interested in two issues that his earlier research methodology had made difficult to access. The first of these was the ways in which the actual practices of watching television at home were difficult to access through groups that were not constituted through shared domestic spaces. The second of these was the question of what people chose to watch in the first place. His 1980 study had assumed that all his groups would be familiar with *Nationwide*; but what if the black students' 'alienated "critique of silence"' was a consequence of their total uninterest in the programme? Thus in *Family Television*, Morley (1986) interviewed eighteen white nuclear families living in south London. All were working class or lower middle class (as defined by Morley using notions of cultural capital rather than income [Morley 1986: 52–3]), all had two adults and at least two children less than 18 years old, and all owned at least one television and one VCR. He used the unstructured interviews (which took place in the family's home and which lasted one or two hours each) to explore how the use of television was embedded in the wider family dynamics. How were televisions and VCRs used? What was watched and with what reaction? How were decisions about what to watch made? Most of his results (again with lots of transcripts reproduced) are recorded family by family, but there is one thematic chapter on television and gendered relations which argues

Figure 9.1

the 'den' of a Manhattan house

(Halle 1993: 95)

that, in these households, the adult men tend to plan the viewing, control the remote control, watch in silence, watch more television than anyone else, prefer more factual programmes, work the VCR and not like admitting to talking about TV programmes.

Morley's move to considering the social practices through which watching television occurs is a shift that many others interested in audiencing have also advocated. As John Fiske (1994: 198) notes, 'audiencing is a variety of practices, an activity', and exploring that activity is of increasing interest to many researchers. However, many of these other writers have also advocated the use of other methods to access those practices. Chief among them is ethnography.

3.2 ethnographies of audiencing

The trajectory followed by Morley's work in the 1980s was to move from asking audiences to talk about a TV programme in an interview situation set up entirely for the purposes of his research project, to investigating TV watching in one of the locations where it is usually done: the family home (see McCarthy 2001 for a discussion of the variety of places televisions are in fact found, and how this influences what they show). For Morley, this trajectory followed a logical line of argument concerning how the decoding of TV programmes should best be examined. However, if the aim is to explore 'the immediate physical and interpersonal contexts of daily media reception' (Moores 1993: 7), then it could be argued that any sort of interview format is inappropriate. Instead, the most appropriate methodology would be to go to those contexts and take a close-up view of TV watching as it actually happens. This logic thus moves away from interviews set up to examine processes of decoding, because interviews are too different from the ways television is watched in practice. Instead, a more ethnographic approach to TV watching is suggested, which can access the complex detail of decoding as it is in the process of occurring.

Like interviewing, ethnography is a method long-established and much discussed in the social sciences, and, again, there are excellent discussions of it elsewhere which I will not repeat here. As Marie Gillespie (2005a) notes, there are different sorts of ethnography, but the method usually entails, first, extended periods of observation 'in the field', and, secondly, unstructured, conversational interviews with those active in that field (for other possible ways of gaining ethnographic data relevant to audience studies, see Silverstone et al. 1991). The aim, as Gillespie describes it, is to access and understand the texture of everyday life:

> Ethnographers expose the features of everyday life (habits, routines and rituals, small talk and gossip) that are taken for granted, commonplace, even trivial. They seek to understand social life through first-hand, direct experience, conducting fieldwork in particular local contexts. They use a plurality of methods and techniques to explore how we construct meaningful social worlds: they participate and observe, listen and talk to people as they go about their everyday lives. (Gillespie 2005a: 151)

For Gillespie, ethnography is thus a window onto 'audiences in their full sociological complexity' (Gillespie 2005a: 152). Because it positions audiences as embedded in complex and fluid social relations and identities, ethnography seems ideally suited as a method for exploring the way the active interpretation of the mass media takes place in the richness of everyday contexts.

However, more recently another logic has begun to advocate ethnographic approaches to audience studies. This logic looks, not at theoretical accounts of how audiences decode the mass media, but at empirical changes in audiences' media environment. Over the past decade, the importance of digital media has, for some people at least, increased exponentially. Many homes now are full of audio-visual media in ways they never have been before: televisions and radios are still there (though they may have gone digital), but so too are mp3 players, DVD players, personal computers and camera-phones.

> My 17-year-old nephew appears to be able to watch a DVD film on TV while receiving and sending text messages on his mobile, and e-mails on the computer. He moves fluidly between these activities, interspersing conversations with his friends about who's been thrown out of *Big Brother* [a television show], all the while practising drum beats or guitar riffs. Last summer he used his mobile phone to download and watch movies, took a picture of the planet

Venus (when it crossed the face of the sun), superimposed his girlfriend's face on it (a work of art in his view), and received the latest Tottenham Hotspur football scores. (Gillespie 2005b: 4).

Some theorists are arguing that the plethora of different media technologies that now saturate some everyday lives has significant implications both for how the 'audience' of such a range of media should be thought of, and how they should be researched. Gillespie (2005b: 4), for example, uses the example of her nephew's media-savvy activities to ask if 'the term audience [is] still appropriate for the kinds of highly individualised pathways that he makes'. Her suggestion is that audience studies are premised on the claim that relationships with, and interpretations of, the messages carried by media are based on some aspect of social identity. But with the media now being so diverse, perhaps that premise no longer holds; perhaps there are now just too many different ways to use various media technologies to make generalizations based on social categories like class or gender valid. On the other hand, Nicholas Abercrombie and Brian Longhurst (1998) suggest that the very pervasiveness of media use actually demands certain sorts of generalizations. They claim, for example, that now, given all the audio-visual technologies that surround so many of us so persistently, 'in contemporary society, everyone becomes an audience all of the time' (Abercrombie and Longhurst 1998: 68). Thus for Abercrombie and Longhurst, the problematic now for audience studies is to examine how these media are making audiencing constitutive of everyday life (see also Alasuutari 1999). While some scepticism towards these claims about 'contemporary society' is surely appropriate (and Abercrombie and Longurst [1998] admit that they have little evidence to back up their assertions), the claim that the media environment in which audiences encounter images has changed is an important one. And both Gillespie (1995, 2005a) and Abercrombie and Longhurst (1998: 161) are clear that ethnography, with its detailed attention to the characteristics of everyday life, is the method most suited to exploring how people engage with a wide range of media images in their everyday lives.

If ethnographic approaches towards (what not everyone is still happy to call) audiences are currently being advocated for both empirical and theoretical reasons, then, it is perhaps surprising to find that there are not, in fact, huge numbers of ethnographies being undertaken by those influenced by the cultural studies approach to audience studies. Ethnography, however, is a particularly demanding research method. Let us get a better sense of what it entails by exploring three, rather different ethnographic case studies of audience decoding.

One reason that ethnographic studies are not more common is that negotiating access to where media decoding goes on can be difficult. This is especially the case if the site chosen is a home. An ethnographic approach to television viewing at home would involve the researcher observing an audience in their homes over an extended period of time, and talking with them about their viewing but probably also about many other things too. Not surprisingly perhaps, examples of this sort of ethnography are rare, because it is difficult to get access to people's houses for the length of time that an ethnographic study requires. However, a self-styled 'ethnographic' study by James Lull (1990: 174–85) offers some pointers for other researchers. Lull (1990: 183) defines ethnographic audiencing research as 'an interpretive enterprise whereby the investigator uses observation and in-depth interviewing to grasp the meaning of communication by analysing the perceptions, shared assumptions, and activities of the social actors under scrutiny'. He suggests that there are four things to consider when planning an ethnographic study of audiencing:

- *access to the audience*. Lull (1990: 175) notes that this is very difficult. He suggests going through the committee or board that runs a local institution such as a school or a church. (He notes that this may involve gaining access only to a specific social group.) Explain what you want to do to them (and Lull suggests keeping this as vague as possible), ask them to give you access to their membership list and then contact the names on that list. He suggests that 25 to 30 per cent of families thus contacted will agree to participate in the study.
- *observation techniques*. Lull (1990: 177) advocates the usual ethnographic means of recording what you see and hear: unobtrusive note-taking.
- *data collection*. Lull (1990: 178–80) suggests that spending between three and seven days with a family is enough to give the researcher access to their usual behaviour, and that during this period there are different stages of data collection. The first one or two days he suggests spending in collecting the more obvious kinds of data: what the house looks like, family history, biographical sketches. The next couple of days should focus on recording the dynamics of the family, especially by participating in its important routines. The final stage is to interview each family member separately.
- *analysing data*. As Lull (1990: 180) comments, ethnographic work generates lots of data. He rather briefly recommends interpreting it by organizing it into internally coherent topics which can be used to illustrate conceptual points. Judith Okely (1994) in her discussion of interpreting ethnographic data is more detailed about the challenges of dealing with observational notes and interview material.

Lull (1990) puts these precepts to work in large-scale studies the aim of which is the objective study of family viewing habits. According to him, 'the observer must create and sustain rapport with family members while maintaining the disinterested eye and ear of the objective observer-reporter' (Lull 1990: 179), and he recommends that the researcher does not reveal at any stage in the process what their real object of interest is: television viewing. This raises an issue concerning the ethics of research however. Ang (1989) has commented that qualitative methods do not necessarily guarantee a critical research methodology, and Lull's discussion of ethnography seems to bear this claim out. In his advocacy of deceiving research subjects in the name of objective research, he shows no concern for the power relations between the researcher and researched. Thus there is no reflexive consideration of how those relations might affect his research findings either.

Another example of ethnographic research of an audience in its home – and one that Lull (1990: 16–17) dismisses for being too personal – is Valerie Walkerdine's (1990) account of watching a family watch a video of *Rocky II*. Walkerdine is certainly very personal in this essay, but she is so in order to explore just those issues that Lull's methodological orientation evades: her own complicity in the power dynamics between an academic researcher and, in this case, a working-class man who cheers as he watches the boxer Rocky smash his opponent into pulp. Walkerdine watched him do this when she was in the family living room, ethnographically observing their activities, and she describes her own revulsion at this scene and also her revulsion at the man's pleasure in it. Later though, she describes how she watched the video herself in the privacy of her office and found herself breaking down in tears as she watched the same scene in another way; this time as a woman herself from a working-class background absolutely at one with Rocky's brutal determination to succeed, to get out, to fight his way free. What her own changed audiencing suggests to Walkerdine is her own complicity with the ways in which the academy so often denigrates working-class understandings. In that living room, she says, she was acting as a feminist academic horrified at male violence, and in that position she could not see any other way; in particular, the class dynamics of the situation were invisible to her.

Lull (1990) and Walkerdine (1990) offer two, very different ways of researching audiencing in homes (and, in Walkerdine's case, reflecting on the academic as an audiencer too). A third model for ethnographic audience studies is offered by Gillespie's (1995) account of television and video use by Asian young people in Southall, London. As I have already noted, Gillespie sees the whole point of ethnography as the exploration of the 'microprocesses of daily uses, interpretations and identifications' of and with the media (1995: 1). She chose to undertake her research in the area of London in which she had already been working for some time as a teacher, and during her fieldwork she lived in Southall with a family. (In fact, she lived there for two years, which poses another question in relation to Lull's [1990] work: is studying a family for at most a week enough to explore adequately the everyday 'microprocesses' of audience activity?) However, Gillespie did not use that family home as the main site of her ethnography. Instead, she used a range of places where young people gathered together – morning registration and classes at school, 'cruising' around Southall at weekends, weddings – as well as a number of family's homes. In all these locations, she listened to how what had been watched on television and video got talked about. And the emphasis of her study is very much on talk about television. In brief, Gillespie

(1995) argues that watching and, crucially, talking about television programmes is a vitally important way in which social identities are made. In particular, the challenge for the young people with which she worked is to become competently 'cosmopolitan' as a means of articulating their diasporic and hybrid cultural identity. For Gillespie, not only does 'the learning and testing of these competences [shape] talk among peers and in families about news on TV' (Gillespie 1995: 21), but "TV talk" – the embedding of TV experiences in conversational forms and flows – becomes 'a feasible object of study only when fully ethnographic methods are used' (Gillespie 1995: 23).

Walkerdine (1990), Gillespie (1995) and Lull (1990) offer rather different models for ethnographic research into audiencing. Walkerdine's account is certainly less methodologically explicit than Lull's, and we certainly cannot generalize from it. But its contribution to a critical visual methodology may nonetheless be greater, because her account is one of the very few sustained reflexive discussions of viewing in the large literature cited in this book. It is not the only one though; Gillespie (1995) also reflects carefully on her position as a white researcher of Irish descent in relation to her research subjects. While not perhaps as powerful or revelatory as Walkerdine's essay, Gillespie's careful discussion nevertheless allows the reader to evaluate the reliability of her account. Gillespie's methodological explicitness is very helpful in establishing the validity of her study too. What it also reveals, however, is the enormous commitment of time and energy that in-depth ethnographies demand: another reason for the rarity of ethnographic audience studies.

---

focus

The previous chapter suggested that very few studies of museums and galleries had paid attention to their visitors.

Consider the museum or gallery you visited for the last chapter, or think about a museum or gallery you are familiar with. In the light of the debates about researching audiencing just discussed, how would you go about exploring what sense various visitors made of that museum or gallery?

---

4 audience studies: an assessment

The work cited here explores an issue mentioned frequently in the preceding chapters of this book but not so far addressed directly. This work takes the site of audiencing as its main focus, and offers a number of theoretical and methodological resources for understanding its dynamics. Clearly, 'audience' is not a simple category: how it is defined (see also Ang 1991), how its social position relates to its interpretive practices, how it might be changing and how best to access its activity are all debated. And questions too have been raised about how this work relates to other aspects of the critical visual methodology that this book has been advocating.

One of these questions concerns that very focus on the site of audiencing alone, and the way in which that site is approached almost exclusively in its social modality in all the audience studies discussed here. Both Mark Jancovich (1992) and Virginia Nightingale (1996) remark that as a consequence of the attention it pays to audiencing, this body of work neglects the image itself and its production. That is, 'the textual processes through which television establishes social, cultural and political agendas' are ignored (Jancovich 1992: 136). As an example of this, Gillespie's (1995) introduction to her ethnography takes thirteen pages to get back to television after its opening mention, discussing in the meanwhile questions of identity, race, hybridity, cosmopolitanism, fieldwork, diaspora, the subaltern and youth culture. While her more detailed discussions do pay attention to specific scenes in tv programmes, her overall approach is very much to subordinate the semiotic detail of the programme to the sociological situation of its audiences. Indeed, the emphasis on the social modality of television watching is so strong in work of this kind that Moores (1993: 54) wonders whether studies that aim to embed television watching firmly in the dynamics of classed, racialized and gendered social relations, end up being more about those relations than about television. Jancovich (1992: 136) pursues this worry when he says that it is not clear in Morley's (1986) study of family television precisely how those dynamics of family interaction affect the decoding of TV programmes. Clearly they do affect crucial aspects of television use, such as who decides to watch what and when; but their effect on who interprets what and how is much less clear.

A related question concerns certain work that takes for granted that audiences will produce viewings subversive of a programme's preferred reading. Fiske (1994: 192), for example, watches a group of teenagers watch a sitcom and decides that they 'produced a cultural experience within which the show, the behaviour of watching it, and the place where it was watched were all mobilized to produce social identities and social relations that were within their control as opposed to, and in emancipation from, those institutionalized for them in the officially approved family'. Maybe for that particular audience that was the case; but to assume it will always be the case neglects the power of visual imagery to exert its own effects, and the effects of its meanings. Other modalities are also neglected in much of this work; if there is little on the compositional modality of television itself, nor is there a great deal on its technological modality (although this absence is beginning to be rectified in work on digital technologies).

Another set of concerns cluster around the reflexivity of this work on audiencing. Ang (1989) argues that much of the early work on audiencing assumed the authoritative researcher who knew more, or better, about tv programmes than the people he or she was interviewing. Moores (1993: 65) responds that some of her critique is misplaced, since authors like Morley (1980) explicitly invited their readers to make their own sense of their interview material by including large amounts of interview transcripts in their accounts. In this way, Morley is somewhat more modest in his interpretive claims than Ang allows, since his reader can reach their own conclusions on the basis of the materials provided by Morley. However, on one point Ang's (1989) critique does seem fair. She says that the assumption that there is a preferred meaning contained in a visual image implies that only the researcher can access it, and that it can act as a kind of baseline from which other audience interpretations can be assessed. Morley (1980: 22) actually deploys a number of ideas from semiology to describe the preferred meanings of *Nationwide*, or, as he puts it, 'to establish provisional readings of their main communicative and ideological structures'. But as Moores (1993: 28) asks of these 'communicative and ideological structures', 'can we be sure we didn't put it there ourselves while we were looking?' Thus the notion of a preferred meaning is vulnerable to the same kind of questioning as all non-reflexive semiological claims to access the hidden meanings in images (see section 5 of Chapter 4). (And recall that similar questions were posed in relation to content analysis and its claim to access the real meanings of images in Chapter 5.)

Another concern about the methods used to access audiencing processes also focuses on the role of the researcher. In relation to interviewing, the issue concerns the impact of the researcher on their research subjects during the interview. As Buckingham (1991: 229) notes, all talk is done in a specific context, and that context affects what sorts of talk is done. This is true of all social interactions, as those discourse analysts discussed in Chapter 7 here insist. However, Buckingham (1991) suggests that those researching audiencing should pay a little more attention to the effects of the interview context on what is said in the interview. I have already suggested that Gray (1992) might have considered this issue when making her decision to interview women VCR users on a one-to-one basis rather than in family groups. Obviously one-to-one interviews have their own specificities (which Gray (1992: 34) does explore), but it is rare to find any consideration of the way the researcher might have affected group or family interviews. The example Buckingham (1991: 229–32) uses is from his own work with school-age children. He notes that he interviewed these children at school and was introduced to them by their teacher, so that the children in those groups most likely associated him with teachers. In the group interviews, the kids were very critical of tv advertising, and also discussed the racism and sexism of some kids' cartoon series; but the question Buckingham asks is, were these children employing an 'interpretative repertoire' that they thought was appropriate to the situation (see Chapter 7 section 4.1), a situation in which an adult was listening to them and when they know many adults, especially teachers, disapprove of television? Buckingham (1991) is not suggesting that the children were not saying what they thought, still less that they were lying; he is simply considering what effect the interview situation itself might have had on the material he gathered there. Again, this is a reflexive strategy rarely deployed in studies of audiencing.

In relation to ethnographic methods, the question of reflexivity is also relevant. This chapter has examined very different approaches to reflexivity, particularly in relation to the ethics of research. While Lull (1990) advocates deceiving the subjects of ethnographic study, both Walkerdine (1990) and Gillespie (1995) advocate full disclosure and the careful, not to say painful, exploration of the researcher's position in relation to those she or he is researching. That position is understood in the same way as the social position or identity of the audience: in terms of class, gender, race and so on. Walkerdine (1990) and Gillespie (1995) use their reflexive self-descriptions in rather different ways, however. For Gillespie, reflecting on her relation to the people and place she studied serves to affirm both the validity of her interpretation and the ethical nature of her project. Walkerdine's essay, instead, seems to me to be conveying a critical theoretical insight into the complex and sometimes ambiguous work of critical interpretation. Reflexivity, then, is not a necessary component of audience studies (it was not part of Hall's [1980] early account of encoding); and when it is used, it is used to various ends.

In sum, this body of work on audiencing strongly emphasizes the importance of the social modality of the audiencing site. However, in terms of a critical visual methodology, it pays little attention to the power of images themselves, and, although it can be strongly and productively reflexive, it is not necessarily so.

summary

- *associated with:*
  The sort of audience studies discussed here have been used most often in relation to the audiences of TV programmes.

- *sites and modalities:*
  This body of work focuses most strongly on the site of audiencing in its social modality.

- *key terms:*
  Key terms include encoding, decoding and hegemony.

- *strengths and weaknesses:*
  Audience studies can explore the richness and complexity of audience's engagements with visual materials while paying attention to social power relations. They can also offer reflexive accounts of the research process. However, the specificity of visual materials can be lost in more sociological accounts of audiencing.

Further reading
Marie Gillespie's edited collection on *Media Audiences* (2005) is a very useful review of this body of work. John Tulloch, in his *Watching Television Audiences: Cultural Theories and Methods* (2000), reflects at length on these various methods of accessing audiences, and Gillespie's own book, *Television, Ethnicity and Cultural Change* (1995), is a fascinating account of her in-depth ethnographic research.

10
an anthropological approach

directly observing the social life of
visual objects

key example the use of some contemporary family photographs.

1 the social life of images: an introduction

The previous chapter discussed a range of audience studies that explore how
specific audiences decode the meanings of visual materials in particular ways.
This chapter also discusses an approach that focuses a good deal of attention
on what various people do with visual materials. However, it comes from a
different theoretical and disciplinary tradition than does audience studies.
Instead of being affiliated with sociology and making use of social theory like
audience studies, the approach discussed in this chapter draws more on anthropology and some of its key theoretical themes. As this chapter will show, while
audience studies and this approach share some common concerns, this
anthropological grounding in the end produces a rather different sort of
methodology for exploring images and other visual objects.

One of the most enduring and theoretically productive of anthropology's
concerns as a discipline has been the practice of exchange. In all human societies, people exchange some things for other things: money for food, or food
for carvings, or carvings for money. These exchanges can take many forms.
Some might consist of gift-giving, and others of trade; and there are different
kinds of gifting and trading, which constitute different relations between
those giving and receiving. So important is the practice of exchange, seen in
this broad way, that anthropologist Nicholas Thomas opens his book on
Entangled Objects by saying that 'exchange relations seem to be the substance of social life' (Thomas 1991: 7).

And if exchange relations are so important to social life, then so too are
the objects that are exchanged. For without things to exchange, the social

relations established by the processes of exchange would not exist. Anthropologists pay careful attention to the particular material qualities of things, though, because it usually matters a good deal exactly what is being exchanged. (As an example, recall Bourdieu's [1984] argument that 'taste' – a liking for certain styles of object over others – is fundamental to producing class distinctions.) So social relations depend in large part on objects; and objects get exchanged (and made, of course) in the context of social relations. Anthropologist Arjun Appadurai, in his essay in the book *The Social Life of Things*, has thus talked about what he calls the 'intercalibration of the biographies of persons and things' (Appadurai 1986: 2). Things, objects, no less than people, argues Appadurai, have a social life (see also Pinney 1997).

All this might seem rather far removed from visual methodologies. However, what happens if, like Appadurai and Thomas among others, we start to think of visual materials less as texts to be decoded for their meaning, and more as objects with which things are done? This is precisely the move made by the anthropologists this chapter will discuss. It is the source of the significant difference between this anthropological body of work, I think, and audience studies. Audience studies are concerned with social identity and its relation to the meaning of images. They explore how that identity affects the decoding of that meaning, and how the process of decoding is itself part of making identity. Their emphasis is thus on the process of interpretation undertaken by audiences on images. The anthropologists under discussion here are rather less concerned with processes of interpretation. What interests them most is what happens when something is *done* with visual materials. They are interested in tracing the social practices within which photographs, for example, are embedded, and they are interested in the effects of such practices. Now, of course, interpreting and making meanings are themselves practices that are done with visual materials. But they are not the only things that get done with images. Sometimes things happen with images which aren't necessarily about meaning; the images may provoke other actions, for example. So Alfred Gell (1998: 6) writes about art objects in particular, arguing that they are 'intended to change the world rather than encode symbolic propositions about it'. Gell continues saying that he is therefore more interested in 'the practical mediatory role of art objects in the social process, rather than with the interpretation of objects "as if" they were texts' (Gell 1998: 6). The anthropologists under discussion here are indeed all interested, to paraphrase Gell, in the practical mediatory role of visual objects in the social process.

This anthropological interest in visual materials as objects with which things are done entails the careful observation of interactions between people and visual objects. Here is Deborah Poole describing what happened when she was asked to take photographs of families who lived in her fieldwork site, the southern highlands of Peru:

> The poses they chose were remarkably uniform. They stood stiffly, with their arms down at the side, facing the camera, with serious faces. Photographs with smiles were usually rejected, as were the unposed, or what we would call 'natural', photographs I took on my own. My subjects were also committed to being photographed in their best clothes. I did a good deal of my interviews and other fieldwork while hanging around houses waiting for them to wash and braid their hair, scrub the baby, and even trim the horse's mane in preparation for the family portrait. (Poole 1997: 5)

Poole is paying careful attention to how certain photographs get made: elsewhere in her study, she traces in detail what happens to photos and other kinds of images once they have been produced. Her questions are, how do those visual objects look? What is done with them? What effects do they have? How are her informants' preferred photos embedded in their everyday lives? What happens because of that embeddedness? In trying to answer these sorts of questions, anthropologists like Poole (1997), Christopher Pinney (1997; 2004) and Laura Lewis (2004) contextualise their informants' understandings of photography in relation to the social identities, practices and relations of their fieldwork places (see also Thomas 1991, 1998; Henare 2005). Photographs and other visual images are not seen as independent of the people who take and display, like and dislike them; rather, like any other object, images are seen as 'unrelentingly and unquestionably social, located in specific, historically constituted worlds' (Myers 2001: 54); and Pinney's (2003: 1) description of photography as a 'globally disseminated and locally appropriated medium' is a reminder that attention should also be paid to the geographical specificities of visual practices.

In their claim that visual objects and the people who do things with them are mutually constitutive (Miller and Slater 2000: 8), these authors are clearly paying careful attention to both the site of the image and of its audiencing (although 'audience' is not a term that this body of work uses generally). They are also reflexive. Poole, for example, uses the description quoted above as a way of asking questions not only about certain Peruvian photographic practices, but also about her own assumptions of what makes a 'good' photograph; Pinney makes a similar move at the beginning of his study of Indian photography (Pinney 1997: 8–9). Thus far, then, this anthropological approach to visual materials would seem to be a candidate for a critical visual methodology. But does it examine the other criterion established in Chapter 1: does it think about the social conditions and effects of visual objects?

It does. Indeed, almost all the authors discussed in this chapter have done significant work on visual images in the context of colonial and postcolonial social relations. Many of their studies have examined photographs produced in the context of colonial and imperial conquest, for example, especially photographs taken by Western explorers, missionaries and colonial adminstrators and investigators of the people being colonised. Scholars such as Elizabeth Edwards (1992; 2001), James Faris (1996), Alison Griffiths (2002) and James Ryan (1997) have clearly demonstrated that many of these photographs of 'others' were given significance by nine-teenth-century discourses and institutions which asserted absolute differ-ences between different 'races', and placed all races in a hierarchy of progress towards the 'civilisation' of the West. Other studies have exam-ined postcolonial constructions of sameness and difference through the contemporary circulation of objects such as Maori cloaks (Henare 2005), Aboriginal art (Thomas 1999; see also Marcus and Myers 1995; Myers 2002) and art photography (Lewis 2004).

This anthropological approach to images therefore has the potential to be an adequately critical visual methodology. This chapter will explore that potential further by doing four things:

- discussing the theoretical understanding of objects and subjects in a little more detail;
- emphasising the empirical bent to the anthropological approach;
- discussing its method;
- assessing its strengths and weaknesses as a critical visual methodology.

2 the social life of things: materiality, materialization and mobility

This anthropological approach to interpreting visual materials – I will explain why I am calling it 'anthropological' in more detail later in this section – has three key characteristics.

First, it treats images as material *objects*. A photo, for example:

> A photograph is a three-dimensional thing, not only a two-dimensional image. As such, photographs exist materially in the world, as chemical deposits on paper, as images mounted on a multitude of different sized, shaped, coloured and decorated cards, as subject to additions to their surface or as drawing their meanings from presentational forms such as frames and albums. Photographs are both images and physical objects that exist in time and space (Edwards and Hart 2004: 1)

Treating photos as objects means paying attention to their specific, physical qualities, their complex sensuality, their **materiality**: how they look and feel, their shape and volume, weight and texture. For these scholars it also implies placing photographs in particular geographical locations and in their social and cultural contexts.

materiality

The second distinctive characteristic of this approach to visual materials is its understanding of how the material qualities of an image intervene in the world, particularly the world of people. The argument here is a performative one. 'Images are not representations in the sense of a screen onto which meaning is projected', notes Pinney (2004: 8); they are instead 'compressed performances'. That is, the significance of an object does not pre-exist its social life. Any object is always actualized in a specific moment of use, which produces both the object and the sort of person looking at it. Appadurai (1986), for example, was interested in how practices of economic exchange bestow certain values on commodities; no thing is a commodity before it is put into specific economic circuits. His more general claim that it is what is done with things that produces their signficance was extended to visual images in Nicholas Thomas's influential book *Entangled Objects* (1991), where Thomas argued that it is what is done with an image, rather than its inherent meaning, that gives it significance. Thomas (1991: 4) remarked there that 'objects are not what they were made to be but what they have become'. An image may have a range of material qualities, but it is only when someone uses the image in some way that any of those qualities become activated, as it were, and significant. It may have a range of potential meanings, but they are latent until mobilized in a specific context. And while a person is a rich and complex subject, they are momentarily shaped by the visual object as they look at it. So, it is only when someone gazes reverently and knowledgably at a painting in an art gallery that the painting becomes art and the person becomes a connoisseur. And it is only when an eclectic mix of photographs from all over the world, taken in a variety of ways for a variety of reasons, become catalogued and stored in particular ways that they become a colonial archive and the person doing the cataloguing becomes an archivist (Edwards 2001, 2002). Pinney (2004: 8) even coins a neologism to emphasize this process: 'corpothetics', where the visual efficacy of an image works only in relation to an embodied observer. This performative understanding of the *co-constitution of image and observer* thus demands a fine-grained analysis of how images and people relate to each other in specific times and places, producing each other in particular ways as they do so.

One aspect of this performative approach to visual materials deserves emphasis because it is another important difference between this approach and that of audience studies. (It also resonates with the debate in visual culture studies, mentioned in Chapter 1 section 4.2 about whether, and how, images exceed the cultural.) The approach to images discussed here emphasizes that the significance of objects is not entirely determined by the meanings people place on them. In his account of the relations between indigenous art and colonial culture in Australia and New Zealand, for example, Thomas (1999) explores the way certain artworks have intervened in the cultural

Figure 10.1

a framed photo of Sitabai's son posing in front of painted studio backdrop (Pinney 1997: 173)

identities of, and relations between, white settlers and indigenous peoples; 'I have presumed that art is effective in defining those relations and meanings, and may radically redefine them', he notes in his introduction (Thomas 1999: 18). More generally, he argues that the agency of objects means that this co-constitution of people and objects is not always a predictable process. 'Objects and contexts not only define each other,' he writes, 'but may change and disrupt each other' (Thomas 1999: 18). And Thomas (1991) strongly advocates the empirical investigation of specific encounters between objects and people in order to delineate properly the effects of those unpredictable encounters.

Indeed, all of the anthropologists I have mentioned so far have developed their arguments on the basis of extensive ethnographic fieldwork, and this is one reason why it has been suggested that this approach to understanding visual materials is above all anthropological. Actually, there are several reasons for my decision to describe this as an anthropological approach to visual materials, which I will pause here for a moment to enumerate. Its commitment to in-depth fieldwork is the first reason, emphasized by Gell (1998) in his effort to develop an anthropological theory of art. He argues that close attention to the 'immediate context of social interactions' of the sort demanded by this approach is typical of anthropologists' in-depth fieldwork practice (Gell 1998: 8). Certainly neither Pinney (1997, 2004) nor Poole (1997) make much reference to theoretical debates in their monographs on Indian or Andean photographs, preferring to let their fieldwork carry their arguments. And while Thomas (1991) draws on Appadurai (1986), as well as the work of other anthropologists of exchange, his point in doing so is to emphasize the need for more 'middle-level accounts' that learn from a range of specific contexts of exchange, rather than to develop further a general theory of exchange, gifts or commodities. A second reason for describing this approach as anthropological is that its concern with the materiality of objects has been central to anthropology as an academic discipline ever since its founding fathers sent objects back to Europe from their fieldwork sites in the late nineteenth and early twentieth centuries, as Henare (2003) points out, and the work discussed here celebrates aspects of that tradition, especially those that refuse a methodology in which 'artefacts are reduced to mere illustration' (Henare 2003: 55). Finally, there is also a commitment among many anthropologists to learning from elsewhere. Thomas (1991) notes that early anthropological theories of exchange were developed in the context of colonialism, and that they suggested – or were taken to suggest – that there was a fundamental distinction between 'us' in the civilized world and 'them' in the colonised world. In that sense, those anthropological theories were complicit with colonialism. Much social theory continues to build implicitly from Western experiences, while claiming to be universal. Pinney (2003) criticizes Barthes's (1982) influential concept of the *punctum* of a photograph – the point at which Barthes claimed that the real erupts through the cultural codes of a photo (see section 3.2, Chapter 5) – on these grounds, suggesting that it is not in fact the characteristic feature of photography in general, as Barthes claimed, but rather is a feature that many Westerners *draw out of* photography. Other understandings prevail in other places, and we might learn from them. This point underpins Poole's story about her surprise at indigenous understandings of photographs; that surprise serves to provincialize anthropologists' understanding of photography and prompts them to investigate photographic practices as local practices rather than universal truths (Chakrabarty 2000). Of course, this is not simple preference for 'empirical reality' over 'Western theory'. Clearly, what Pinney (2004) has learnt from Melanesia, for example, has come from the anthropological work of Marilyn Strathern there; and Thomas (1991: 38) suggests that his empirical specificity is simply a new way of approaching some old and still important analytical questions. Nonetheless, advocating 'an anthropological position of direct observation' of place-specific practices (Edwards 2002: 69) is another characteristic feature of this approach to interpreting images. Hence my decision to use the label 'anthropological' to describe the approach to visual images that this chapter discusses.

To return to the three key characteristics of this anthropological approach: it thinks of photographs, then, or other visual objects, as both material – as physical entities with specific properties in particular locations – and as materialized – they have agency in the specific, performative social situations of those locations. The third important aspect of this approach to the social life of images is that they are also understood as *mobile*. Many visual objects travel, and this is perhaps especially true of photographs. Photos are made in one place and displayed or stored in another; and they are also very easily sent or taken yet somewhere else. And a visual object's value or significance often changes as it makes those various moves through time and across space. This is because, as Appadurai (1986) makes clear, although in theory any meaning could be given to any object, in practice the play of meanings is constrained by the cultural context in which an image is placed, and these are (somewhat) different in different places and periods. The importance of that context lies both in its shaping of an object's value and in what is done with a visual object. This claim allows Thomas (1991) to emphasize the **recontextualization** of objects. In its social life and travels, an object passes through different cultural contexts which may modify or even transform what it means. 'What we are confronted with is never more or less than a succession of uses and recontextualizations' (Thomas 1991: 29), and Myers (2001: 54) suggests that recontextualization has become a 'reigning concept' for this anthropological approach to visual objects. What Thomas (1991: 28) called the 'mutability of things in recontextualization' is the theme of much anthropological work on visual objects, commodified or otherwise.

    recontextualization

So things not only have social lives, according to Appadurai (1986), they also have biographies. This interest in the history and circulation of things is in part a result of Appadurai's engagement with anthropological theories of exchange; in the case of Thomas (1991, 1999) it is also a consequence of his empirical interest in the specific exchanges of many sorts of objects that happened when European explorers arrived at various Pacific islands in the eighteenth century. The concern with how objects travel is an important part of the methodology of this anthropological approach to images, however, because of the assumption that when things travel, the meanings and values that attach to objects become particularly evident.

> We have to follow the things themselves, for their meanings are inscribed in their forms, their uses, their trajectories. It is only through the analysis of these trajectories that we can interpret the human transactions and calculations that enliven things. Thus, even though from a *theoretical* point of view human actors encode things with significance, from a *methodological* point of view it is the things-in-motion that illuminate their human and social context. (Appadurai 1986: 5)

Following how things move is argued to give especially effective access to their significance and effects, then.

visual economy

Poole's (1997) study of various kinds of images of the Peruvian Andes provides a good example of this anthropological approach to images in action. Her book examines what she calls the 'Andean image world' from the seventeenth century to the twentieth, and her notion of an 'image world' refers to the complex circulation of images about the Andes between Europe, Andean South America and North America. To discuss how this image world produced various subjectivities constituted in relation to each other, Poole (1997: 9) deploys the term **visual economy**. She does so, she says, because the notion of an 'economy' of visual images – in which photographs were central – conveys a sense of both the circulation of images between places and the structured effects of that circulation. In particular, Poole talks about a 'modern visual economy' which developed from the mid-nineteenth century. It produced and circulated image objects and visual experiences, provided in particular by photos of people and places, through which human subjectivity was reorganized through categories of racialized difference.

Poole's (1997) study also confirms the importance of the specific material qualities of the visual things that travelled through the visual economy. For what we can see from her work is that, although the circulation of photos produced social identities, it did so only because the particular qualities of some photographs were seen in particular ways. Certain qualities of photographs seemed to have been valued more than others. Poole (1997) pays particular attention to the importance of a type of photograph called a *cartes de visite*. Patented in 1854, *cartes de visite* were small and cheap photos of people, from friends to celebrities to racialized 'types', which were immensely popular. They were produced commercially in huge numbers and given away, bought, swapped, collected and put in albums designed especially for them. Poole (1997: 107) suggests that their visual equivalence helped to establish the importance of recognizable racialized types to the modern visual economy.

So, this anthropological approach to images suggests that visual objects are material, that they are materialized, and that they are mobile. The next section will explore the methodological implications of these claims by discussing a particular kind of photograph: family snaps. These are informal photos, taken by members of a family, and mostly looked at only by members of that same family. These photos have been given fairly short shrift by many visual culture critics. Family photos are described as having 'an astonishingly narrow' range of subject matter (Halle 1993: 104) which produces an 'overwhelming sense of similarity and redundancy' (Chalfen 1987: 142), and it is in family photography, apparently, that 'the most stultified and stereotyped repertoire of composition, subject matter and style resides' (Evans 2000: 112). Despite these critical verdicts, family snaps remain a very popular form of visual imagery, and in 2000, I conducted a number of interviews with a group of women, all of whom had small children, in their homes in two towns in south-east England, about (and with) their family photos. Although there are several studies available which make claims about what family snaps mean (see, for example, Bourdieu 1990; Chalfen 1987; Evans

2000), I was more interested in finding out what these mothers did with their photos – and then, as the interviews were under way, what their photos did for them (Rose 2003, 2004, 2005; see also Csikszentmihalyi and Rochberg-Halton 1981; Halle 1993; Jacobs 1981). Inspired by the anthropologists whose work I have been discussing in this chapter, I was interested in how these women, in their specific cultural location, appropriated photographic technology and made particular use of it, making their lives as mothers in part with the photographs they took of their children. This project, along with some other work on family photos in similar cultural contexts, will provide the methodological case study that I work through in the next section.

3 how to observe the social life of images

The methods used by the anthropological approach to images are diverse. Historical studies of the circulation of images and objects depend on work in archives, tracking the movement of objects and exploring how objects' significance changed as they changed geographical and cultural context; they often use versions of discourse analysis to achieve this. Nicholas Thomas (1991), for example, in his discussion of 'the European appropriation of indigenous things' in the Pacific during the eighteenth century, examines the notion of 'curiosity' that was prevalent in the records of explorers, colonial officials and missionaries as a way of labelling both objects and a certain attitude towards those objects. He did this by using discourse analysis I, looking for themes that recur through a range of diaries, journals and letters, concluding that:

> An attempt to map European interests in artifacts in the period could thus take seriously the idea that a collection of curiosities in some sense stood for the objectification of the culturally and historically specific form of intellectual and experiential desire which 'curiosity' alluded to. (Thomas 1991: 127).

Here, 'curiosity', as a specific form of desire, is seen as represented both by the objects and by the word 'curiosity'. Thomas also notes how, as the eighteenth century gave way to the nineteenth, curiosity was increasingly understood as an inferior form of knowledge, prevalent among sailors for example rather than officers, and what were seen as more scientific and judgemental modes of knowing became dominant.

Archival work poses its own challenges. Contemporary anthropological work relies on more familiar social science methods: ethnography and interviews. This section will examine less the detail of any of these methods than the kinds of questions they set out to answer. These questions address four areas: the materiality of an image, what is done with it, how it has travelled and what its effects are. Each of the sub-sections below examines one of these areas. However, it is important to note that the four sub-sections do not represent four sequential stages of empirical research. Whether you are undertaking an ethnography or interviews, you will find that the evidence to answer these questions is all tangled up. And, of course, it would be. The claim that images and their viewers are co-constituted through what is done with images does not allow for the neat separation of any one of these things from the others. The four questions here are thus artificial cuts into the mutually constituting relations between objects and people. Nonetheless, providing their artificiality is not forgotten, these four questions provide useful ways of untangling the evidence generated by interviews and ethnography. We will examine their utility by seeing how they work in relation to a discussion of how photos of family members come to do different things as they are seen, displayed and circulated in various ways.

3.1 finding your images

Before that, though, a word about finding your visual objects. This anthropological approach to images is not worried about finding representative samples of images to interpret. Instead, it simply chooses to work with images it thinks have effects in the world. In the case of my research on family photographs and middle-class mothers in south-east England, the objects seemed self-evident: all those family snaps, whether in envelopes, boxes, albums and frames, or just tucked or propped somewhere, that were in every room of the houses I visited.

However, it does seem to me that there are some limits to the sorts of images that this approach is able to examine. The anthropological approaches to images I am discussing in this chapter need to examine images that are constituted as objects. More specifically, they focus on solid objects that don't usually change form as they travel. The fact that much of this work has focused on photography, with fine art objects a close second, is perhaps no coincidence here. Norman Bryson (2001: 3) remarks that a painting is 'built to travel away both from its maker and from its original context, carried by the frame into different times and places', and Fred Myers's (2002) work on Australian Aboriginal art, for example, is driven by tracking artworks as they move through art markets. Photographs, too, travel. Most photographs are small, easy to hold and easy to transport to other places. Indeed, photographs have travelled ever since photography was invented (Osborne 2000), and this is as true of ordinary family photographs as it is of photos made in colonial contexts; nineteenth century immigrants to cities carried photos of the families they had left behind across countrysides and oceans, and Stuart Hall (1991) describes how immigrants to London in the 1950s sent photos home. Sending family snaps to other family members is a continuing obligation in many families (Rose 2003).

But other sorts of images are less amenable to being thought of as objects in this way. Is a film an object? Well yes, we can think of the reel of film in its can, travelling around as it is projected in different places. But are adverts? Adverts certainly have material qualities which depend on their context: an ad in a newspaper is not the same as an ad in a glossy magazine. But is the ad itself an object? Or would the paper or magazine be the proper focus of study? And what about the digital images dispersed across various screens that the previous chapter suggested were now so prevalent in some parts of the world – can an image circulating between the web, a camera-phone and a computer be thought of as an object? It may be the case that the anthropological approach to images is better suited to examining the effects of some sorts of images than others.

So, assuming you have found some images that seem thinkable as objects, here are four aspects of them to examine. The discussion in the following four sub-sections, based as it is on some of my own research, is going to sound rather different from other chapters' discussions of methods, where I was examining the work of others. I am probably going to sound much less critical! However, I chose to use my work rather than, say, Poole's (1997) or Pinney's (1997, 2004) because I imagine that most readers of this book are more likely to be able to conduct a series of interviews using this anthropological approach than they would be able to conduct ethnographic fieldwork over a period of years, and thus will find an example based on interviews more useful to think through.

3.2 the materiality of the visual object

The assertion that material objects have their own particular physical properties is one place to start an anthropological study of visual objects. Edwards (2002) suggests that there are three aspects to their materiality:

1 *visual form*, or content. This refers to what the image shows.
2 *material form*, or the physical qualities of the visual object itself. In the case of a photograph, we can think about the paper it's printed on, whether it's glossy or matt, its size, whether it's cut or torn or worn.
3 *presentational form*, or the particular way in which an image is presented to the person looking at it. Photographs always come presented to their viewers in some specific way. Sometimes a family photo is put into a frame, or an album, a box, or stuck under a fridge magent. And Geoffrey Batchen (2001: 59) has emphasized what he calls 'the photograph's morphological possibilities', for photos that don't stay on paper: the ones that get printed onto mugs and bags, or made into calendars, for example, or enameled as memorials for gravestones.

focus

Choose a visual object that isn't a photo, and try to describe it using the three sorts of form listed here. How easy was this? Did you notice any aspects of its materiality that were difficult to describe using these three forms? Do these forms depend too much on photos as a particular kind of visual object?

One way to elaborate on these material properties would be to use compositional interpretation; that is, to take a visual object and subject it to a detailed description using the sort of vocabulary examined in Chapter 3. While doing that might sensitize you to the particular material qualities of the specific photo you were interested in, it is not quite the approach invited by this anthropological approach to images. Since the visual object and viewer are co-constituted, it is more important to pay attention to those material qualities that the viewers emphasize or enact.

For example, in the case of family photographs, the important aspect of their visual form to my interviewees was not their composition or technical prowess, but who they showed. This was clear from our interview talk, and another very important quality of photographs which my interviewees emphasized was their realism. They were seen as being accurate descriptions of what people looked like. They were frequently used as objective evidence of children's growth and development, because they were seen as far more accurate than the mother's own experience or memory. It was also important that the photographs were small and robust enough to be picked up and touched. This became clear as I talked with these women about their photos: framed photos were taken down off shelves so I could see them, photos were taken out of album pages to be held while they were looked at. Finally, in terms of their presentational form, what seemed to be important was that lots of photos were put together. So as well as albums, several of the women had made collages of what looked like hundreds of baby photos, cut out and stuck together in one big frame, and large frames with holes cut out to put different photos behind were also very popular.

3.3 what is done with a visual object in a particular location

The materiality of an image in context is in part about how its 'objectness' is constructed by those people doing things with it. Another set of questions addresses what is actually done with a specific visual object.

> How are photographs actually used as objects in social space? How are they
> acquired and accumulated? By whom? How are they displayed? Where? To
> whom? Which remain in small private worlds intentionally hidden? How do
> these link with ... frames and albums? (Edwards 2002: 70)

It is important to consider how an individual image is placed in relation to
other objects. For example, is that mug with the printed photo put in a
china display cabinet with other precious things, or is it kept in a kitchen
cupboard or dishwasher with other mugs? In my own study, I noticed
that framed photos were very often displayed in groups, either standing on
mantelpieces or televisions, for example, or hung together on walls. Other
accounts of family photos *in situ* remark on the same thing (Halle 1993; and
see Figure 9.1).

It is also important to consider how images are looked at in that
context – which most likely involves a lot more than just looking. Are they
gazed at reverently, glanced at and thrown away, carefully stored, seen but
not really taken in? What else is going on when images are seen in some way?
Are they touched, torn, scrawled over? A great many things are done with
family photos, for example. Once the photos are back from the printers, they
are dated and sorted. Some may then be put into some more or less organized
form of storage, while others will be chosen for display in the house. Some
are glanced at and forgotten, others kept in fire-proof boxes and looked at in
moments of introspection; others hang in hallways rarely actually studied but
nonetheless having a necessary presence.

Who does what with visual objects can be important to explore. For
example, the social life of family photos, at least in my research project, was
highly gendered: almost all the things done with family snaps were done by
the mothers I interviewed rather than by their husbands. They sorted and
displayed their photos. And they emphasized certain things about that
doing: that the dating was really important, for example. Another very obvious finding from the interviews was that one thing was hardly ever done
with family snaps of children: they were never thrown away. Disposing of a
photo of your own child was beyond the pale for my interviewees (but
whether the same taboo applies to deleting photos on the screen of a digital
camera remains to be seen: none of the women had a digital camera when I
interviewed them). And three of my interviewees told me the same story:
that they had put a photo of their own parents' wedding in a frame and put
it on a wall in their house; the next time their husband's parents had visited,
their husband's mother had noticed this and soon afterwards had sent the
interviewee a photo of her husband's parents' wedding to display in the
house as well.

Clearly, what I was seeing and hearing in these interviews were both
the 'local appropriations', if you like, of the photographic medium by these
women and some of the rules and conventions that governed those

appropriations. This is part of the cultural context that for Thomas (1991) as for Appadurai (1986) shapes the biographies of objects.

3.4 the mobility of the visual object: where it travels

As section 2 of this chapter noted, the anthropological approach to images suggests that tracking objects as they move is a particularly fruitful way of accessing their significance.

Family photographs certainly move. Some may only move relatively small distances from their first place of display: the first photo of a first grandchild may gradually lose its central position in a cluster of frames as other photos and other grandchildren arrive; photos of spouses get removed from displays after divorce (Halle 1993). Other movements are over long distances. Photos are sent to relatives (especially grandparents, and grandmothers in particular, I found), and sometimes, but much less often, to friends. Again, there are clear conventions shaping this movement, just as there were in the display of photos in houses.

Sometimes the geographical move made by a family photograph is also a significant change in the meaning of the photo, as suggested by this anthropological approach to photos. This is true of photos that are sold off after the death of their owner, or photos that move from houses to archives. Andrew Blaikie (2001) examines this latter journey in relation to family photos now stored in archives in Scotland. He suggests that the move to the archive has recontextualized those photos and that 'in the very creation of display, indigenous readings have been elided' (Blaikie 2001: 346). He also notes, though, that local people use archived photos for their own efforts at affirming the solidarities of kin and association, and the photos are sometimes contextualized yet again in this process. Photos can also leave the archive for which they were produced and become recontextualized as family photos. Jo-Anne Driessens (2003) recounts finding a photograph of her great-grandfather Charlie Chambers, taken by an expedition of anthropologists in Australia, in the 1930s, in a state library archive; she describes the photograph as 'very controlled and impersonal' but says that nonetheless, as a piece of scarce evidence about her Aboriginal family, 'it plays a very important part of my life' (Driessens 2003: 22).

3.5 the effect of the visual object: putting it all together

Examining the effects of these materialities, performances and mobilities is complex. At the level of discourse, ethnographic fieldnotes or interview materials can be interpreted using discourse analysis I, and this is how I chose to work with the interviews about family photos that I carried out. I transcribed the interviews and then worked with them, working outwards from what I was told about the things that were done with photos, and gradually finding recurring themes and taken-for-granted assumptions which I felt were the meanings of the photos in this phase of their existence.

However, when I was talking with my interviewees about their photos, I also tried to be as observant as I could about what they were doing as we talked, and when we stopped talking, I tried just to look. I also tried to observe the materialities of the photos, especially their presentational form. So as well as the interviews, I had the notes I made after each interview that described how the photos were displayed, how I was shown them, when our conversation halted over them. In doing this, I also had to reflect on my own role in the interview. As I have already suggested, doing family photographs is quite a regulated affair, with various conventions about what photos to display and who to send them to. Viewing them is also conventionalized: and although an interview with a stranger is not the same as showing the latest set of pictures to your mum, nonetheless I did my best to observe the way I was also 'doing' the photos, not only as an interviewer with certain academic interests but also as a mother who takes her own photos and displays them in her house, and sees the similar displays of friends who are parents.

Putting these self-reflections together with interview material and observational notes to reach conclusions about the effects of these photographs as the women I spoke with did various things with them, was a complex process of working with the range of materials until some robust findings began to emerge.

One of the most important ways in which the photographs and my interviewees co-constituted each other, I found, was the way in which these photos helped to produce a relation of 'togetherness' (Rose 2004). Many of the things that were done with photos were about using them to show familial togetherness. So my interviewees preferred photos whose visual content showed family members together; and modes of presentation were often about that too, with the frames or albums used to display photos being presents from family members. Arranging photographs in groups was also about using photographs to 'do togetherness', and so too were the ways in which photos were seen, which was most often with children or other relatives, sharing the images and their memories.

And when these particular photographs travelled, they appeared to be sent to distant relatives in order to extend that togetherness. Family photos were posted to family in order to include them in a familial relation that stretched long distances; indeed, some albums were doubled up, with one mother I interviewed sending a copy of every one of her photos to her own mother, who in turn made an album with them. This sort of travelling, however, suggests that mobile objects do not in fact always change as they travel, as Appadurai (1986) argues (and see Myers 2001); sometimes the purpose of their mobility is to extend a meaning or value attached to an object in one place, to another place. The notion of family togetherness articulated by the photos I saw was thus made to reach from the towns in south-east England where I did the interviews, to Scotland, Australia and the USA. This difference between what I think the objects I was examining in the family photography research did when they travelled and what Appadurai (1986) suggests happens is exactly why Thomas (1991) and Pinney (2003) are so resistant to what they see as theory-driven accounts of images. My empirical results differ somewhat from Appadurai's generalization, and perhaps shed some light on the ways in which affluent Western families can extend their identities and relations globally.

A different moment for the mothers I interviewed came with the way the photos offered their own intervention into their interview talk. Interviews, as a research strategy, tend to ask interviewees to interpret their lives, to make meaning out of them, to tell a story. I tried to counteract this by doing things with my interviewees as well as talking with them; in particular, I asked them to show me photographs as we talked. I was always shown hundreds, and often given a tour around their house too, to see the photos on display there. But sometimes, the talk and stories faltered. In particular, they faltered around pictures of newborn babies. In these moments, I felt that my interviewees were focusing on the unmediated reality carried by the photos – the reality of their tiny newborn's skin or hair or size – and that the extraordinary reality of that body as marked on the photographic paper interrupted our talk with an awe and amazement that words could not convey. The photos disrupted our talk, silenced us (Rose 2003, 2005). I understood these moments using Barthes's (1982) notion of the *punctum*, trying to deploy that concept as a local one that made sense of some moments of looking at photographs in which the photographs threw something back at their viewers, producing feelings beyond expression.

There is more to be said about the co-constitution of these mothers and their photos of their children, and I have discussed my findings at greater length elsewhere (Rose 2005). However, I hope I have said enough to suggest that using the anthropological approach in relation to family snaps is quite different from the many studies that choose to interpret their meaning in isolation from how they work in domestic settings. Those studies, as I have already noted, see family snaps as signifying little more than a certain familial ideology. My work suggested that, to the extent that that characterization is accurate, it is not only because of what the photos show, but also because of what is done with them (all that happy togetherness). But I think my study also demonstrated that 'togetherness' is not all that family photos do. Family photos are also especially important to mothers because of the way they allowed moments of intense emotion in relation to their children to play out. And it was only by looking at their photos with those women, experiencing what they did as well as what they said, that such an insight became possible.

3.6 reflexivity and the anthropological approach to images

My interest in what mothers get out of family photos, as opposed to how the institution of the family benefits from them, was prompted in particular by a certain moment in the analysis of the interviews. In that moment, I properly noticed two things. The first was that in all our interview talk about the photos, the children who were the subjects of so many of the photos were only rarely discussed by their mothers and me in terms of whether they liked being photographed or not. And secondly, it had taken me a couple of months of working with the transcripts to notice the children's absence, as active subjects of photographs, from their mother's accounts. It was not only their absence from the talk of their mothers that made me begin to think that the active subject consituted by this photographic work was not the ostensible subjects of the photos at all (the children), but rather the person doing so many things with the photos (the mother); it was also my complicity with that absence as I worked with the transcripts for so long without really noticing it. As a mother, I reflected, perhaps I too photographed my kids more for me than for them, or for the friends and relations I sent their pictures to; or perhaps it was for both me and those other family members. That moment of self-reflection prompted a specific analytical move in my particular study of family photos, towards thinking about photos in relation to mothering in particular.

The ongoing reflection on their position of the anthropologists with which this chapter opened also encouraged them to analyse photos in a particular way; they too chose to think, from their own experiences, about photos in relation to a specific situation rather than to photography in general. None of them offers full biographical accounts in order to do that though; rather, as we noted, they offer a specific aspect of their research practice as a point from which to reflect on the partiality and locatedness of knowledge. In their case, like mine, it was what they did with photos. Thomas (1999) adopts a somewhat similar strategy in his study of 'indigenous art/colonial culture' in Australia and New Zealand. After describing his own position as a white Australian, and admitting that his account must therefore be selective and partial, like any other account, he suggests that it is not in fact this personal biography that matters in relation to how he can interpret the significance of the visual objects he will discuss in his book. Rather, it is how his specific cultural context will inflect his account of that same context as it shapes, and is shaped by, art objects:

> I am not so much concerned to 'come to terms' with this in a personal sense as to illustrate why the region's history makes 'coming to terms' always an incomplete business: one that is necessary, awkward, rewarding and also improbable. (Thomas 1999: 19)

The reflexivity of this approach is thus of a particular kind. It might be described as less autobiographical and more situational. It works from specific moments of relation or surprise between the researcher and the researched, in order to mark the constructed nature of the researcher's account.

4 the anthropological approach: an assessment

It is rather tricky to assess fairly the strengths and weaknesses of an approach that I have used myself. Nonetheless, the anthropological approach does have some limitations, which I will discuss after I have briefly rehearsed its advantages.

This anthropological approach to visual objects is clearly a prime candidate for a critical visual methodology. It pays careful attention to the specifics of images; indeed, in its interest in their materiality it might be argued to pay more attention to the full range of qualities possessed by visual objects than do several other methods discussed elsewhere in this book. The concept of recontextualization was intended by Thomas (1991) precisely to enable the discussion of power relations as they play out through the movement of objects. His particular interest, remember, was in the exchanges of objects between indigenous peoples and European travellers on various Pacific islands in the eighteenth and nineteenth centuries, which in the context of colonialism were often appropriations by the latter of the former's objects. And this approach's embeddedness in anthropology means that reflexivity is a taken-for-granted aspect of its practice. That reflexivity is quite specific, as we have seen, but nonetheless serves to mark the agency of the researcher.

Another obvious advantage of the anthropological method is that it pays attention to several sites and modalities. In its concern with the materiality of the image, it examines its technological and compositional modality. Its focus on the social life of images means that the social modality of the image is also key, as is the site of audiencing. The site of production is also relevant; both Pinney (1997) and Poole (1997) spend some time exploring the photographic studio as a key site for the production of images.

This latter advantage, though, can also be a disadvantage for this anthropological approach. Clearly, given enough time and resources, a researcher can explore all these sites and modalities in great detail, examining their co-constitution and the working of recontextualization across them. The richness of the work of Pinney, Poole and Thomas is enviable. But researchers with less time and resources will not have the luxury of extended, close-up ethnographic observation, and they will therefore have to make choices about what aspect of the social life of their chosen images they wish to concentrate on. For example, in my own work, I chose to concentrate mostly on how family photographs were displayed in houses. I did not undertake a careful survey of their visual content (as did, for example, David Halle [1993] with two research assistants to help him), but instead I assumed that the surveys carried out by others like Halle (1993) and Chalfen (1987) were more or less accurate. I have to admit that this was a short cut, and a more thorough study would have carefully examined the visual content of the thousands of family photos I was shown. Although I saw nothing to contradict those surveys' claims that family photos are most often of family members together, happy and at leisure, maybe there was something in that content that I missed and which could have altered my conclusions. Nor did I follow any of the photos I was told all my interviewees had sent elsewhere. I therefore did not develop any claims about the recontextualization of the images I was interested in. Time and resource constraints placed these limits on my study, but I imagine that such constraints affect many researchers. And since the quality of the findings of this approach does depend on detailed and extensive empirical evidence, such constraints may affect this method more perhaps than others this book has discussed.

The importance of empirical evidence to this approach is also double-edged in another way. On the one hand, it is clearly a strength of this kind of anthropological work; detailed studies of specific practices are fascinatingly complex and subtle in and of themselves and, as Thomas (1991) demonstrates, can contribute to wider understandings of how images work. However, there is also perhaps a danger of empiricism in this approach. That is, while the anthropologists discussed here have good reason to be suspicious of over-arching theories ungrounded in any detailed context, plunging into the specificities of case studies without considering their wider theoretical relevance is an equally limited tactic. I wonder if this empirical bent is responsible for the equation of exchange with mobility and recontextualization. Both Appadurai (1986) and Thomas (1991) build their theoretical statements in large part from empirical anthropological studies of exchange. It seems to me, though, that they both generalize from certain, empirically specific aspects of particular examples of exchange, to the circulation of objects in general. In particular, there is an assumption (which I think is more than just a methodological convenience, as Appadurai [1986: 5] claims) that when an object moves, it is also recontextualized. Now, in the instances Thomas (1991) was most concerned with, that was undoubtedly the case: when Europeans took objects from Papua New Guinea, or when Papuans took European objects, those objects began a new stage in their biographies. However, it seems to me that not all images get so radically recontextualized when they move. Indeed, the effect of some objects moving may be to carry certain effects from one place to another, in the way that the 'togetherness' of family photos is extended over long distances when photos are circulated between family members. Images as objects are mobile, for sure, but whether they are also always recontextualized when they travel needs to be established rather than assumed.

Finally, I have already mentioned one other difficulty with this work – which is that not all visual materials are equally thinkable as objects.

summary

- *associated with:*
  Photographs and art objects, most often.

- *sites and modalities:*
  This method can in principle address all three sites of production, image and audiencing, and pay attention to all their modalities.

- *key terms:*
  Key terms include materiality, recontextualization and mobility.

- *strengths and weaknesses:*
  The method can be a comprehensive approach to the socialities in which visual objects participate. Its weaknesses include the resources needed to fulfil its potential, its preference for empirical work over theory, and its suitability for all images.

Further reading

Christopher Pinney's (2003) polemical introduction to an edited collection of essays is a bracing introduction to this work, and Nicholas Thomas's (1991) book *Entangled Objects* is a very helpful, more sustained argument for it.

11
making photographs as part of a research project
photo-elicitation, photo-documentation
and other uses of photos

key examples this chapter explores a range of methods, and so discusses several examples. All of them use photographs, made either by the researcher or the people they are researching, which in some way or another form part of the researcher's analysis.

1 making photographs as part of a research project: an introduction

This chapter looks at a range of methods attracting more and more attention in social sciences such as sociology and human geography. These methods are distinct from all the other approaches to visual materials discussed in this book so far, because they do not work with 'found' images that already exist distinct from a research project: Hollywood films or family snaps, for example. Instead, they work with images that are made as part of a research project. The images can be made by the researcher, or they can be made by the people they are researching; and they can take the form of film or still photos, maps or diagrams (Latham 2003; Young and Barrett 2001) or drawings (Guillemin 2004; Kearney and Hyle 2004). Importantly, these are not images that simply illustrate some aspect of the research project: what Marcus Banks (2001: 144) calls a 'largely redundant visual representation of something already described in the text'. Instead, in these methods, the images are used actively in the research process, alongside other sorts of evidence generated usually by interviews or ethnographic fieldwork.

This chapter focuses on the making of just one sort of image as a visual research tool, however: photographs. This is partly because photographic images, whether moving or still, are currently the most popular sort of image being created by social scientists. And while there is a long tradition in visual anthropology of making films in order to answer research questions, this is a highly specialized and technically demanding method which is less likely to be accessible to readers of this book. (Full accounts of ethnographic film-making are available elsewhere; see, for example, Banks 2001; Barbash and Taylor 1997; Pink 2006) Photos, then, are both popular and more easily made than films, and this chapter will focus on them.

Many of the methods discussed so far in this book flow directly from a clear theoretical position. Semiology, psychoanalysis, discourse analysis I and II and audience studies in particular are clearly predicated on specific theoretical frameworks that understand the visual in particular ways. This is somewhat less true of the anthropological approach discussed in Chapter 10; its theoretical bases are materiality, performativity and mobility rather than visuality. The methods discussed in this chapter are also less engaged with theories of visuality or of visual objects. Rather, they use images to address questions and issues generated in a wide range of theoretical contexts. This has encouraged the editors of a recent collection of essays on using visual methods for social research, Caroline Knowles and Paul Sweetman (2004), to claim that they are uninterested in theorizing exactly what photography in general is or does. Instead, they suggest that the photographs used by social science researchers are simply means to certain ends. They emphasize 'the analytical and conceptual possibilities of visual methods' in terms of 'what it is that visual methods are able to achieve' (Knowles and Sweetman 2004: 6), rather than in terms of what photographs inherently are.

Nonetheless, Knowles and Sweetman (2004) are convinced that such photographic work is worthwhile because, they argue, photos can achieve something that methods relying only on speech and writing cannot. Many researchers agree, arguing that photographs in particular are unique sources of evidence in social science research. One of the first to argue for the use of photographs alongside interviews – John Collier – claimed that 'photographs are precise records of material reality' (Collier 1967: 5) and that their value lay in the way this precision provided data for analysis. John Grady (2004: 20) agrees: 'pictures are valuable because they encode an enormous amount of information in a single representation', he says. Photos are valuable too for the way they convey 'real, flesh and blood life', according to Howard Becker (2002: 11), making their audiences 'bear witness' to that life (Holliday 2004: 61). As well as providing data and evidence in this way, they also give research participants a means to reflect on aspects of their lives that they may usually give little thought to (Blinn and Harrist 1991; Holliday 2004; Latham 2003). Hence photos are used by these social scientists because they can carry or evoke three things – information, affect and reflection – particularly well. As a result, photos can be described as 'a more transparent representation of the life experiences of participants in [a] study' (Dodman 2003: 294).

Thus, despite Knowles and Sweetman's (2004) protestations to the contrary, this body of work does indeed cleave to a broad conceptualization of what photographs are and what therefore they can do in social science research. How to explore, then, the range of ways this conceptualization has encouraged social scientists to use photographs in their work?

As Becker (2004) remarks, there is no clearly established methodological framework to discuss the uses of photography in social science research. My approach here is to create two groups of methods, distinguished by the way in which the qualities attributed to photographs are put to work in a research project. In the first of these groups, photos are *subordinated* in some way to the researcher's interpretations; they are worked over for what they offer in the way of evidence to answer a resarch question. In the second, in contrast, they are used because they are seen as *excessive* to the researcher's interpretive work. The first of these I call *supporting* and the second *supplemental*. Most of what are called *photo-elicitation* studies fall into the first of these categories, because photo-elicitation uses photos to encourage interview talk that would not be possible without the photos, and the photos and the talk are then interpreted by the researcher. Using photographs as documentary evidence – what I am calling *photo-documentation* – is also part of this first group of methods, again because the photographs only become meaningful through the interpretive work of the researcher. The second group of methods I discuss includes studies where the specific visual qualities of photos are allowed to display themselves rather more on their own terms, thus acting as a visual supplement to the written text of the researcher.

The fact that these methods use photos made for a research project provokes a rather different inflection to the question of whether they constitute a critical visual research methodology. Clearly, the criterion that images must be considered carefully, and as having their own agency, seems to be met by this work, which either scrutinizes photos for the information they carry, or pays careful attention to their specific effects. The second criterion – that the research considers the social conditions and effects of visual objects – needs approaching rather differently when considering these methods, however. Most of the studies I will discuss in this chapter use photographs, but not usually in order to examine the social effects of imagery. Usually, the photos are made in relation to other things: the aestheticization of contemporary workplaces, for example (Warren 2002), or the use of urban public space (Latham 2003, 2004). While these topics may touch on questions of visuality, the methods are not always directed at examining the social effects of visual materials in the same way as many of the other methods in this book are. Nonetheless, the question of the social effects of the visual images remains relevant to these methods: not in relation to what their images do in the wider social world, but in relation to the social relations embedded in the research process itself. That is, the social effects of images with which these methods are most concerned centre on the relations between the researcher, those people they are researching and the photos. And this means, as Samantha Warren (2002: 240) points out, that the question of **research ethics** is much **research ethics** more overt in these methods than in others. Research ethics is precisely about ensuring that the social relations of a research project are ethical. A consequence of this concern with research ethics is that the third criterion for a critical visual methodology – reflexivity – is also usually quite central to research projects using photographs. Just how reflexivity has been argued to be part of ethical research practices using photographs will be examined more carefully in section 4 of this chapter.

In order to assess the usefulness of these methods in relation to this, slightly modified, understanding of a critical visual methodology, this chapter will:

- examine the use of photos as supportive of a researcher's text;
- examine the use of photos as excessive to the words of the researcher;
- examine the research ethics of such studies;
- and assess the strengths and weaknesses of these approaches.

2 using photos to support social science research

This section examines two sorts of uses of photographs, in which the rich visual information provided by the photograph is interpreted by the researcher. As we will see, that interpretation almost always works with other sources of evidence as well, particularly interviews or ethnographic data.

2.1 photo-elicitation

Photo-elicitation is, as one of its prime exponents notes, 'based on the simple idea of inserting a photograph into a research interview' (Harper 2002: 13). The photo can be taken either by the researcher or the researched. The point of doing this rests on that interpretation of photographs outlined in section 1: photographs offer 'an opportunity to gain not just more but different insights into social phenomena, which research methods relying on oral, aural or written data cannot provide' (Bolton et al. 2001: 503). In the case of photo-elicitation, it is argued that while ordinary interview talk can explore many issues, discussing a photograph with an interviewee can prompt much more talk about different things. Indeed, Collier's early argument for photo-elicitation claimed that it is only through interviewing that the information carried by a photo can be accessed by the researcher (Collier 1967: 49). It can also prompt talk in different registers. Namiko Kunimoto (2004), for example, was researching the experience of Japanese-Canadians interned during and after the Second World War. Although not strictly a photo-elicitation study, her essay demonstrates especially clearly how photos can evoke quite different kinds of memories in her interviews. She recounts that at the beginning of an interview, things would feel rather restrained and formal – until she asked to see any photographs from the internment camps that her interviewee had.

Once the photos were retrieved, she found the whole interview changing, becoming much more intense and emotional as the photos stirred deep and often painful memories. Alan Latham used photo-elicitation differently again (Latham 2003, 2004). In a project interested in how urban public life gets done, he asked his interviewees to make a photo-diary for a week. He then interviewed them about their diary. He argues that discussing the diary and its photos – in which people were often mucking around, performing for the camera – gave his interviewees some distance from their ordinary routines and enabled them to articulate some of the taken-for-granted practical knowledges with which they negotiated public space (see also Holliday 2004). Photographs, then, whether taken by the researcher or the researched, can alter both the quantity and the nature of interview material.

As with any simple idea, there are endless possible permutations, but the conventional way of doing photo-elicitation has six stages, once the initial research question has been formulated (see also Banks 2001; Harper 2002; Latham 2003; McIntyre 2003; Warren 2002). I will discuss them using Lynn Blinn and Amanda Harrist's (1991) study of women going back to university as mature students as an example. Blinn and Harrist (1991: 175) were interested in creating 'an emic view of what it is like to be a female re-entry college student'. That is, like many users of photo-elicitation, they asked the people they were studying to take photographs and assumed that the photographs would express their experiences, feelings and preferences. They recruited 27 women for their study, 16 of whom were married with children and all of whom were middle-class; all but one were white. They then went through the six basic stages of photo-elicitation:

1   An initial interview, or series of interviews, is conducted with interviewees as part of the research project. This initial interview usually will not address the question of photographs; rather, it will focus on the questions that the photographs are going to contribute to answering.
2   Interviewees are then given a camera, and some guidance about what sort of photographs to take and how many. Blinn and Harrist (1991) made sure all their interviewees were comfortable using the Polaroid cameras they were giving them, and then asked each one to take ten photos representing her experiences as a re-entry student (Blinn and Harrist 1991: 179–80). Alternatively, the researcher decides what sort of photos to take themselves, based on their interpretation of the initial interview stage.
3   The photos are developed and interviewees may be asked to write something about the photos before they meet the researcher again. The women in Blinn and Harrist's study were each given a sheet to fill in after they had taken each photo: it asked for a title and a description of each photo, and a description of the thoughts and feelings each photo evoked in them and in their family members. Blinn and Harrist (1991: 189) suggest that, in studies where interviewees are taking their own photos, this moment of reflection on the photos is very helpful in making the next stage of the research fruitful.

4   The researcher then conducts another interview (or interviews) with the interviewees, discussing the photos with them in detail. All researchers using this method agree that this stage is vital in clarifying what photos taken by interviewees mean to them. For example, many of the women in Blinn and Harrist's study took photos which, to the women, represented the support they got from their family while they studied. These photos, however, usually took the form of simple portraits of husbands and children, and Blinn and Harrist (1991: 184) remark that it would have been very difficult for them as researchers to know what these photos were representing if they had not also talked with the women about them (and read the sheets accompanying these photos).

5   The interview material and photographs are then interpreted using conventional social science techniques (see also Collier 2001). Blinn and Harrist (1991) analysed their interview transcripts using the software package Ethnograph, and they used content analysis on the photos and written sheets since they had 257 of them to interpret. It is not unusual for photo-elicitation studies to make use of content analysis to interpret informants' photos if there are lots of them. Dodman (2003) had 838 photos, for example, taken by school pupils in Kingston, Jamaica, showing what they liked and disliked about the city. He used content analysis but developed its coding categories by discussing the photos with the children. Blinn and Harrist's content analysis used the written texts to make sense of the content of the photos. This demonstrated to them that the two key themes that the photos were showing were the women's guilt and lack of time: the guilt felt by the women at no longer being able to do all that they had done for their family before they went to college, and the relative lack of time they now had to spend with their families and to do domestic labour. Blint and Harrist expand on the notion of time in their discussion of their interview material, suggesting that the temporalities of the women's life-cycle stage, the academic year and of everyday rhythms are a useful lens through which to understand the women's experiences as returning college students.

6   The finished research tends to be presented such that the talk about the photos between the researcher and the researched takes precedence over the photos themselves. Blinn and Harrist's (1991) study is quite revealing in this regard, since they do not actually reproduce any of the photos taken by their informants. The photos are represented in their paper by a combination of their own analyses, their interpretation of their informants' self-reflection, and a table showing the result of their content analyses of the photos. This is unusual, and most photo-elicitation studies do reproduce some of their informant's photos. But their absence from Blinn and Harrist's essay does confirm that, in photo-elicitation, the researcher's text tends to dominate the photographs.

Blinn and Harrist (1991) conclude by emphasizing two of the reasons why combining photos with interviews offers a particularly insightful research method: first, because it gives detailed information about how informants see their world; and second, because it allows interviewees to reflect on things they do not usually think about.

2.2 photo-documentation

In this method, photos are made systematically by the researcher in order to provide data that the researcher then analyses. A good example of this approach is Charles Suchar's work on gentrification in the neighbourhods of Lincoln Park in Chicago and Jordaan in Amsterdam (1997, 2004). Gentrification is a process of change in long-established, rather run-down but quite central urban neighbourhoods; new people, attracted by relatively low house prices and the centrality of the location, start to move in, with subsequent changes to a range of the neighbourhood's features. Suchar's earlier work was interested in the detailed physical, social and cultural changes that gentrification brought to the urban environment, both externally, to the streets and gardens, and to the internal decoration of homes. It focused on the individuals who moved into the areas recently as well as on long-term residents, using photographs of shops, roads, buildings and homes as well as portraits of individuals.

Key to the successful use of photo-documentation, as Jon Rieger (1996) makes clear, is the careful conceptualization of the link between the research topic – in Suchar's case, those changes associated with gentrification – and the photographs being taken. Suchar (1997) achieves this by using what he calls 'shooting scripts'. Shooting scripts depend on the initial research question being addressed. They are lists of sub-questions, if you like, generated by that overall question, and they guide a first go at taking photographs relevant to the research question. Suchar (1997: 34) uses scripts so that the 'information within [a photo] can be argued as putative facts that are answers to particular questions'. For example, one of the things that changes when an urban area is undergoing gentrification are the shops. They often go more upmarket, or more trendy. So the list of questions Suchar (1997: 37) set himself in relation to the aspect of gentrification was:

- What variety of shops is found in the different neighbourhood areas?
- What do they sell, or what services do they provide?
- Who are the customers? Are they locals or do they come from outside the neighbourhood?
- Who works in, owns or manages these shops?

While Suchar does not discount taking photos in a more intuitive kind of way, a shooting script of this sort guides what photographs he takes and, most importantly, why he takes them: Suchar rightly insists that to serve as evidence for social science research, the photos must be clearly connected to a research question, and in his work this is achieved by the shooting script.

Such an initial shooting script guides the first stage of taking photographs. The photographs thus made, however, do not speak for themselves.

To further develop their links to the research question, Suchar (1997) adds fieldnotes to each photo he takes. This includes factual information (date, time, location for example), but also a paragraph or two of commentary on how each photo relates to the shooting script questions. Suchar also attaches labels to each photo which he describes as a kind of coding (Suchar 1997: 38).

The second stage of the process then begins. Attaching codes to his photos allows Suchar to begin to compare photographs. He could compare the same sorts of store, and compare different kinds of store; he evaluated their storefronts, advertising and clientele. And from this process of comparision, facilitated by the first stage of coding, further codes begin to emerge. These codes might contribute to answering the research question; but they might themselves require further exploration. Suchar (1997: 39) also says that the photos themselves might throw up interesting issues that the questions of the initial shooting script did not address. So a third stage of this process is to develop a second shooting script, to develop and refine the insights generated by the first.

Suchar (1997) develops his method by comparing it to a grounded theory approach to social science research (on grounded theory, see Strauss and Corbin 1999). Grounded theory builds iteratively from detailed field evidence, and this is exactly Suchar's approach to using photographs as evidence; he says that he finds 'that reference to very detailed visual documents, and the information they contain, allows for a closer link between the abstractive process of conceptualizing and experientially derived observations' (Suchar 1997: 52). And although the photographs show him patterns that would not otherwise be evident, their significance depends on Suchar's systematic coding of what they show. They are used as descriptive devices, the meaning of which must be established by the researcher. For example, although his photos of gentrifiers' houses allowed him to establish the importance of a certain style of their housing which he called 'urban romantic', the significance of that style in terms of its relation to social change is established by the interpretive work he does with the photos (and with photo-elicitation interviews with residents [Suchar 1997]). The supportive status of the photographs is clear in Suchar's (1997, 2004) published accounts of his work, where his photos are presented as illustrations of typical changes in these two urban neighbourhoods. They have captions explaining what they show, but those captions usually downplay any peculiarity in favour of presenting each photo as a typical example of the wider changes with which he is concerned (see Figure 11.1 reproduced here with its original caption). In his published work therefore, his photos serve to confirm and validate his analysis of gentrification.

Thus, although photo-documentation and photo-elicitation appear to be quite different methods in terms of their procedures, I am suggesting that they are similar in that they use photographs to the same ends: as evidence to be interpreted. It is that interpretation that then takes precedence in the researcher's argument.

Figure 11.1
from Suchar's study of gentrification in Chicago. The original caption reads '900 W. block of Concord Place. A typical collection of older cottages and new construction/ housing units that have replaced the torn-down structures. Spring 2001.' (Suchar 2004: 158)

---

focus

You know that a local town always has a lantern parade down its high street three weeks before Christmas each year, to coincide with the Christmas lights being switched on. You are also interested in notions of 'community', a key term in the social sciences from their foundation in the late nineteenth century to today. Develop a shooting script that would begin to answer the question: does that parade generate a sense of community among its participants?

Things you need to consider include what theorization of community you will be working with, what the visible effects of such a parade are, and how they might relate to that theorization. You also need to think about what information and evidence you need about the parade and how you will get it: will you need to do interviews, for example, or participate in the local workshop events where the lanterns get made?

Finally, how does Suchar's iterative approach to photo-documentation work when you're interested in a one-off event?

---

3 using photos to supplement social science research

The distinction I am making between two approaches to working with photographs as part of the research process is that, while the methods just discussed in section 2 generally use photos as evidence to be interpreted by the researcher (often in conjunction with interviewees), the methods to be discussed now give more space to the photographs themselves to have their own, perhaps rather unpredictable, effects in the research process. I would suggest that there are two things that photos can be asked to do: what Becker (2002) calls 'specified generalization'; and what Latham (2003: 2009) calls 'texture'.

3.1 photographs as 'specified generalization'

Becker uses the phrase 'specified generalization' to talk about a book written by John Berger and heavy with photographs by Jean Mohr, called *A Seventh Man* (Berger and Mohr 1975). The book is about experiences of men migrating from poorer to more affluent parts of Europe. In 'A Note to the Reader' at the beginning of the book, Berger says that 'the book consists of images and words' and that 'both should be read on their own terms'; 'only occasionally is an image used to illustrate the text' (Berger and Mohr 1975: 7). The photos are never referred to directly by the text, and their minimal captions are listed at the end of the book rather than next to the relevant photo.

The differences between the deployment of photographs in this book, and the use (or non-use) of photos in Blinn and Harrist's (1991) photo-elicitation and Suchar's (1997, 2004) photo-documentation is obvious immediately. Far from being subordinated to the interpretive work of the researcher, Mohr's photos are intended as a parallel source of understanding to Berger's account, to be 'read on their own terms'.

Becker (2002) points out that Berger's text relies on a range of evidence to make its arguments about the exploitation of migrant workers, including social theory, narrative and statistics. This range of sources helps to persuade the reader that Berger's account is a truthful one. And so do Mohr's photos, suggests Becker, for similar reasons: there are enough of them, from different places and showing different things, to give an impression of properly comprehensive coverage. The photos ask the reader to work to make sense of them; they are not all easy to respond to; there is a depth to the engagement they invite that again suggests a seriousness of purpose to Mohr's work. And while Becker (2002: 10) admits that the work asked of the reader/viewer of *A Seventh Man* may produce interpretations of what is pictured that differ from Berger's, he argues nevertheless that Mohr's photographs actively confirm Berger's account by reassuring us that the things referred to in Berger's account do indeed exist.

Becker (2002) thus calls Mohr's photographs 'specified generalizations'. They add something to Berger's generalizations about migration and its effects: they specify them. They show what they really are, what they look like, what they do – they make them believable. The photos of a broiler processing factory in Maine, USA, taken by Cedric Chatterley, work similarly, it seems to me; they are particularly effective at conveying the complex ambivalence felt by an interviewee when the factory closed and she lost her unpleasant, low-paid job (Mauad et al. 2004). And it is the peculiar ability of photos to do this, to show 'flesh and blood' as if for real, claims Becker:

> What can you do with pictures that your couldn't do just as well with words (or numbers)? The answer is that I can lead you to believe that the abstract tale I've told you has a real, flesh and blood life, and therefore is to be believed in a way that is hard to do when all you have is the argument and some scraps and can only wonder if there really is anyone like that out there. (Becker 2002: 11)

Becker is arguing that the effect of Mohr's photos is, in the end, to affirm the veracity of Berger's text. The photos are not used as evidence for the researcher's arguments, as they are in photo-documentation or photo-elicitation projects; they work more actively to convince us that those arguments are correct. The visual qualities of the photographs are being used to make the reader believe what the text of the book is telling us.

Becker (2002) makes this argument in relation to a researcher's photographs. But his analysis of why photos work as part of research would seem to hold whether it refers to photos made by a researcher, or by the researched. It is their effect that matters, not their source.

3.2 photographs that capture 'texture'

One theme that recurs in discussions about making photos as part of social science research projects is that photos are particularly good at capturing the 'texture' of places. Whether the place is the homes and classrooms of Blinn and Harrist's (1991) study of women returning to college, or the gentrified neighbourhoods of Suchar's (1997, 2004) studies, or the borders, hostels and factories of Berger and Mohr's (1975) book, photos can convey the 'feel' of specific locations very effectively. This is partly because photos can carry so much visual information; they can show us details in a moment that it would take pages of writing to describe.

Photographs can also show us things that are hard to describe in writing at all. Geographers have long been interested in the elusive qualities that define sense of place, and some are now using photography deliberately to convey it (see for example Goin 2002). More recently, there has been some interest across the social sciences in things that writing and words cannot convey, or find very hard to do so (or at least the conventional social science kinds of writing). There is a lot of interest in the emotional, for example, and in how some emotions evade verbal or written expression; there is also much interest in the materiality of social life, and in how objects intervene in social life and in how the things that are done with them are not always consciously reflected upon and given meaning. The anthropologists discussed in Chapter 10 here are part this wider turn towards materiality and practice, and there is also some connection, I would suggest, between this interest and the debates in visual culture studies, mentioned in section 4.2 of Chapter 1, about the ability of (some) visual images to exert their own agency. And some researchers interested in precisely how the practices within which the materiality of social life is embedded can exceed their spoken or written expression have turned to photography as a means of evoking such excess.

Tim Edensor's (2005) study of industrial ruins is exemplary here. Edensor argues that ruins are spaces into which powerful efforts to order social life extend only sporadically; hence industrial ruins are condemned as useless and ugly wasteland while also harbouring a range of less-than-conventional activities. Edensor also suggests that they offer a very different set of sensory experiences than do the organized and sanitized spaces in which so much of social life is conducted, so that ruins can surprise, confound, scare and amaze. Thus, for Edensor, ruins exceed dominant cultural meaning in two ways: first by offering zones where other, sometimes oppositional meanings can be practised, and secondly by making a range of experiences available that are otherwise difficult to find. And Edensor uses photographs throughout his book to evoke these various, excessive qualities of ruins. In fact, he uses photographs in two ways. First, he records ruins themselves, before they are demolished or renovated or disintegrate entirely, noting that photos 'can reveal the stages and temporalities of decay' (Edensor 2005: 16). Secondly, he suggests that photographs convey some of the experiential qualities peculiar to ruins:

> Photographs are never merely visual but in fact conjure up synaesthetic and kinaesthetic effects, for the visual provokes other sensory responses. The textures and tactilities, smells, atmospheres and sounds of ruined spaces, together with the signs and objects they accommodate, can be empathetically conjured up by visual material. (Edensor 2005: 16)

Occasionally, the ruins' decay seems to have infected the form of Edensor's photos. They too sometimes lose definition and meaning, and it is impossible to make out what they are 'of' (for example, see Figure 11.2). Edensor also induces the feel and texture and strange obscurity of ruins by inserting the photos uncaptioned into his text. There they work as a kind of visual

Figure 11.2   *From Edensor's study of industrial ruins 2005: 121*

supplement to his arguments, hanging there, unreferenced, perhaps 'utilised as an alternative source of information independent from the text' (Edensor 2005: 16), and in any case always suggesting that there is more to ruins than Edensor's interpretation can convey. Like Berger and Mohr (1975), Edensor (2005) is concerned to allow photographs to do work that could not be done by other means.

Finally, as well as using photographs to act as supplements to a written text, some critics have made essays entirely out of photographs. Given my conviction that images only make sense in a wider context that will always include written text, I have my doubts about how effectively photo-essays can carry an argument. However, both John Berger (1972) and Griselda Pollock (1988) have made photo-essays, and Marcus Banks (2001: 145–71) discusses them as a potentially productive research method.

3.3 some practical considerations
Whether supportive of or supplemental to the researcher's text, using photographs in the way discussed in this section depends on two practical considerations. First, the photos used need to be – well, good. Although 'good' is a rather hard quality to define, it does seem to me that these methods

require a fairly high level of photographic skill really to be effective. While this is a skill that can be developed and improved (Grady 2004), there is no doubt that some researchers are just better at taking the sort of photos that work well in these sorts of project than others. If in your heart of hearts you know you are not one of them, then you would need to think seriously about undertaking a project that relied on photographs in this way.

Secondly – and in the social sciences this is not a minor point – both these methods require good quality reproduction. While this is now easier than ever in dissertations and theses, when it comes to publishing research with images it is more difficult; most social science journals have lamentable standards of photographic reproduction. It is very rare to find colour reproduction available (indeed, it was only in its fifth year of publication that the *Journal of Visual Culture* finally got colour pages), and even black and white photos can be blurred and grey when published. This is a significant problem for these supplemental strategies in particular, which rely on the power of visual images to do work. Indeed, Warren (2002), only half-jokingly, suggests that this is in fact the major reason why social scientists have been so slow to explore visual methods of research: they just can't get their photos published properly. She also points out, though, that this may change as more journals move from being print-based to web-based, since high-definition and colour images are much easier to reproduce on the web.

Finally, I want to suggest that supplemental uses of photographs – photographs as 'specified generalizations' and photographs as 'texture' – carry a certain risk. The risk is that the readers/viewers of the work that contains this sort of photo will simply be baffled by the photos, rather than convinced by them or moved by them or amazed by them or whatever. Leaving aside questions about the quality of the photographs and the overall execution of the research, writers on visual methods often complain about the inability of most social scientists to work with visual materials and studies in the same way that they are happy to work with written evidence. This is an oft-repeated lament in the literature that I have drawn on for this chapter. Having myself had a journal invent from thin air captions for the photos I had deliberately left uncaptioned in a paper, it is a lament with which I have some sympathy. Nonetheless, it is also true, I think, that in order to make sense – or for their supplemental non-sense to be contextualized – photos need accompanying text. As I noted in the preface to this book, interpreting images is not an easy task. Photo-essays without text are very hard to make head or tail of (and Banks [2001: 139–51] confirms this). Without wanting to undermine the valid point that images can do work that written text cannot, readers still need some guidance on how to treat the images that they are being offered. If they are not, there is a much higher risk than usual that the images will be ignored or else read in ways entirely different from those intended by the researcher.

4 research ethics and reflexivity when making images as part of a research project

Of the studies discussed so far in this chapter, only Edensor's (2005) contains no photographs of people. All the others do. And when photographs are made of people in a research project, specific ethical issues arise in relation to the photos that are distinct from the ethical considerations attaching to the other elements of the project (see Banks 2001: 128–35; Lewis 2004; Warren 2002). The Economic and Social Research Council, which is a major funder of social science research in the UK, recently defined ethical research as having six key principles. Here they are (ESRC 2006: 1):

- ethical research should have integrity and quality;
- it should inform all research staff and subjects fully about the purposes, methods and intended possible uses of the research, what their participation involves, and any possible risks;
- all information supplied by informants should be confidential, and all informants guaranteed anonymity (in the case of photographs, this would entail ensuring that no individuals were identifiable, by blurring faces digitally, for example);
- all participants should participate voluntarily, free from coercion;
- harm to research participants should be avoided;
- the research should be independent, and any conflicts of interest should be made explicit.

Guidelines such as these have been criticized for being too rigid (Thrift 2003). It is certainly easy to imagine circumstances in which at least some of these principles might not hold; for example, in many of the projects discussed in section 4.1 below, the empowerment felt by the individuals participating might well be decreased if they had to adopt pseudonyms in order to have their anonymity guaranteed. It is also possible to wonder whether any researcher is truly in a position, certainly before research begins, to tell their informants *fully* about *any* possible risks their participation might entail.

Nonetheless, it is clear that doing research with photos means making a record of identifiable people doing specific things. How that record is made and what is then done with it therefore matters. Research that treats both research subjects and their photos ethically can be straightforward to formulate, but research ethics are more often subtly complicated; and there is no one set of rules that can guarantee ethical research in any circumstances. But some of the issues at least can be explored under four headings: reflexivity, collaborative research, permissions, copyright and returning images.

4.1 collaborative research

Collaborative research (that is also reflexive) is what Banks (2001) recommends as a strategy for ethical research. Collaborative research means doing research *with* your respondents or informants, rather than *on* them. It means acknowledging their own skills and understandings and being open to those skills and understandings mediating and altering your own.

Banks (2001: 112) suggests that visual research may even be inherently collaborative, because making images always entails some sort of negotiated relationship between those making the images and those being pictured. He elaborates this point: as a researcher picks up a camera and prepares to shoot, it is obvious that she is about to take a picture, and 'in some contexts people will actively encourage the researcher to create images, in others they will appear indifferent, and in others they will more or less politely tell her to stop or evade the lens' (Banks 2001: 113). Thus the very act of taking a photograph creates an opportunity for some sort of collaboration. Laura Lewis (2005) offers a salutary tale, though, of the limits of such 'collaboration', in her discussion of the photographs taken by Maya Goded of the inhabitants of a village in Guerrero, Mexico. Goded visited the village in the early 1990s and took many portrait photographs, obviously with the permission of the villagers. But when the photos appeared in a book and exhibition some time later, the villagers barely recognized themselves in the photos. They had been pictured in ways that they found degrading and inappropriate, while Goded's career advanced. Lewis (2004: 491) describes this as an unethical 'optical violence' inflicted upon them. Clearly the process of collaboration has to extend beyond the site and moment of producing an image, to the sites of its content and audiencing as well.

Banks (2001) also discusses more sustained forms of collaboration in the context of anthropological film-making, however, when researchers seek to involve their subjects in decisions about what to shoot and how; another example of a fuller collaboration between researcher and researched in the production of images is when subjects are given cameras themselves and asked to photograph what they think is most appropriate. Alice McIntyre (2003) discusses an example of this kind of participatory research in depth. Many photo-elicitation studies fall into this category, of course, if they are based on asking informants to picture themselves and their worlds on their terms. Researchers who have undertaken such work suggest that it is empowering to interviewees; it allows them a degree of autonomous self-expression they are rarely allowed otherwise. For some researchers, this self-expression is simply a more-or-less straightforward articulation of an existing social identity (Dodman 2003; McIntyre 2003); for others, such as Holliday (2004) and Latham (2003), who work with more relational and performative understandings of subjectivity, visual images allow a performance of identity, with the researcher as its audience, which is also an exploration of identity. Both positions, though, rely on the veracity of the visual to convey aspects of identity, a veracity which, according to Holliday (2004: 62) 'prevents a total appropriation of the meanings of [informants'] accounts'.

4.2 reflexivity

Effective collaboration requires reflexive vigilance, however. For many researchers using visual methods, reflexivity is thus a prerequisite for ethical research. By this they simply mean the careful and consistent awareness of what the researcher is doing, why, and with what possible consequences in terms of the power relations between researcher and researched.

Holliday (2004) has argued that using visual methods like photo-elicitation offers opportunities for a particular sort of reflexivity. She shares the scepticism of various post-structuralist schools of thought about forms of reflexivity that involve the researcher reflecting on his or her position and identifying its effects, a reflexivity that assumes a stable identity that can be reflected upon (Holliday 2004: 56; Rose 1997). Instead, she argues that both researcher and researched are positioned by discourses external to themselves; and, moreover, in relation to each other. While this is a differentiated relationship, it is also one that is visible to a more sustained kind of scrutiny than texts authored by the researcher alone because the voices and the images of the research subjects are there to 'talk back', as it were, from their photos. Holliday (2004: 60) says that 'their reflections seem to be much more present within the authorial text I have constructed through video than if I were simply reciting their accounts in my own words'. It is as if the veracity of the visual demands that due attention be paid to the research participants. So for Holliday it is the particular quality of the visual that allows such an explicit playing out of reflexivity.

4.3 permissions

Permissions are a more specific technique for ensuring that research is ethical, and they should be used in the context of ongoing reflection on research strategies. Permissions can be of two sorts: one at the site of image production involves getting permission to take photographs, whether they are being taken by the researcher or those they are researching, and the other involves permission to reproduce photographs at sites of audiencing.

Permission to take photographs might involve getting permission to take photographs in a particular place (a shopping mall, for example, or museum); it might involve getting permission to take photographs of something or someone; or it might involve both of these. Permission to photograph people is quite common in the sorts of research discussed here. As Banks (2001: 131) notes, permission can range from a casual verbal request before a camera starts to snap, to written permission granted only after extensive discussion. Usually, as the ESRC guidelines suggest, it is considered good practice for the researcher to be as open as possible about the aims and intentions of the research. However, Chapter 9 has already discussed one example of covert research where this was not done: Lull's (1990) study of home television watching. There may be circumstances in which such covert research is appropriate, but they are likely to be rare.

Getting permission to reproduce photographs is also important. You need to be clear where you want to reproduce your images, and also why. You will need permission from the copyright holder (see section 4.4), but you may also feel you want to get permission from the person pictured in a photo if they are not the copyright holder.

4.4 copyright

Copyright is a legal term and refers to who owns the photographs. Generally, unless they are subsequently sold to someone else, the person who took the photo is the person who owns it. If the photos in your research project were taken by the people you were researching, they are the copyright owners and you will need to seek their permission to reproduce the photos in any presentations or publications. However, if you took the photos you are the copyright owner and you can use them how you want. At least, that is the legal position. However, as section 4.3 hinted, you may feel that even though you are legally entitled to use the photos as you wish, nevertheless you want to ask permission from whoever you photographed too.

4.5 returning images

Another aspect of ethical research practice in relation to images often mentioned by practioners is giving a copy of whatever photographs have been taken back to the research informants. This gesture may be appreciated or not: the anthropological literature is rife with examples of informants actually not liking the photographs taken of them by Western anthropologists, remember! However, it does seem appropriate that if someone agreed to be photographed, or indeed took photographs themselves, they should be given a copy to do with what they will.

focus

Think again about a plan to use photographs as evidence to explore whether a town's annual lantern parade creates a sense of community among the parade's participants. Are there any ethical questions raised by what you plan to photograph, how you plan to photograph it and what you plan to do with the photographs you make?

5 making photographs as part of a research project: an assessment

This chapter has discussed a range of methods that depend on making photographs as part of the research process, rather than using found images as the focus of research. Most discussions of these sorts of methods lump them together in a rich but rather ragbag kind of way, refusing to systematize across their individual contributions (for example van Leeuwen and Jewitt 2001; Knowles and Sweetman, 2004; Prosser 1998). I have attempted to be rather more systematic, identifying the characteristics of photos that these researchers put to work, and looking at how those characteristics are related to the researcher's arguments and knowledge claims. Are the photos used as evidence and then reproduced as supportive of those arguments and claims? Or are the photos allowed some sort of agency, either to affirm the researcher's argument or to exceed it?

This distinction is not meant to imply that images and words are two separate things that can be bolted together by the researcher in various combinations. To the contrary: images and words only become significant in relation to each other in the work discussed here, and Warren (2002) draws on W.J.T. Mitchell's (1994) notion of the image-text to develop her sense of their interdependency. This interdependency points to a certain paradox at the heart of this body of work, though, which is that while it advocates the unique abilities of visual materials to convey information or affect in ways that words find hard or impossible, those visual materials still need some written context to make their effects evident.

Choosing to group these methods in this way has had certain consequences for my discussion. It depends on the effect of the use of photographs (or other images) rather than the procedures of their use, and so it is possible envisage a photo-elicitation study in which the photos are not subordinated to the researcher's argument and instead exceed it in some way to become supplemental. But how are those effects to be established? As the authors discussed in Chapter 9 insisted, readers/viewers bring all sorts of ways of looking to visual images. So, do the readers/viewers of work using these various methods see the photos doing the work that the researcher intended? And a question prompted by the previous chapter's emphasis on the agency of objects might be added here, too: do photos necessarily do what the researcher wants? None of the methods discussed here addresses these questions. Banks (2001: 140–1) points this out in relation to ethnographic filmmaking too; he could locate only one study that explored how undergraduate anthropology students actually reacted to seeing specific films. Thus, although great care is often taken in terms of how the research informants relate to photos, the other audience for the photos – the audience when the research is presented – is rarely considered in this work (for an exception, see Holliday 2004).

If the site of audiencing is only selectively considered in these methods, however, the site of production is much more fully part of them, since much care goes into the making of the photos or other sorts of images, whether by the researcher or the researched. These methods also demand that the researcher pay careful attention to images, either as evidence or for their effects, and this brings us to their potential as part of a critical visual methodology. These methods do pay careful attention to the images they produce, and they may well be deployed in order to examine social power relations. They also often entail careful reflection on the ethics of research. They are therefore candidates for critical visual research methods. In particular, it seems to me that they are especially effective when they engage with something that is itself visual. Whether that is the aesthetics of a work environment (Warren 2002), the texture of a place (Edensor 2005) or social identity theorized as itself increasingly visibilized (Abercrombie and Longhurst 1998; Holliday 2004), photos do analytical work most helpfully when they are used to evoke something that is itself visual, at least in part.

summary

- *associated with:*
  These methods usually use either documentary-style photographs taken by the researcher, or images – which might be photos but could also be drawings or maps, for example – made by the research subjects.

- *sites and modalities:*
  These methods usually pay careful attention to the sites of production, image and audiencing in relation to research participants, although the audiences for the finished research are somewhat neglected.

- *key terms:*
  There are no key terms.

- *strengths and weaknesses:*
  Images can present things that words cannot and can therefore be used as evidence to develop and support, or to supplement, research findings. Nonetheless, images still need to be contextualized to some degree by words.

Further reading
The recent collection edited by Caroline Knowles and Paul Sweetman (2004) offers a range of case studies that use a variety of these sorts of methods, and Marcus Banks (2001) gives a good overview of the issues, concentrating mainly on ethnographic film-making but with generous discussion of photography too.

12
visual methodologies
a review

1 introduction

This chapter concludes the book by rehearsing its central themes. Each chapter has explored a particular method for working with a particular kind of visual imagery, and the first section of this chapter will compare the methods a little more systematically than previous chapters have done. For each of these methods has its strengths and weaknesses not only in relation to the criteria for a critical visual methodology laid out in Chapter 1, but also in terms of what it is most effective in exploring empirically. These empirical foci do not concern the kinds of visual images on which each method can be deployed; although most chapters have concentrated on only one sort of visual image, every method discussed here can be applied to images other than the sort discussed in that method's chapter. Rather, the specificity of the empirical orientations of these methods concerns the sites and modalities of visual meaning-making, and this specificity leads to the other topic of this chapter: the possibility of mixing methods, in order to broaden the empirical scope of a study.

Thus this chapter will:

- briefly rehearse the arguments of Chapter 1 concerning the sites and modalities of the meanings of visual images, and place the methods so far discussed in relation to them;
- discuss the merits of mixing methods.

2 sites, modalities and methods

Chapter 1 commented that the large body of work exploring the meanings of found visual images suggests that there are three sites at which their meanings are made: the site of *production*, the site of the *image or object itself* and the site of its *audiencing*. That is, how an image is made, what it looks like and how it is seen are the three crucial ways in which a visual image has cultural and other effects. (I use the term 'image' in this discussion, but that should also imply the notion of a visual 'object', as discussed in Chapter 11, too.) Chapter 1 also suggested that each of those three sites could be understood in terms of three modalities, which it termed the *technological*, the *compositional* and the *social*. The technological concerns the tools and equipment used to make, structure and display an image; the compositional concerns the visual construction, qualities and reception of an image; and the social concerns the social, economic, political and institutional practices and relations that produce, saturate and interpret an image.

Clearly, these three sites and modalities are in practice often difficult to distinguish neatly one from another. Because of that, Figure 1.4 is an image that draws boundaries between things that are rarely so neatly divided one from another. Its lines are misleadingly solid; and, if you have been reading steadily through this book, by this point you may feel that a list of questions like the one that follows is a more appropriate way of approaching the complexity and richness of meaning in a visual image than the demarcated fields offered in Figure 1.4.

some questions about the production of an image:

- when was it made?
- where was it made?
- who made it?
- was it made for someone else?
- what technologies does its production depend on?
- what were the social identities of the maker, the owner and the subject of the image?
- what were the relations between the maker, the owner and the subject?
- does the genre of the image address these identities and relations of its production?
- does the form of the image reconstitute those identities and relations?

some questions about the image:

- what is being shown? what are the components of the image? how are they arranged?
- what is its material form?
- is it one of a series?
- where is the viewer's eye drawn to in the image, and why?
- what is the vantage point of the image?
- what relationships are established between the components of the image visually?
- what use is made of colour?
- how has its technology affected the text?
- what is, or are, the genre(s) of the image? Is it documentary, soap opera, or melodrama, for example?
- to what extent does this image draw on the characteristics of its genre?

- does this image comment critically on the characteristics of its genre?
- what do the different components of an image signify?
- what knowledges are being deployed?
- whose knowledges are excluded from this representation?
- does this image's particular look at its subject disempower its subject?
- are the relations between the components of this image unstable?
- is this a contradictory image?

some questions about audiencing:

- who were the original audience(s) for this image?
- where and how would the text have been displayed originally?
- how is it circulated?
- how is it stored?
- how is it re-displayed?
- who are the more recent audiences for this text?
- where is the spectator positioned in relation to the components of the image?
- what relation does this produce between the image and its viewers?
- is the image one of a series, and how do the preceding and subsequent images affect its meanings?
- would the image have had a written text to guide its interpretation in its initial moment of display, for example a caption or a catalogue entry?
- is the image represented elsewhere in a way that invites a particular relation to it, in publicity materials for example, or in reviews?
- have the technologies of circulation and display affected the various audiences' interpretation of this image?
- what are the conventions for viewing this technology?
- is more than one interpretation of the image possible?
- how actively does a particular audience engage with the image?
- is there any evidence that a particular audience produced a meaning for an image that differed from the meanings made at the site of its production or by the image itself?
- how do different audiences interpret this image?
- how are these audiences different from each other, in terms of class, gender, 'race', sexuality and so on?
- how do these axes of social identity structure different interpretations?

Such a long list of questions addressed to a particular visual image may be a useful starting point for your study. It may prompt new ideas because the questions ask about something you have not thought about before; or your image may suggest other questions to you that become more interesting by their absence from this list.

However, this list of questions is very eclectic. It does not suggest that any one series of questions is any more important than any other. And the usefulness of Figure 1.4 was precisely to suggest that the theoretical debates in which many of the methods discussed in this book are embedded are important because they do claim that certain sites or certain modalities are more fundamental for understanding the meaning of an image than others. That is, they suggest that some questions in that list are more important than others. So, as Chapter 1 also insisted, you need to engage with these more theoretical debates about how images mean, or how they do things, before deploying any of the methods discussed in this book.

Since many of the methods discussed here are related to specific arguments about how images become significant, it is not surprising that many of them produce quite specific empirical foci when they are used, as well as implying their own conceptual understanding of imagery. Figure 1.4 suggests what these empirical foci are – although, as section 2 in Chapter 2 noted, in some cases these foci are more a matter of what has been done so far by those researchers interested in visual matters than what the method itself might allow. This is the case, for example, in relation to the neglect of audiencing by the second type of discourse analysis discussed in Chapter 8; there does not seem to be anything in the founding arguments of that kind of discourse analysis that precludes exploring the site of audiencing, but very few of its proponents have carried out that kind of research. Instead, those sort of discourse analysts have focused on the institutional sites of image production, use and display, and on particular genres of images. On the other hand, semiology (particularly its earlier manifestations) and much psychoanalysis also neglect to explore the processes of audiencing, but this is because both claim that it is the image itself that produces its audiences' positions. Since both these theories conceptualize the image as productive of spectatorship, both have developed complex and elaborate ways of interpreting what their proponents argue are the effects of those images by looking only at the images in question. The notion that different audiences might react differently to the same image is not acknowledged conceptually, and the methodologies that flow from that conceptualization therefore also neglect the processes of audiencing. Hence it would be very difficult, using either of those methods, to explore how actual audiences make sense of images.

These sorts of considerations suggest that mixing one method with another is a useful strategy for widening the empirical focus of a research project. Whether this is in fact the case is considered in the next section.

2 mixing methods

Each of the methods discussed in this book, then, has been applied, either necessarily or contingently, on only one of the sites at which the meanings of images are made (see Figure 1.4 again). This raises the question of mixing different methods to explore more fully the range of meanings invested in an image at its different sites.

This book has already mentioned some studies that choose to use more than one method in order precisely to explore the diverse meanings that particular images carry at their various sites of production, image and reception. Catherine Lutz and Jane Collins (1993), for example, used several methods to access each of these three sites in their study of the photographs of the *National Geographic* magazine. At the site of the photographs' production, they studied the archives of the magazine and interviewed editors, journalists and photographers. At the site of the photographs themselves, they used content analysis, as Chapter 4 examined. And at the audiencing site, they used group interviews, showing different groups the same few key photographs and examining their reactions. Similarly, in her study of an exhibition in a museum, Henrietta Lidchi (1997) suggests using discourse analysis II to interpret the institutional processes that produced the exhibition's effects, and semiology for interpreting the effects of the technologies of display. We have also noted that advocates of photo-elicitation studies use content analysis to interpret their informants' photographs and then use qualitative methods on the transcripts of their interviews.

Using more than one method in this manner clearly has benefits. It allows a richly detailed picture of images' significance to be developed, and in particular it can shed interesting light on the contradictory meanings an image may articulate. The visualities articulated by producers, images and audiences may not coincide, and this may in itself be an important issue to address. Moreover, making images (as well as studying them) as part of research into the workings of visual culture could be a very productive research strategy. However, simply discovering that different sites produce different meanings may also be a rather obvious finding. And that kind of argument can easily shift into a claim that 'everyone sees things in their own way', a claim that obscures the very real power relations in which visual images – and all social life – participate. As Ang (1989: 107) argues in the context of audience studies, the critical task is to assess what the significance of diverse audience interpretations might be, not simply to mark their existence. Here, the emphasis on mobility in the anthropological approach to interpreting visual materials discussed in Chapter 10 is obviously useful. Instead of just pointing to the existence of three different sites, that approach focuses precisely on the movements of specific visual objects between different locations, which could include the sites of production and audiencing, and it examines the consequences of their effects as they travel. It is perhaps therefore better equipped to respond to Ang's (1989) concern than some more eclectic methodologies.

My assessments of methods in this book have depended on this argument about the power relations articulated through visual images. Hence the critique of compositional interpretation, mentioned in section 4.5 of Chapter 3, which in its turn to universalized notions of Art and Genius ignores the social modality of art entirely. Hence too the critique, mentioned in section 4 of Chapter 9, that studies of creative audiences often neglect the powerful effects of images' ways of seeing. And hence too the problems with Lutz and Collins's (1993) use of content analysis (discussed in section 3 of Chapter 4), where their advocacy of that method as the most 'objective' means of avoiding the unconscious interpretation of images implies that researchers are more analytically powerful than other sorts of audiences. These criticisms all depend for their force on an abiding concern for the power relations that saturate all ways of seeing: producers', images' and audiences', including researchers like us. This is important to bear in mind when mixing methods, then. Be methodologically eclectic or, even better, methodologically innovative; but do so bearing in mind the power relations that structure the connections between the different sites and modalities you want to bring together.

Finally then, I would like to reiterate the implications of the critical visual methodology outlined in Chapter 1. Precisely because images matter, because they are powerful and seductive, it is necessary to consider them critically. Whatever method you choose to use, make sure that your account acknowledges the differentiated effects of both an image's way of seeing and your own.

useful reading on visual media

picture archives and libraries

Evans, H. and Evans, M. (2001) *Picture Researcher's Handbook: An International Guide to Picture Sources and How to Use Them*, 7th edition. Leatherhead: Pira International.

fine art

Carr, D.W. and Leonard, M. (1992) *Looking at Paintings: A Guide to Technical Terms*. London: J. Paul Getty Museum in association with the British Museum Press.

Jones, A. (2006) *A Companion to Contemporary Art since 1945*. Oxford: Blackwell.

Pollard, E.B. (1986) *Visual Arts Research: A Handbook*. London: Greenwood Press.

Turner, J. (ed.) (1996) *The Dictionary of Art*, 34 vols. London: Macmillan.

Roberts, H.E. (ed.) (1998) *Encyclopedia of Comparative Iconography: Themes Depicted in Works of Art*, 2 vols. London: Fitzroy Dearborn.

Van Straten, R. (1994) *An Introduction to Iconography* (translated by P. de Man). Yverdon: Gordon and Breach.

photography

Barthes, R. (1982) *Camera Lucida: Reflections on Photography* (translated by R. Howard). London: Jonathan Cape.

Pinney, C. (2003) 'Introduction: how the other half ... photography's other histories', in C. Pinney and N. Peterson (eds) *Photography's Other Histories*. Durham, NC: Duke University Press, pp. 1–14.

Wells, L. (2004) (ed.) *Photography: A Critical Introduction*, 3rd edition. London: Routledge.

Wright, T. (1999) *The Photography Handbook*. London: Routledge.

film

Arroyo, J. (ed.) *Action/Spectacle Cinema: A Sight and Sound Reader*. London: British Film Institute.

Bordwell, D., Staiger, J. and Thompson, K. (1988) *The Classical Hollywood Cinema: Film Style and Mode of Production to 1960*. London: Routledge.

Ellis, J. (1992) *Visible Fictions: Cinema, Television, Video*, revised edition. London: Routledge.

Hayward, S. (2006) *Cinema Studies: Key Concepts*. London: Routledge.

Monaco, J. (2000) *How to Read a Film: Movies, Media, Multimedia*, 3rd edition. London: Oxford University Press.

Neale, S. and Smith, M. (eds) (1998) *Contemporary Hollywood Cinema*. London: Routledge.

Nelmes, J. (2003) *An Introduction to Film Studies*, 2nd edition, London: Routledge.

Turner, G. (2006) *Film as Social Practice*. London: Routledge.

The British Film Institute publishes a series of books on individual films and directors. You can check the full list at www.bfi.org.uk.

advertising

Botterill, J., Jhally, S., Kline, S. and Leiss, W. (2005) *Social Communication in Advertising*, 3rd edition. London: Routledge.

Dyer, G. (1982) *Advertising as Communication*. London: Methuen.

Goldman, R. (1992) *Reading Ads Socially*. London: Routledge.

McKay, J. (2005) *The Magazine Handbook*. London: Routledge.

television

Bignell, J. and Orlebar, J. (2005) *The Television Handbook*. London: Routledge.

Ellis, J. (1992) *Visible Fictions: Cinema, Television, Video*, revised edition. London: Routledge.

Miller, T. (ed.) (2000) *Television*. London: Routledge.

Silverstone, R. (1994) *Television and Everyday Life*. London: Routledge.

Williams, R. (1989) *Raymond Williams on Television: Selected Writings* (edited by A. O'Connor). London: Routledge.

The British Film Institute publishes a series of books on British television series. You can check the full list at www.bfi.org.uk.

video

Ellis, J. (1992) *Visible Fictions: Cinema, Television, Video*, revised edition. London: Routledge.

Monaco, J. (2000) *How to Read a Film: Movies, Media, Multimedia*, 3rd edition. London: Oxford University Press.

maps

Cosgrove, D. (ed.) *Mappings*. London: Reaktion Books.

Harley, J.B. (1992) 'Deconstructing the map', in T.J. Barnes and J.S. Duncan (eds) *Writing Worlds: Discourse, Text and Metaphor in the Representation of Landscape*. London: Routledge, pp. 231–47.

medical images

Cartwright, L. (1995) *Screening the Body: Tracing Medicine's Visual Culture*. Minneapolis: Minnesota University Press.
McGrath, R. (2002) *Seeing Her Sex: Medical Archives and the Female Body*. Manchester: Manchester University Press.

visualizing data

Tufte, E.R. (1990) *Envisioning Information*. Cheshire: Graphics Press.
Tufte, E.R. (1997) *Visual and Statistical Thinking: Displays of Evidence for Making Decisions*. Cheshire: Graphics Press.

references

Abercrombie, N. and Longhurst, B. (1998) *Audiences: A Sociological Theory of Performance and Imagination*. London: Sage.
Acton, M. (1997) *Learning to Look at Paintings*. London: Routledge.
Adler, J. (1989) 'Origins of sightseeing', *Annals of Tourism Research* 16, 7–29.
Alasuutari, P. (1999) 'Introduction: three phases of reception studies', in P. Alasuutari (ed.) *Rethinking the Media Audience: The New Agenda*. London: Sage, pp. 1–21.
Alpers, S. (1983) *The Art of Describing: Dutch Art in the Seventeenth Century*. London: John Murray.
Andersen, N.A. (2003) *Discursive Analytical Strategies: Understanding Foucault, Koselleck, Laclau, Luhmann*. Bristol: Policy Press.
Andrews, S. (1995) *Story and Space in Renaissance Art*. Cambridge: Cambridge University Press.
Ang, I. (1985) *Watching Dallas*. London: Methuen.
Ang, I. (1989) 'Wanted: Audiences. On the politics of empirical audience studies', in E. Seiter, H. Borchers, G. Kreutzner and E.-M. Warth (eds) *Remote Control: Television, Audiences, and Cultural Power*. London: Routledge, pp. 96–105.
Ang, I. (1991) *Desperately Seeking the Audience*. London: Routledge.
Appadurai, A. (1986) 'Introduction: commodities and the politics of value', in A. Appadurai (ed.) *The Social Life of Things: Commodities in Cultural Perspective*. Cambridge: Cambridge University Press, pp. 3–63.
Armstrong, C. (1996) 'Visual culture questionnaire', *October* 77, 26–8.
Armstrong, C. (1998) *Scenes in a Library: Reading the Photograph in the Book*. London: MIT Press.
Arroyo, J. (2000) 'Mission: sublime', in J. Arroyo (ed.) *Action/Spectacle Cinema: A Sight and Sound Reader*. London: British Film Institute, pp. 21–5.
Back, L. and Quaade, V. (1993) 'Dream utopias, nightmare realities: imagining race and culture within the world of Benetton', *Third Text* 22, 65–80.
Bal, M. (1991) *Reading Rembrandt: Beyond the Word–Image Opposition*. Cambridge: Cambridge University Press.
Bal, M. (1996) *Double Exposures: The Subject of Cultural Analysis*. London: Routledge.
Bal, M. and Bryson, N. (1991) 'Semiotics and art history', *Art Bulletin* 73, 174–208.

Bal, M. (2003) 'Visual essentialism and the object of visual culture', *Journal of Visual Culture* 2, 5–32.

Ball, M.S. and Smith, G.W.H. (1992) *Analysing Visual Data*. London: Sage.

Banks, M. (2001) *Visual Methods in Social Research*. London: Sage.

Bann, S. (1998) 'Art history and museums', in M.A. Cheetham, M.A. Holly and K. Moxey (eds) *The Subjects of Art History: Historical Objects in Contemporary Perspective*. Cambridge: Cambridge University Press, pp. 230–49.

Barbash, I. and Taylor, L. (1997) *Cross-Cultural Filmmaking: A Handbook for Making Documentary and Ethnographic Films and Video*. Berkeley, CA: California University Press.

Barker, E. (ed.) (1999) *Contemporary Cultures of Display*. London: Yale University Press in association with The Open University.

Barnard, M. (2001) *Approaches to Understanding Visual Culture*. Houndmills: Palgrave.

Barrett, M. (1991) *The Politics of Truth: From Marx to Foucault*. Cambridge: Polity Press.

Barthes, R. (1973) *Mythologies* (translated by A. Lavers). London: Paladin.

Barthes, R. (1977) *Image–Music–Text* (edited and translated by S. Heath). London: Fontana.

Barthes, R. (1982) *Camera Lucida: Reflections on Photography* (translated by R. Howard). London: Jonathan Cape.

Batchen, G. (2001) *Each Wild Idea: Writing, Photography, History*. Boston, MA: MIT Press

Battersby, C. (1994) *Gender and Genius: Towards a Feminist Aesthetics*. London: Women's Press.

Baudrillard, J. (1988) *Selected Writings*. (edited by M. Poster). Cambridge: Polity Press.

Baxandall, M. (1972) *Painting and Experience in Fifteenth Century Italy: A Primer in the Social History of Pictorial Style*. Oxford: Oxford University Press.

Becker, H. (1982) *Art Worlds*. Berkeley, CA: University of California Press.

Becker, H. (1998) 'Visual sociology, documentary photography and photojournalism: it's (almost) all a matter of context', in J. Prosser (ed.) *Image-Based Research: A Sourcebook for Qualitative Researchers*. London: Falmer Press, pp. 84–96.

Becker, H. (2002) 'Visual evidence: a Seventh Man, the specified generalization, and the work of the reader', *Visual Studies* 17, 3–11.

Becker, H. (2004) 'Afterword: photography as evidence, photographs as exposition', in C. Knowles and J. Sweetman (eds) *Picturing the Social Landscape: Visual Methods and the Sociological Imagination*. London: Routledge, pp. 193–7.

Bedaux, J.B. (1986) 'The reality of symbols', *Semiolus* 16, 5–28.

Bell, P. (2001) 'Content analysis of visual images', in T. van Leeuwen and C. Jewitt (eds) *Handbook of Visual Analysis*. London: Sage, pp. 10–34.

Bennett, T. (1995) *The Birth of the Museum: History, Theory, Politics*. London: Routledge.

Berger, J. (1972) *Ways of Seeing*. London: British Broadcasting Association, and Harmondsworth: Penguin.

Berger, J. and Mohr, J. (1975) *A Seventh Man*. Harmondsworth: Penguin.

Bird, J. et al. (eds) (1996) *The BLOCK Reader in Visual Culture*. London: Routledge.

Bird, J., Curtis, B., Mash, M., Putnam, T., Robertson, G., Stafford, S. and Tickner, L. (eds) (1996) *The BLOCK Reader in Visual Culture*. London: Routledge.

Blaikie, A. (2001) 'Photographs in the cultural account: contested narratives and collective memory in the Scottish Highlands', *Sociological Review* 49, 345–67.

Blinn, L. and Harrist, A.W. (1991) 'Combining native instant photography and photo-elicitation', *Visual Anthropology* 4, 175–92.

Bolton, A., Pole, C. and Mizen, P. (2001) 'Picture this: researching child workers', *Sociology* 35, 501–18.

Bolton, R. (1989) 'In the American West: Richard Avedon Incorporated', in R. Bolton (ed.) *The Contest of Meaning: Critical Histories of Photography*. London: MIT Press, pp. 261–82.

Bordo, S. (1993) *Unbearable Weight: Feminism, Western Culture, and the Body*. Berkeley, CA: California University Press.

Bourdieu, P. (1984) *Distinction: A Social Critique of the Judgement of Taste* (translated by R. Nice). London: Routledge and Kegan Paul.

Bourdieu, P. and Darbel, A. with Schnapper, D. (1991) *The Love of Art: European Art Museums and Their Public*. Cambridge: Polity Press.

Bourdieu, P., with Boltanski, L., Castel, R., Chamboredun, J.-C. and Schnapper, D. (1990) *Photography: A Middle-Brow Art* (translated by S. Whiteside). Cambridge: Polity Press.

Bowie, M. (1991) *Lacan*. London: Fontana.

Brennan, T. and Jay, M. (eds) (1996) *Vision in Context: Historical and Contemporary Perspectives on Sight*. London: Routledge.

Bronfen, E. (1992) 'Castration complex', in E. Wright (ed.) *Feminism and Psychoanalysis: A Critical Dictionary*. Oxford: Blackwell, pp. 41–5.

Brooker, W. and Jermyn, D. (2003) *The Audience Studies Reader*. London: Routledge.

Bruno, G. (1993) *Streetwalking on a Ruined Map: Cultural Theory and the City Films of Elivira Notari*. Princeton, NJ: Princeton University Press.

Bruno, G. (2002) *Atlas of Emotion: Journeys in Art, Architecture and Film*. London: Verso.

Bryson, N. (1988) 'The gaze in the expanded field', in H. Foster (ed.) *Vision and Visuality*. Seattle, WA: Bay Press, pp. 87–108.

Bryson, N. (1991) 'Semiology and visual interpretation', in N. Bryson, M.A. Holly and K. Moxey (eds) *Visual Theory: Painting and Interpretation*. Cambridge: Polity Press, pp. 61–73.

Bryson, N. (2001) 'Introduction: art and intersubjectivity photography's centrality to various colonial and imperial projects', in M. Bal and N. Bryson, *Looking In: The Art of Viewing*. London: Routledge, pp. 1–39.

Bryson, N., Holly, M.A. and Moxey, K. (1994) 'Introduction', in N. Bryson, M.A. Holly and K. Moxey (eds) *Visual Culture: Images and Interpretations*. London: Wesleyan University Press of New England, pp. xv–xxix.

Buckingham, D. (1987) *Public Secrets: East Enders and Its Audience*. London: British Film Institute.

Buckingham, D. (1991) 'What are words worth? Interpreting children's talk about television', *Cultural Studies* 5, 228–45.

Burgin, V. (1986) *The End of Art Theory: Criticism and Postmodernity*. Basingstoke: Macmillan.

Burgin, V. (1992) 'Fantasy', in E. Wright (ed.) *Feminism and Psychoanalysis: A Critical Dictionary*. Oxford: Blackwell, pp. 84–8.

Butler, J. (1990) *Gender Trouble: Feminism and the Subversion of Identity*. London: Routledge.

Celant, G. (1996) 'A visual machine: art installation and its modern archetypes', in R. Greenberg, B.W. Ferguson and S. Nairne (eds) *Thinking About Exhibitions*. London: Routledge, pp. 371–86.

Chakrabarty, D. (2000) *Provincialising Europe: Postcolonial Thought and Historical Difference*. Princeton, NJ: Princeton University Press.

Chalfen, R. (1987) *Snapshot Versions of Life*. Bowling Green, OH: Bowling Green State University Popular Press.

Cheetham, M.A., Holly, M.A. and Moxey, K. (2005) 'Visual studies, historiography and aesthetics', *Journal of Visual Culture* 4, 75–90.

Cherry, D. (2005) *Art : History : Visual : Culture*. Oxford: Blackwell.

Cohan, S. and Hark, I.R. (eds) (1993) *Screening the Male: Exploring Masculinities in Hollywood Cinema*. London: Routledge.

Collier, J. (1967) *Visual Anthropology: Photography as a Research Method*. New York: Holt, Rinehart and Winston.

Collier, M. (2001) 'Approaches to analysis in visual anthropology', in T. van Leeuwen and C. Jewitt (eds) *Handbook of Visual Analysis*. London: Sage, pp. 35–60.

Coombes, A. (1994) *Reinventing Africa: Museums, Material Culture and Popular Imagination in Late Victorian and Edwardian England*. London: Yale University Press.

Cooper, M.G. (2002) 'Narrative spaces', *Screen* 43, 139–57.

Copjec, J. (1989) 'The orthopsychic subject: film theory and the reception of Lacan', *October* 49, 53–72.

Corbett, D.P. (2005) 'Visual culture and the history of art', in C. van Eck and E. Winters (eds) *Dealing with the Visual: Art History, Aesthetics and Visual Culture*. Aldershot: Ashgate, pp. 17–36.

Court, E. (1999) 'Africa on display: exhibiting art by Africans', in E. Barker (ed.) *Contemporary Cultures of Display*. London: Yale University Press in association with The Open University, pp. 147–73.

Cowie, E. (1990) 'Fantasia', in P. Adams and E. Cowie (eds) *The Woman in Question: m/f*. London: Verso, pp. 149–96.

Cowling, M. (1989) *The Artist as Anthropologist: The Representation of Type and Character in Victorian Art*. Cambridge: Cambridge University Press.

Crary, J. (1992) *Techniques of the Observer: Vision and Modernity in the Nineteenth Century*. London: MIT Press.

Csikszentmihalyi, M. and Rochberg-Halton, E. (1981) *The Meaning of Things: Domestic Symbols and the Self*. Cambridge: Cambridge University Press.

Curtis, L.P. (2001) *Jack the Ripper and the London Press*. London: Yale University Press.

Dayan, D. and Katz, E. (1992) *Media Events: The Live Broadcasting of History*. Cambridge, MA: Harvard University Press.

De Lauretis, T. (1994) *The Practice of Love: Lesbian Sexuality and Perverse Desire*. Bloomington, IN: Indiana University Press.

De Lauretis, T. (1995) 'On the subject of fantasy', in L. Pietropaulo and A. Testaferri (eds) *Feminisms in the Cinema*. Bloomington, IN: Indiana University Press, pp. 63–5.

Debord, G. (1977) *Society of the Spectacle*. Detroit, IL: Black and Red.

Deutsche, R. (1991) 'Boys town', *Environment and Planning D: Society and Space* 9, 5–30.

Dey, I. (1993) *Qualitative Data Analysis: A User-Friendly Guide for Social Scientists*. London: Routledge.

Dikovitskaya, M. (2005) *Visual Culture: The Study of the Visual After the Cultural Turn*. Boston, MA: MIT Press.

Doane, M.A. (1982) 'Film and the masquerade: theorising the female spectator', *Screen* 3, 74–87.

Doane, M.A. (1987) *The Desire to Desire: The Woman's Film of the 1940s*. Bloomington, IN: Indiana University Press.

Doane, M.A. (1991) *Femmes Fatales: Feminism, Film Theory, Psychoanalysis*. London: Routledge.

Dodman, D.R. (2003) 'Shooting in the city: an autophotographic exploration of the urban environment in Kingston, Jamaica', *Area* 35, 293–304.

Doisneau, R. (1990) *Renault: In the Thirties* (edited by M. Koetzle). London: Dirk Nishen.

Doisneau, R. (1991) *Robert Doisneau: Interview with Robert Doisneau by Sylvain Roumette*. London: Thames & Hudson.

Driessens, J.-A. (2003) 'Relating to photographs', in C. Pinney and N. Peterson (eds) *Photography's Other Histories*. Durham, NC: Duke University Press, pp. 17–22.

Duncan, C. (1993) *The Aesthetics of Power: Essays in Critical Art History*. Cambridge: Cambridge University Press.

Duncan, C. (1995) *Civilising Rituals: Inside Public Art Museums*. London: Routledge.

Dyer, G. (1982) *Advertising as Communication*. London: Methuen.

Dyer, R. (1982) 'Don't look now: the male pin-up', *Screen* 23, 61–73.

Dyer, R. (1990) *Now You See It: Historical Studies on Lesbian and Gay Film*. London: Routledge.

Dyer, R. (1997) *White*. London: Routledge.

Eakins, R. and Loving, E. (1985) *Picture Sources UK*. London: MacDonald.

Edensor, T. (2005) *Industrial Ruins: Space, Aesthetics and Modernity*. Oxford: Berg.

Edgerton, S.Y. (1975) *The Renaissance Rediscovery of Perspective*. New York: Harper and Row.

Edwards, E. (2001) *Raw Histories: Photographs, Anthropology and Museums*. Oxford: Berg.

Edwards, E. (2002) 'Material beings: objecthood and ethnographic photographs', *Visual Studies* 17, 67–75.

Edwards, E. (ed.) (1992) *Anthropology and Photography, 1860–1920*. London: Yale University Press and the Royal Anthropological Institute.

Edwards, E. and Hart, J. (2004) 'Introduction: photographs as objects', in E. Edwards and J. Hart (eds) *Photographs Objects Histories: On the Materiality of Images*. London: Routledge, pp. 1–15.

Elkins, J. (1991) 'On the *Arnolfini Portrait* and the *Luca Madonna*: did Jan van Eyck have a perspectival system?' *Art Bulletin* LXXIII, 53–62.

Elkins, J. (1994) *The Poetics of Perspective*. Ithaca, NY: Cornell University Press.

Elkins, J. (1998) *On Pictures and the Words That Fail Them*. Cambridge: Cambridge University Press.

Ellis, J. (1992) *Visible Fictions: Cinema, Television, Video*, revised edition. London: Routledge.

Emmison, M. and Smith, P. (2000) *Researching the Visual: Images, Objects, Contexts and Interactions in Social and Cultural Inquiry*. London: Sage.

ESRC (2006) *Research Ethics Framework*. www.esrcsocietytoday.ac.uk/ESRCInfo Centre/Images/ESRC_RE_Ethics_Frame_tcm6-11291.pdf. (Accessed 29 March 2006.)

Evans, J. (2000) 'Photography', in F. Carson and C. Pajaczkowska (eds) *Feminist Visual Culture*. Edinburgh: Edinburgh University Press, pp. 105–20.

Evans, J. (2006) *Visual Culture*. London: Sage.

Evans, J. and Hall, S. (1999) *Visual Culture: The Reader*. London: Sage in association with The Open University.

Evans, H. and Evans, M. (2001) *Picture Researcher's Handbook: An International Guide to Picture Sources and How to Use Them*, 7th edition. Leatherhead: Pira International.

Fairclough, N. (1995) *Critical Discourse Analysis: The Critical Study of Language*. London: Longman.

Fanon, F. (1986) *Black Skin, White Masks*. New York: Grove Press.

Faris, J. (1996) *Navajo and Photography*. Albuquerque, NM: University of New Mexico Press.

Fernie, E. (1995) *Art History and Its Methods: A Critical Anthology*. London: Phaidon.

Fishman, W.J. (1988) *East End, 1888*. London: Duckworth.

Fiske, J. (1994) 'Audiencing', in N.K. Denzin and Y.S. Lincoln (eds) *Handbook of Qualitative Methods*. London: Sage.

Foster, H. (1988a) 'Preface', in H. Foster (ed.) *Vision and Visuality*. Seattle, WA: Bay Press, pp. ix–xiv.

Foster, H. (ed.) (1988) *Vision and Visuality*. Seattle, WA: Bay Press.

Foster, H. (1996) 'The archive without museums', *October* 77, 97–119.

Foucault, M. (1972) *The Archaeology of Knowledge* (translated by A.M. Sheridan Smith). London: Tavistock Publications.

Foucault, M. (1977) *Discipline and Punish: The Birth of the Prison* (translated by A. Sheridan). London: Allen Lane.

Foucault, M. (1979) *The History of Sexuality, Volume I: An Introduction* (translated by R. Hurley). London: Allen Lane.

Fyfe, G. and Law. J. (1988) 'Introduction: on the invisibility of the visible', in G. Fyfe and J. Law (eds) *Picturing Power: Visual Depiction and Social Relations*. London: Routledge, pp. 1–14.

Fyfe, G. and Ross, M. (1996) 'Decoding the visitor's gaze: rethinking museum visiting', in S. MacDonald and G. Fyfe (eds) *Theorizing Museums*. Blackwell: Oxford, pp. 127–50.

Gage, J. (1993) *Colour and Culture: Practice and Meaning from Antiquity to Abstraction*. London: Thames & Hudson.

Gaines, J. (1988) 'White privilege and looking relations: race and gender in feminist film theory', *Screen* 29, 12–27.

Gell, A. (1998) *Art and Agency: An Anthropological Theory*. Oxford: Clarendon Press.

Gilbert, R. (1995) *Living With Art*, 4th edition. London: McGraw Hill.

Gill, R. (1996) 'Discourse analysis: practical implementation', in J.T.E. Richardson (ed.) *Handbook of Qualitative Methods for Psychology and the Social Sciences*. Leicester: British Psychological Society, pp. 141–56.

Gillespie, M. (1995) *Television, Ethnicity and Cultural Change*. London: Routledge.

Gillespie, M. (ed.) (2005) *Media Audiences*. Maidenhead: The Open University Press.

Gillespie, M. (2005a) 'Television drama and audience ethnography', in M. Gillespie (ed.) *Media Audiences*. Maidenhead: The Open University Press, pp. 137–82.

Gillespie, M. (2005b) 'Introduction', in M. Gillespie (ed.) *Media Audiences*. Maidenhead: The Open University Press, pp. 1–8.

Gilman, S. (1985) *Difference and Pathology: Stereotypes of Sexuality, Race and Madness*. Ithaca, NY: Cornell University Press.

Gilman, S. (1990) '"I'm down on whores": race and gender in Victorian London', in D. Goldberg (ed.) *The Anatomy of Racism*. Minneapolis, MN: Minnesota University Press, pp. 146–70.

Gilroy, P. (1987) *There Ain't No Black in the Union Jack: The Cultural Politics of Race and Nation*. London: Hutchinson.

Goin, P. (2002) 'Where the pavement ends', *Geographical Review* 92, 545–55.

Goldman, R. (1992) *Reading Ads Socially*. London: Routledge.

Goodwin, C. (2001) 'Practices of seeing visual analysis: an ethnomethodological approach', in T. van Leeuwen and C. Jewitt (eds) *Handbook of Visual Analysis*. London: Sage, pp. 157–82.

Grady, J. (2004) 'Working with visible evidence: an invitation and some practical advice', in C. Knowles and J. Sweetman (eds) *Picturing the Social Landscape: Visual Methods and the Sociological Imagination*. London: Routledge, pp. 18–32.

Graham-Brown, S. (1988) *Images of Women: The Portrayal of Women in Photography of the Middle East, 1860–1950*. London: Quartet.

Gray, A. (1992) *Video Playtime: The Gendering of a Leisure Technology*. London: Routledge.

Green, N. (1990) *The Spectacle of Nature: Landscape and Bourgeois Nature in Nineteenth-Century France*. Manchester: Manchester University Press.

Greenberg, R., Ferguson, B.W. and Nairne, S. (eds) (1996) *Thinking About Exhibitions*. London: Routledge.

Griffiths, A. (2002) *Wondrous Difference: Cinema, Anthropology and Turn-of-the-Century Visual Culture*. New York: Columbia University Press.

Grunenberg, C. (1999) 'The modern art museum', in E. Barker (ed.) *Contemporary Cultures of Display*. London: Yale University Press in association with The Open University, pp. 26–49.

Guillemin, M. (2004) 'Understanding illness: using drawings as a research method', *Qualitative Health Research* 14, 272–89.

Hall, E. (1994) *The Arnolfini Betrothal*. Berkeley, CA: California University Press.

Hall, S. (1980) 'Encoding/decoding', in Centre for Contemporary Cultural Studies *Culture, Media, Language: Working Papers in Cultural Studies*. London: Hutchinson, pp. 128–38.

Hall, S. (1991) 'Reconstruction work: images of post-war black settlement', in J. Spence and P. Holland (eds) *Family Snaps*. London: Virago.

Hall, S. (1996) 'Introduction: who needs identity?', in S. Hall and P. du Gay (eds) *Questions of Cultural Identity*. London: Sage, pp. 1–17.

Hall, S. (1997a) 'Introduction', in S. Hall (ed.) *Representation: Cultural Representations and Signifying Practices*. London: Sage, pp. 1–12.

Hall, S. (1997b) 'The work of representation', in S. Hall (ed.) *Representation: Cultural Representations and Signifying Practices*. London: Sage, pp. 13–74.

Hall, S. (1999) 'Introduction: looking and subjectivity', in J. Evans and S. Hall (eds) *Visual Culture: The Reader*. London: Sage, pp. 309–14.

Halle, D. (1993) *Inside Culture: Art and Class in the American Home*. Chicago, IL: Chicago University Press.

Hamburger, J.F. (1997) *Nuns as Artists: The Visual Culture of a Medieval Convent*. Berkeley, CA: California University Press.

Hamilton, P. (1997) 'Representing the social: France and Frenchness in post-war humanist photography', in S. Hall (ed.) *Representation: Cultural Representations and Signifying Practices*. London: Sage, pp. 75–150.

Haraway, D. (1989) *Primate Visions: Gender, Race, and Nature in the World of Modern Science*. London: Routledge.

Haraway, D. (1991) *Simians, Cyborgs, and Women: The Reinvention of Nature*. London: Free Association Books.

Harper, D. (2002) 'Talking about pictures: a case for photo-elicitation', *Visual Studies* 17, 13–26.

Harvey, D. (1989) *The Condition of Postmodernity*. Oxford: Blackwell.

Henare, A. (2003) 'Artefacts in theory: anthropology and material culture', *Cambridge Anthropology* 23, 54–66.

Henare, A. (2005) *Museums, Anthropology and Colonial Exchange*. Cambridge: Cambridge University Press.

Hetherington, K. (1997) 'Museum topology and the will to connect', *Journal of Material Culture* 2, 199–218.

Hodge, R. and Kress, G. (1988) *Social Semiotics*. Cambridge: Polity Press.

Holliday, R. (2004) 'Reflecting the self', in C. Knowles and J. Sweetman (eds) *Picturing the Social Landscape: Visual Methods and the Sociological Imagination*. London: Routledge, pp. 49–64.

Holly, M.A. (1996) *Past Looking: Historical Imagination and the Rhetoric of the Image*. Ithaca, NY: Cornell University Press.

Hooper-Greenhill, E. (1992) *Museums and the Shaping of Knowledge*. London: Routledge.

Hooper-Greenhill, E. (1994) *Museums and Their Visitors*. London: Routledge.

Howells, R. (2003) *Visual Culture*. Cambridge: Polity Press.

Iginla, B. (1992) 'Black feminist critique of psychoanalysis', in E. Wright (ed.) *Feminism and Psychoanalysis: A Critical Dictionary*. Oxford: Blackwell, pp. 31–3.

Irigaray, L. (1985) *This Sex Which is Not One* (translated by C. Porter). Ithaca, NY: Cornell University Press.

Iversen, M. (1986) 'Saussure v. Pierce: models for a semiotics of visual art', in A.L. Rees and F. Borzello (eds) *The New Art History*. London: Camden Press, pp. 82–94.

Jacobs, D.L. (1981) 'Domestic snapshots: towards a grammar of motives', *Journal of American Culture* 4, 93–105.

Jameson, F. (1984) 'Postmodernism, or the cultural logic of late capitalism', *New Left Review* 146, 53–92.

Jancovich, M. (1992) 'David Morley, The *Nationwide* studies', in M. Barker and A. Beezer (eds) *Reading into Cultural Studies*. London: Routledge, pp. 134–47.

Jay, M. (1993) *Downcast Eyes: The Denigration of Vision in Twentieth-Century French Thought*. Berkeley, CA: California University Press.

Jenks, C. (1995) 'The centrality of the eye in Western culture', in C. Jenks (ed.) *Visual Culture*. London: Routledge, pp. 1–12.

Jewitt, C. and Oyama, R. (2001) 'Visual meaning: a semiotic approach', in T. van Leeuwen and C. Jewitt (eds) *Handbook of Visual Analysis*. London: Sage, pp. 134–56.

Jones, G.S. (1976) *Outcast London: A Study in the Relationship between Classes in Victorian Society*. London: Peregrine Books.

Jones, G.S. (1989) 'The 'cockney' and the nation, 1780–1988', in D. Feldman and G.S. Jones (eds) *Metropolis London: Histories and Representations since 1800*. London: Routledge, pp. 272–324.

Kearney, K.S. and Hyle, A.E. (2004) 'Drawing out emotions: the use of participant-produced drawings in qualitative inquiry', *Qualitative Research* 4, 361–82.

Keating, P. (1976) 'Introduction', in P. Keating (ed.) *Into Unknown England, 1866–1913: Selections from the Social Explorers*. London: Fontana, pp. 11–32.

Kendall, G. and Wickham, G. (1999) *Using Foucault's Methods*. London: Sage.

Knowles, C. and Sweetman, P. (2004) 'Introduction', in C. Knowles and J. Sweetman (eds) *Picturing the Social Landscape: Visual Methods and the Sociological Imagination*. London: Routledge, pp. 1–17.

Kress, G. and van Leeuwen, T. (1996) *Reading Images: The Grammar of Visual Design*. London: Routledge.

Krippendorf, K. (1980) *Content Analysis: An Introduction to its Methodologies*. London: Sage.

Kunimoto, N. (2004) 'Intimate archives: Japanese-Canadian family photography, 1939–49', *Art History* 27, 129–55.

Lacan, J. (1977) *The Four Fundamental Concepts of Psychoanalysis* (translated by A. Sheridan). London: Hogarth Press.

Lalvani, S. (1996) *Photography, Vision and the Production of Modern Bodies*. Albany, NY: SUNY Press.

Latham, A. (2003) 'Research, performance, and doing human geography: some reflections on the diary-photograph, diary-interview method', *Environment and Planning A* 35, 1993–2017.

Latham, A. (2004) 'Research and writing everyday accounts of the city: an introduction to the diary–photo–diary–interview method', in C. Knowles and J. Sweetman (eds) *Picturing the Social Landscape: Visual Methods and the Sociological Imagination*. London: Routledge, pp. 117–31.

Leiss, W., Kline, S. and Jhally, S. (1986) *Social Communication in Advertising: Persons, Products and Images of Well-Being*. London: Methuen.

Lewis, L.A. (2004) 'Modesty and modernity: photography, race and representation on Mexico's Costa Chica (Guerrero)', *Identities: Global Studies in Culture and Power* 11, 471–99.

Lidchi, H. (1997) 'The poetics and politics of exhibition in other cultures', in S. Hall (ed.) *Representation: Cultural Representations and Signifying Practices*. London: Sage, pp. 151–222.

Lister, M. and Wells, L. (2001) 'Seeing beyond belief: cultural studies as an approach to studying the visual', in T. van Leeuwen and C. Jewitt (eds) *Handbook of Visual Analysis*. London: Sage, pp. 61–91.

Livesy, R. (2004) 'Reading for character: women social reformers and narratives of the urban poor in late Victorian and Edwardian London', *Journal of Victorian Culture* 9, 43–67.

Livingstone, S. (2005) 'Media audiences, interpreters and users', in M. Gillespie (ed.) *Media Audiences*. Maidenhead: Open University Press, pp. 9–50.

Luke, T.W. (2002) *Museum Politics: Power Plays at the Exhibition*. Minneapolis, MN: Minnesota University Press.

Lull, J. (1990) *Inside Family Viewing: Ethnographic Research on Television's Audiences*. London: Routledge.

Lutz, C.A. and Collins, J.L. (1993) *Reading National Geographic*. Chicago, IL: University of Chicago Press.

Lyman, C.M. (1982) *The Vanishing Race and Other Illusions: Photographs of Indians by Edward S. Curtis*. Washington, DC: Smithsonian Institute.

Lyotard, J.-F. (1996) 'Les immaterieux', in R. Greenberg, B.W. Ferguson and S. Nairne (eds) *Thinking About Exhibitions*. London: Routledge, pp. 113–31.

Marcus, G.E. and Myers, F.R. (eds) (1995) *The Traffic in Culture: Refiguring Art and Anthropology*. Berkeley, CA: California University Press.

Mauad, A.M., Rouverol, A.J. and Chatterley, C.N. (2004) 'Telling the story of Linda Lord through photographs', in C. Knowles and J. Sweetman (eds) *Picturing the Social Landscape: Visual Methods and the Sociological Imagination*. London: Routledge, pp. 178–94.

Mayne, J. (1993) *Cinema and Spectatorship*. London: Routledge.

McCarthy, A. (2001) *Ambient Television: Visual Culture and Public Space*. Durham, NC: Duke University Press.

McIntyre, A. (2003) 'Through the eyes of women: photovoice and participatory research as tools for reimagining place', *Gender, Place and Culture* 10, 47–66.

McQuail, D. (1997) *Audience Analysis*. London: Sage.

Miles, M.B. and Hubermann A.M. (1994) *Qualitative Data Analysis: An Expanded Source Book*, 2nd edition. London: Sage.

Miller, D. and Slater, D. (2000) *The Internet: An Ethnographic Approach*. Oxford: Berg.

Mirzoeff, N. (1998) 'What is visual culture?', in N. Mirzoeff (ed.) *The Visual Culture Reader*. London: Routledge, pp. 3–13.

Mirzoeff, N. (1999) *An Introduction to Visual Culture*. London: Routledge.

Mitchell, J. (1974) *Psychoanalysis and Feminism*. London: Allen Lane.

Mitchell, T. (1988) *Colonising Egypt*. Cambridge: Cambridge University Press.

Mitchell, W.J.T. (1994) *Picture Theory: Essays on Verbal and Visual Representation*. Chicago: Chicago University Press.

Mitchell, W.J.T. (1996) 'What do pictures *really* want?' *October* 77, 71–82.

Modleski, T. (1986) 'Feminism and the power of interpretation', in T. de Lauretis (ed.) *Feminist Studies/Critical Studies*. Basingstoke: Macmillan.

Modleski, T. (1988) *The Women Who Knew Too Much: Hitchcock and Feminist Theory*. London: Methuen.

Monaco, J. (2000) *How to Read a Film: Movies, Media, Multimedia*, 3rd edition. London: Oxford University Press.

Moores, S. (1993) *Interpreting Audiences: The Ethnography of Media Consumption*. London: Sage.

Morley, D. (1980) *The Nationwide Audience: Structure and Decoding*. London: British Film Institute.

Morley, D. (1986) *Family Television*. London: Routledge.

Morley, D. (1992) *Television, Audiences and Cultural Studies*. London: Routledge.

Morley, D. and Robins, K. (1995) *Spaces of Identity: Global Media, Electronic Landscapes and Cultural Boundaries*. London: Routledge.

Mulvey, L. (1989) *Visual and Other Pleasures*. London: Macmillan.

Myers, F.R. (2001) 'Introduction: the empire of things', in F.R. Myers (ed.) *The Empire of Things: Regimes of Value and Material Culture*. Oxford: James Currey, pp. 3–61.

Myers, F.R. (2002) *Painting Culture: The Making of Aboriginal High Art*. Durham, NC: Duke University Press.

Myers, K. (1983) 'Understanding advertisers', in H. Davis and P. Walton (eds) *Language, Image, Media*. Oxford: Blackwell, pp. 205–23.

Nead, L. (1988) *Myths of Sexuality: Representations of Women in Victorian Britain*. Oxford: Blackwell.

Nead, L. (2000) *Victorian Babylon: People, Streets and Images in Nineteenth-Century London*. London: Yale University Press.

Neale, S. (1983) 'Masculinity as spectacle', *Screen* 24.

Neuendorf, K.A. (2002) *The Content Analysis Guidebook*. London: Sage.

Nightingale, V. (1996) *Studying Audiences: The Shock of the Real*. London: Routledge.

Nochlin, L. (1989) *Women, Art and Power and Other Essays*. London: Thames & Hudson.

O'Doherty, B. (1996) 'The gallery as gesture', in R. Greenberg, B.W. Ferguson and S. Nairne (eds) *Thinking About Exhibitions*. London: Routledge, pp. 321–40.

O'Toole, M. (1994) *The Language of Displayed Art*. Leicester: Leicester University Press.

Okely, J. (1994) 'Thinking through fieldwork', in A. Bryman and A. Burgess (eds) *Analysing Qualitative Data*. London: Routledge, pp. 18–34.

Osborne, P. (2000) *Travelling Light: Photography, Travel and Visual Culture*. Manchester: Manchester University Press.

Panofsky, E. (1953) *Early Netherlandish Painting: Its Origin and Character, Volume I*. Cambridge, MA: Harvard University Press.

Panofsky, E. (1957) *Meaning in the Visual Arts*. New York: Doubleday Anchor.

Phillips, N. and Hardy, C. (2002) *Discourse Analysis: Investigating Processes of Social Construction*. London: Sage.

Pink, S. (2006) *Doing Visual Ethnography: Images, Media and Representation in Research* 2nd edition. London: Sage.

Pinney, C. (1997) *Camera Indica: The Social Life of Indian Photographs*. London: Reaktion Books.

Pinney, C. (2003) 'Introduction: how the other half ... photography's other histories', in C. Pinney and N. Peterson (eds) *Photography's Other Histories*. Durham, NC: Duke University Press, pp. 1–14.

Pinney, C. (2004) *'Photos of the Gods': The Printed Image and Political Struggle in India*. London: Reaktion Books.

Pollock, G. (1988) *Vision and Difference: Femininity, Feminism and the Histories of Art*. London: Routledge.

Pollock, G. (1992) 'Art', in E. Wright (ed.) *Feminism and Psychoanalysis: A Critical Dictionary*. Oxford: Blackwell, pp. 9–16.

Pollock, G. (1994) '"With my own eyes": fetishism, the labouring body and the colour of its sex', *Art History* 17, 342–82.

Poole, D. (1997) *Vision, Race and Modernity: A Visual Economy of the Andean Image World*. Princeton, NJ: Princeton University Press.

Potter, J. (1996) 'Discourse analysis and constructionist approaches: theoretical background', in J.T.E. Richardson (ed.) *Handbook of Qualitative Methods for Psychology and the Social Sciences*. Leicester: British Psychological Society, pp. 125–40.

Potter, J. and Wetherell, M. (1987) *Discourse and Social Psychology*. London: Sage.

Potter, J. and Wetherell, M. (1994) 'Analysing discourse', in A. Bryman and R.G. Burgess (eds) *Analysing Qualitative Data*. London: Routledge, pp. 47–66.

Pratt, M.L. (1992) *Imperial Eyes: Travel Writing and Transculturation*. London: Routledge.

Preziosi, D. (1989) *Rethinking Art History: Meditations on a Coy Science*. London: Yale University Press.

Preziosi, D. and Farago, C.J. (eds) (2004) *Grasping the World: The Idea of the Museum*. Aldershot: Ashgate Press.

Prosser, J. (ed.) (1998) *Image-Based Research: A Sourcebook for Qualitative Researchers*. London: Falmer.

Pryce, D. (1997) 'Surveyors and surveyed: photography out and about', in L. Wells (ed.) *Photography: A Critical Introduction*. London: Routledge, pp. 55–102.

Rajchman, J. (1988) 'Foucault's art of seeing', *October* 44, 89–117.

Ramamurthy, A. (1997) 'Constructions of illusion: photography and commodity culture', in L. Wells (ed.) *Photography: A Critical Introduction*. London: Routledge, pp. 151–98.

Rampley, M. (2005) *Exploring Visual Culture*. Edinburgh: Edinburgh University Press.

Reynolds, A. (1995) 'Visual stories', in L. Cooke and P. Wollen (eds) *Visual Display: Culture Beyond Appearances*. Seattle, WA: Bay Press, pp. 82–108.

Rieger, J.H. (1996) 'Photographing social change', *Visual Sociology* 11, 5–49.

Riviere, J. (1986) 'Womanliness as masquerade', in V. Burgin, J. Donald and C. Kaplan (eds) *Formations of Fantasy*. London: Methuen, pp. 35–44.

Roberts, H.E. (ed.) (1998) *Encyclopedia of Comparative Iconography: Themes Depicted in Works of Art*, 2 vols. London: Fitzroy Dearborn.

Rogoff, I. (1998) 'Studying visual culture', in N. Mirzoeff (ed.) *The Visual Culture Reader*. London: Routledge, pp. 14–26.

Rorty, R. (1980) *Philosophy and the Mirror of Nature*. Oxford: Blackwell.

Rose, G. (1997) 'Situating knowledges: positionality, reflexivities and other tactics', *Progress in Human Geography* 21, 305–20.

Rose, G. (2000) 'Practising photography: an archive, a study, some photographs and a researcher', *Journal of Historical Geography* 26, 555–71.

Rose, G. (2003) 'Domestic spacings and family photography: a case study', *Transactions of the Institute of British Geographers* 28, 5–18.

Rose, G. (2004) '"Everyone's cuddled up and it just looks really nice": the emotional geography of some mums and their family photos', *Social and Cultural Geography* 5, 549–64.

Rose, G. (2005) '"You just have to make a conscious effort to keep snapping away, I think": a case study of family photos, mothering and familial space', in S. Hardy and C. Wiedmer (eds) *Motherhood and Space: Configurations of the Maternal through Politics, Home, and the Body*. Palgrave: Macmillan, pp. 221–40.

Rose, J. (1986) *Sexuality in the Field of Vision*. London: Verso.

Rothenberg, M. (2003) 'Museum Politics: Power Plays at the Exhibition', *ISIS: Journal of the History of Science in Society*, 94, 504–5.

Ryan, J. (1997) *Picturing Empire: Photography and the Visualisation of the British Empire*. London: Reaktion Books.

Seidel, L. (1993) *Jan van Eyck's Arnolfini Portrait: Stories of an Icon*. Cambridge: Cambridge University Press.

Sekula, A. (1986) 'Reading an archive: photography between labour and capital', in P. Holland, J. Spence and S. Watney (eds) *Photography/Politics: 2*. London: Comedia, pp. 153–61.

Sekula, A. (1989) 'The body and the archive', in R. Bolton (ed.) *The Contest of Meaning: Critical Histories of Photography*. London: MIT Press, pp. 342–88.

Sherman, D.J. and Rogoff, I. (1994) *Museum Culture: Histories, Discourses, Spectacles*. London: Routledge.

Shohat, E. and Stam, R. (1998) 'Narrativizing visual culture: towards a polycentric aesthetic', in N. Mirzoeff (ed.) *The Visual Culture Reader*. London: Routledge, pp. 27–49.

Silverman, K. (1988) *The Acoustic Mirror: The Female Voice in Psychoanalysis and Cinema*. Bloomington, IN: Indiana University Press.

Silverman, K. (1992) *Male Subjectivity at the Margins*. London: Routledge.

Silverman, K. (1996) *The Threshold of the Visible World*. London: Routledge.

Silverstone, R., Hirsch, E. and Morley, D. (1991) 'Listening to a long conversation: an ethnographic approach to the study of information and communication technologies in the home', *Cultural Studies 5*, 204–27.

Slater, D. (1983) 'Marketing mass photography', in H. Davis and P. Walton (eds) *Language, Image, Media*. Oxford: Blackwell, pp. 245–63.

Slater, D. (1995) 'Photography and modern vision: the spectacle of "natural magic" ', in C. Jenks (ed.) *Visual Culture*. London: Routledge, pp. 218–37.

Slater, D. (1998) 'Analysing cultural objects: content analysis and semiotics', in C. Seale (ed.) *Researching Society and Culture*. London: Sage, pp. 233–44.

Smith, L. (1998) *The Politics of Focus: Women, Children and Nineteenth-Century Photography*. Manchester: Manchester University Press.

Sontag, S. (1978) *On Photography*. Harmondsworth: Penguin.

Stafford, B.M. (1984) *Voyage into Substance: Art, Science, Nature and the Illustrated Travel Account, 1760–1840*. Cambridge, MA: MIT Press.

Stafford, B.M. (1991) *Body Criticism: Imaging the Unseen in Enlightenment Art and Science*. London: MIT Press.

Stafford, B.M. (1996) *Good Looking: Essays on the Virtue of Images*. London: MIT Press.

Staniszewski, M.A. (1998) *The Power of Display: A History of Exhibition Installation at the Museum of Modern Art*. London: MIT Press.

Starn, R. (2005) 'A historian's brief guide to new museum studies', American Historical review 110, 68–98.

Strauss, A. and Corbin, J. (1999) *Basics of Qualitative Research: Techniques and Procedures for Developing Grounded Theory*, 2nd edition. London: Sage.

Sturken, M. and Cartwright, L. (2001) *Practices of Looking: An Introduction to Visual Culture*. Oxford: Oxford University Press.

Suchar, C. (1997) 'Grounding visual sociology in shooting scripts', *Qualitative Sociology* 20, 33–55.

Suchar, C. (2004) 'Amsterdam and Chicago: seeing the macro-characteristics of gentrification', in C. Knowles and J. Sweetman (eds) *Picturing the Social Landscape: Visual Methods and the Sociological Imagination*. London: Routledge, pp. 147–65.

Sunderland, J. (2004) *Gendered Discourses*. Basingstoke: Palgrave Macmillan.

Swan-Jones, L. (1999) *Art Information and the Internet: How to Find It, How to Use It*. London: Fitzroy Dearborn.

Tagg, J. (1988) *The Burden of Representation: Essays on Photographies and Histories*. London: Macmillan.

Taylor, J.C. (1957) *Learning to Look: A Handbook for the Visual Arts*. Chicago, IL: Chicago University Press.

Thomas, N. (1991) *Entangled Objects: Exchange, Material Culture and Colonialism in the Pacific*. London: Harvard University Press.

Thomas, N. (1999) *Possessions: Indigenous Art/Colonial Culture*. London: Thames and Hudson.

Thornham, S. (1997) *Passionate Detachments: An Introduction to Feminist Film Theory*. London: Arnold.

Thrift, N. (2003) 'Practising ethics', in M. Pryke, G. Rose and S. Whatmore (eds) *Using Social Theory: Thinking Through Research*. London: Sage, pp. 105–21.

Titus, S.L. (1976) 'Family photographs and the transition to parenthood', *Journal of Marriage and the Family* 38, 525–30.

Tonkiss, F. (1998) 'Analysing discourse', in C. Seale (ed.) *Researching Society and Culture*. London: Sage, pp. 245–60.

Tufte, E.R. (1983) *The Visual Display of Quantitative Information*. Cheshire, CT: Graphics Press.

Tulloch, J. (2000) *Watching Television Audiences: Cultural Theories and Methods*. London: Arnold.

Urry, J. (1990) *The Tourist Gaze: Leisure and Travel in Contemporary Societies*. London: Sage.

Van Alphen, E. (2005) 'What history, whose history, history to what purpose?' *Journal of Visual Culture* 4, 191–202.

Van Eck, C. and Winters, E. (2005) 'Introduction', in C. van Eck and E. Winters (eds) *Dealing with the Visual: Art History, Aesthetics and Visual Culture*. Aldershot: Ashgate, pp. 1–13.

Van Leeuwen, T. (2001) 'Semiotics and iconography', in T. van Leeuwen and C. Jewitt (eds) *Handbook of Visual Analysis*. London: Sage, pp. 92–118.

Van Leeuwen, T. and Jewitt, C. (eds) (2001) *Handbook of Visual Analysis*. London: Sage.

Van Straten, R. (1994) *An Introduction to Iconography* (translated by P. de Man). Reading: Gordon and Breach.

Vergo, P. (ed.) (1989) *The New Museology*. London: Reaktion Books.

Virilio, P. (1994) *The Vision Machine*. London: British Film Institute.

Walkerdine, V. (1990) *Schoolgirl Fictions*. London: Verso.

Walkowitz, J. (1992) *City of Dreadful Delight: Narratives of Sexual Danger in Late-Victorian London*. London: Virago.

Warren, S. (2002) 'Show me how it feels to work here', *Ephemera: Critical Dialogues on Organisation* 2, 224–65 (www.ephemeraweb.org).

Waterfield, G. (1991) *Palaces of Art: Art Galleries in Britain, 1790–1990*. London: Dulwich Picture Gallery.

Weber, R.P. (1990) *Basic Content Analysis*. London: Sage.

Wells, L. (1992) 'Judith Williamson, *Decoding Advertisements*', in M. Barker and A. Beezer (eds) *Reading into Cultural Studies*. London: Routledge, pp. 165–80.

Westerbeck, C. and Meyerowitz, J. (1994) *Bystander: A History of Street Photography*. London: Thames & Hudson.

White, P. (1995) 'Governing lesbian desire: *Nocturne*'s Oedipal fantasy', in L. Pietropaulo and A. Testaferri (eds), *Feminisms in the Cinema*. Bloomington, IN: Indiana University Press, pp. 86–105.

Whitely, N. (1999) 'Readers of the lost art: visuality and particularity in art criticism', in I. Heywood and B. Sandywell (eds), *Interpreting Visual Culture: Explorations in the Hermeneutics of the Visual*. London: Routledge, pp. 99–122.

Williams, R. (1976) *Keywords: A Vocabulary of Culture and Society*. London: Croom Helm.

Williamson, J.E. (1978) *Decoding Advertisements: Ideology and Meaning in Advertising*. London: Marion Boyars.

Wollen, P. (1970) *Signs and Meaning in Cinema*. London: British Film Institute and Thames & Hudson.

Young, L. (1996) *Fear of the Dark: 'Race', Gender and Sexuality in the Cinema*. London: Routledge.

Young, L. and Barrett, H. (2001) 'Adapting visual methods: action research with Kampala street children', *Area* 33, 141–52.

list of key terms

index

Page numbers in *italics* refer to illustrations

Index by Margaret Binns